AN INTRODUCTION
TO THE MUSIC OF
MILTON BABBITT

AN INTRODUCTION TO THE MUSIC OF MILTON BABBITT

Andrew Mead

PRINCETON UNIVERSITY PRESS

PRINCETON, NEW JERSEY

PUBLISHED BY PRINCETON UNIVERSITY PRESS, 41 WILLIAM STREET,

PRINCETON, NEW JERSEY 08540

IN THE UNITED KINGDOM: PRINCETON UNIVERSITY PRESS, CHICHESTER, WEST SUSSEX

LIBRARY OF CONGRESS CATALOGING-IN-PUBLICATION DATA

MEAD, ANDREW WASHBURN.

AN INTRODUCTION TO THE MUSIC OF MILTON BABBIT/ANDREW MEAD.

P.   CM.

DISCOGRAPHY :

INCLUDES BIBLIOGRAPHICAL REFERENCES AND INDEX.

ISBN 0-691-03314-5

1. BABBIT, MILTON, 1916–   —CRITICISM AND INTERPRETATION.

2. TWELVE-TONE SYSTEM.   I. TITLE.

ML410.B066M4   1994   780'.92—dc20   92-37178

CHARTS IN EXAMPLES 1.26, 1.27, AND 3.27a ORIGINALLY APPEARED IN "ABOUT *ABOUT
TIME*'S TIME" BY ANDREW MEAD, *PERSPECTIVES OF NEW MUSIC* 25 (1987): 182–235.

THIS BOOK HAS BEEN COMPOSED IN LINOTRON PALATINO

PRINCETON UNIVERSITY PRESS BOOKS ARE PRINTED
ON ACID-FREE PAPER AND MEET THE GUIDELINES FOR
PERMANENCE AND DURABILITY OF THE COMMITTEE ON
PRODUCTION GUIDELINES FOR BOOK LONGEVITY
OF THE COUNCIL ON LIBRARY RESOURCES

PRINTED IN THE UNITED STATES OF AMERICA

1   3   5   7   9   10   8   6   4   2

For Amy

. . . a world perfect for getting lost in . . .

—Richard Powers, *The Gold Bug Variations*

CONTENTS

ACKNOWLEDGMENTS

I AM INDEBTED to a number of friends, both colleagues and students, for their help and support of the present volume. Richard Swift has been of inestimable help through his extensive conversations and insights on Babbitt's music, and his willingness to share rare materials. Joseph Dubiel has also been particularly helpful in conversation, as have Stephen Peles, Bruce Samet, and Robert Morris. David Smalley prepared the examples, and his intimate knowledge of Babbitt's works was invaluable. Brian Jagger provided much-needed last-minute help. My students William Lake, Dave Hollinden, and Nancy Rao have made major contributions as well. William Lake and Anna Ferenc performed much of the research for the preparation of the bibliography and discography. I am grateful to the Office of the Vice President in charge of Research, University of Michigan, for underwriting the production of the examples. I am also especially grateful to Elizabeth Powers and Lauren Oppenheim, whose patience and editorial insight have made the book possible.

Last but not least, I must also thank Milton Babbitt, who, while always willing to entertain my questions about his music, has consistently prodded me with answers that raise still more and deeper questions.

AN INTRODUCTION
TO THE MUSIC OF
MILTON BABBITT

PROLOGUE

MILTON BABBITT has been a central figure in contemporary American music for most of the past forty years. As a teacher and a writer he has influenced two generations of students, including such notable musicians as Stephen Sondheim and Donald Martino. His years at Princeton University helped establish the study of composition and music theory as serious academic pursuits, and his articles on Schoenberg, Stravinsky, and the twelve-tone system form the foundation of an extensive body of research by a wide variety of scholars. But Milton Babbitt is first and last a composer, and all his words about music have been secondary to his central endeavor: the creation of a large body of complex, demanding, but ultimately rewarding compositions.

This volume is a celebration of Milton Babbitt the composer and of his music. It is addressed to anyone enthusiastic or curious about contemporary music and is conceived as a guide to a more informed hearing of Babbitt's work. Make no bones about it, I enjoy this music, and it is my hope that the following remarks will increase others' enjoyment as well.

In keeping to this particular goal, I have had to omit a great deal about Babbitt. This is not a biographical study, nor does it attempt to place Babbitt in a historical context, except, incidentally, as an heir to the insights of Arnold Schoenberg and Anton Webern, among others. Although Milton Babbitt was a major figure in the development of electronic music in the United States, I have chosen not to emphasize his work with the synthesizer in a special way, because the music he composed for that medium raises essentially the same problems of comprehension for the listener as his compositions for more conventional ensembles. Similarly, I have not included commentary on his *Three Theatrical Songs*, part of an early musical theater work, *Fabulous Voyage* (1946); these works partake of an entirely different world from that of the rest of Babbitt's music, though it is possible to hear the ghosts of jazz and American popular song lurking beneath the surfaces of his most abstract compositions.

The pleasure I derive from Babbitt's music is not merely some intellectual satisfaction at teasing out a complex puzzle. Nevertheless, the strong emotional and expressive charge of his music is deeply rooted in the ways notes and rhythms work together to create webs of association and connection over ever-larger spans of time. To appreciate fully the music's expressivity, we must be able to follow its structure.

And while his musical surfaces revel in great sensuous beauty, they can only grant us incidental gratification unless we attempt to hear the ways they reveal the underlying long-range motion through the background structure that forms the lasting emotional drama of his compositions.

The trick to this, of course, is learning what to listen for and how to understand it in context. The best way to do this is to listen to a lot of music and to listen to the same pieces many times. It is still helpful, however, to have some guidelines, and it is toward this end that I have written this volume. Much of what follows is technical, but it is always offered to elucidate ways of hearing that will lead the listener to a greater appreciation of a rich and rewarding musical world. Despite a reputation to the contrary, Babbitt's music is truly music to be heard, and it yields up beauty upon beauty to the engaged listener.

1

MILTON BABBITT'S

COMPOSITIONAL WORLD

Introduction

IMMERSION in the music of Milton Babbitt leaves one with an impression of overwhelming variety. From the compact intensity of *Post-Partitions* to the broad lyricism of *Philomel* or *The Joy of More Sextets*, from the intimacies of *The Widow's Lament in Springtime* to the vast canvases of *Relata* or the Piano Concerto, we are constantly invited to explore new realms of musical expression, to try out new ways to listen. Nor does this variety partake merely of the intellectual or the purely experimental. There can be an enormous visceral excitement in a live performance of *Reflections*, while the text setting of *A Solo Requiem* can touch our gravest emotions.

Our appreciation of the range and subtlety of Babbitt's music, however, depends on our ability to perceive the underlying structure behind the local details, to follow events below the surface. Once we can recognize the significance of various changes in intervallic patterns, rhythms, or instrumentation, we can begin to assimilate the wealth of surface detail as the most immediate manifestation of larger patterns of transformation and recurrence that add up to our sense of the overall unfolding of a composition. This is what leads us to the vital center of his music, the source that animates the farthest reaches and ramifications of the sounding surface.

As the preceding might imply, the expressive power of Babbitt's music is inextricably entwined with its structure, and, as is true to varying degrees of any body of work based on a highly consistent, richly elaborate self-contained system of relationships, a lack of comprehension or a superficial acquaintance can level the greatest distinctions and render even the most emphatic expression obscure. This problem is not unique to Babbitt, or to twentieth-century music in general; for various groups of people at various times, the same could be said of High Baroque, bebop, or South Indian music.

What has perhaps contributed to the situation with Babbitt's music is that the composer has to a remarkable degree questioned the underlying assumptions of how music goes, has gone, or could go, based on its principles for assembling sounds in time. Most habits of musical construal forged by extensive exposure to tonal music will be of little use with Babbitt's compositions, just as they can be misleading with music by Schoenberg or any number of other recent composers, but Babbitt goes farther than most in pursuing the ramifications of his particular chosen set of compositional constraints. The notions of large-scale form, continuity, and surface gesture adapted from tonal practice that can ease our way into the more radically different pitch worlds of Schoenberg or Webern are less helpful as an entré to Babbitt's music.

This is not to say that Babbitt's music lacks form or continuity, or that his surfaces are without a wealth of compelling gesture; quite the opposite is true, but the ways that immediate moments compound in a continuity, and the means by which he shapes that continuity into the whole, single complex gesture that is a complete piece, differ radically from those that evolved in the works of the tonal masters. At the heart of this difference is Babbitt's wholehearted embrace of Arnold Schoenberg's revolutionary invention, the twelve-tone system. With joy, rigor, and relentless energy Babbitt has explored the implications of twelve-tone composition throughout his career, and they have ramified into every dimension of his music. Form, continuity, and gesture in his compositions all have their source in the principles underlying relationships determined by the twelve-tone system.

Alas, to many, twelve-tone composition seems an artificial technique for generating music without the interposition of a composer's humanity. For some, twelve-tone relationships are unhearable, and compositions so structured acquire musical value in spite of their twelve-tone aspects.[1] Others fear that dabbling in what seems to them a mechanistic approach to composing will rob their own music of originality, and to avoid contamination they have steered clear even of the twelve-tone musical repertoire, let alone the underlying theory.

The twelve-tone system, however, when properly understood, is no more prescriptive than tonality, and its consequences no less hearable. Nor does working within the constraints of twelve-tone relationships and their extensions either obscure a composer's individual voice or remove his or her responsibility for a composition's ultimate qualities. All the many disparate approaches loosely embraced by the phrase "twelve-tone composition" seek to understand and exploit the definable laws of intervallic relationships within the equal-tempered twelve-note universe. A composer working within the chromatic universe is constrained by those relationships, whether or not he or she is aware of them.

Milton Babbitt is, indeed, a twelve-tone composer, unabashedly so, and it is precisely his profound understanding of Arnold Schoenberg's epochal insight that gives Babbitt's music its special quality. By examining the underlying principles of twelve-tone composition, and by understanding the ways Babbitt has extended Schoenberg's thought as a way of making music, we can begin to appreciate Babbitt's music on its own terms, as a richly varied yet unified body of work.

Babbitt is unusual in today's musical world in his decision to pursue exclusively the ramifications of a single compositional concept. His development has been accretive: in even the most recent work one can perceive the presence of his earliest attitudes exerting a powerful influence. These modes of thinking, derived from his insights into the implications of the twelve-tone system, inform his music on a wide variety of levels. Nevertheless, it is these very restrictions that provide the source of the variety and individuality of his compositions. Babbitt's compositional technique is not simply a matter of metier, a dependable method of turning out a proven commodity; nor is his music merely the sterile embodiment of theoretical precepts. Babbitt's remarkable achievement is his creation of a musical world within which to *be* creative. His constraints are his freedoms: by hewing to a particular perspective of the chromatic universe, Babbitt has entered a landscape with discernable distances and directions, recognizable features, and varied terrain. Within this world Babbitt's compositions move with a wonderful balance of spontaneity and inevitability.

Just as it is useful to think of his music existing in a metaphorical world, so it is helpful to think of his compositions themselves as built up of different combinations of musical genes. Each composition can be conceived as a new recombination of a rather small number of practices and predilections found throughout his career, much as Babbitt's complete oeuvre can be seen to develop from certain first principles, constantly reinterpreted and reembodied. These compositional genes are not totally determinate; rather, they endow a composition with certain attributes that will affect and guide its progress, yet allow for the flexibility within the compositional process that gives Babbitt's music its immediacy. Each work moves like a living being through Babbitt's compositional world, affording us its unique perspective on the chromatic universe.

Some of Babbitt's compositional genes are of a technical nature, and we will explore them during the course of this volume, but others are as simple as a preference for certain instruments or an affection for the female voice. His four published string quartets span his career and embody all his principal compositional techniques. Running like a sparkling thread through his life is a series of brilliant solo piano pieces, and each compositional phase contains a major work for soprano, accompanied variously by different favored instruments or ensembles. This particular predilection blossoms forth in *An Elizabethan Sextette*.[2] In contrast to the timbral homogeneity of strings or piano, Babbitt has also written a series of works for mixed ensembles. The quartet of flute, clarinet, violin, and cello, initially appearing together in the Composition for Four Instruments at the beginning of his career, returns whole or in part along with piano, voice, viola, or percussion in a number of pieces. Babbitt's pioneering electronic work, first emerging in solo compositions, eventually joins various favored live instruments and ensembles. Looming behind the wealth of chamber, vocal, and solo music is a mountain range of vast orchestral works, alas but dimly perceived due to their infrequent performance. This, at present, culminates in two enormous peaks—the Piano Concerto of 1985 and *Transfigured Notes* of 1986. The former conjoins Babbitt's virtuosic piano writing with his lapidary orchestral textures, while the latter is the apotheosis of the string ensembles found in the quartets and *Correspondences* for string orchestra and tape (1967). Each of his compositions represents in both obvious and more subtle ways the recombination of instrumental and compositional preferences found in embryo at the outset of his career. In a very real sense, Babbitt's whole body of work can be heard as a single gigantic composition, emerging intermittently and in different guises like an intricate shoreline seen through mist.

Babbitt's music is not static, however. Listening to one of his compositions is akin to seeing nature in all its richness. All the immediacy and individuality of light falling through thick forest growth or the play of waves in a tidal rip derive from the interactions of simpler, more universal underlying forces, and it is the complexity of their interaction that causes the enormous wealth of variety in their manifestation. By understanding the principles guiding the growth of trees or the interactions of wind and water we can better appreciate the dialectic of singularity within the totality, the moment in the flow of time. So too it is with Babbitt's music. Its dynamic qualities depend on a series of dialectics between the surface moments of a piece and their source in its underlying structures, between a structure's compositional interpretation and its abstract properties, between particular abstract structures and Babbitt's habitual corners of the chromatic universe, and ultimately between Babbitt's preferred perspective of the chromatic universe and the chromatic universe itself. It is from an awareness of the dynamic tension found at each level that we can build an appreciation of the balance between communality and individuality that makes Milton Babbitt's compositions such a rich and extensive body of work.

In the following pages we shall begin to explore Babbitt's compositional world. In the remainder of this chapter we shall investigate a number of the principles underlying Babbitt's music and describe the major features of his pitch and rhythmic languages as they have developed through his career. The subsequent chapters contain discussions of selected works from each of Babbitt's three compositional periods. These divisions of his oeuvre are distinguished by certain technical developments.[3] I have endeavored to choose compositions not only for their illustrative power but also according to their availability on recording, as noted in the discography. After all, this is music to be known by hearing, and for all that one can say about it, the best introduction to Babbitt's music is to listen.

The Twelve-Tone System

Fundamental to any discussion of Milton Babbitt's music is the question of twelve-tone composition, as virtually every aspect of his musical world derives from principles inherent in Schoenberg's radical reinterpretation of musical primitives. As a young man, Babbitt was quick to realize that despite its surface similarities to tonal forms, Schoenberg's twelve-tone music represented a fundamental music-syntactic and perceptual shift from tonal composition.[4] That twelve-tone compositions could effectively be made to behave in ways similar to tonal works was a reflection of Schoenberg's yearning for the syntactical power of Mozart's and Brahms's language in a music that would employ the sorts of materials he had explored in his contextual works.[5] Babbitt, however, saw that although twelve-tone syntax can support the dramatic strategies of tonal forms, it may also lead to entirely new compositional strategies vibrant and musically compelling in themselves. No matter how it is used, though, the twelve-tone system depends on ways of construing the basic elements of music that are fundamentally different from those we use to listen to tonal music.

What is this fundamental difference and how should it affect the way we listen to twelve-tone music? A proper answer requires a brief consideration of tonal hearing. Tonal music's hierarchies emerge from the subtle and extensive intervallic properties of the diatonic collection, the collection that underlies the major scale. We can tell where we are in tonal music through our ability to differentiate among the different steps of the scale. This is possible because each member of the underlying diatonic collection has a different inventory of intervals between it and each of the other members of the collection, allowing each scale degree a unique position with regard to all the others.

Two other related properties of the diatonic collection are also of crucial importance. First, each type of interval (or its complement to within the octave) is represented a unique number of times in the collection. Thus any diatonic collection contains two minor seconds (or major sevenths), five major seconds (or minor sevenths), four minor thirds (or major sixths), three major thirds (or minor sixths), six perfect fourths (or perfect fifths), and one augmented fourth (or diminished fifth). This means that each intervallic distance (to within octave complementation) between two major scales will yield a unique number of notes held in common: scales a perfect fourth (or perfect fifth) apart will share six notes in common, while scales a minor second (or major seventh) apart will only contain two notes in common. Second, each type of interval (or its complement) is found at only one distance between scale degrees. Thus, for example, minor seconds (or major sevenths) only occur between adjacent scale degrees, as do major seconds, while thirds, both major and minor, can only be obtained by skipping over a scale degree.[6] In this way, sets of intervals are assigned unique roles in tonal music.

These properties have an enormous effect on the way we think about tonal music, from our technical terminology to the underlying metaphors we use to talk about music and how we experience it. Our familiar note names—the seven letters A, B, C, D, E, F, G plus their chromatic inflections—reflect the primacy of the diatonic collection in so much of our musical thinking. The similarity between major and minor intervals of a given size containing different absolute numbers of half-steps depends on their shared scale degree difference. Given notes can take on different degrees of stability based on what scale degree they represent, and the interplay of changing scale degree significance for a particular note over different spans of time or levels of structure is central to our construal of tonal music. Our ability to recognize our place within the diatonic collection allows us additionally to recognize the placement of notes outside the collection. Thus we can recognize chromatic inflections within a given key, or the temporary establishment of a new key in tonal music. One of our fundamental metaphors to describe music is motion. We tend to describe musical lines as "moving" from place to place, displaced from one position to another based on the various strengths and tendencies of scale degrees and their combinations.

All of the preceding properties and their interpretations depend on the fact that a major scale is based on a collection that may be usefully construed as a subset of the totality of twelve distinct notes, or pitch classes, in the equal-tempered system. The diatonic collection is the largest sort of subset of the chromatic totality that has all of these powerful properties. If we attempt to enlarge the collection, we disturb those properties that underlie tonal music.

In twelve-tone music an entirely different situation obtains.[7] Twelve-tone music—particularly Schoenberg's and, in turn, Babbitt's—is based on concatenated presentations of *aggregates*, the general term in twelve-tone theory to denote a single presentation of the twelve pitch classes, without regard to order. Composing music that proceeds in aggregates poses a problem. In aggregate music that does not employ elements of tonal syntax to maintain our tonal interpretations, the musical fabric no longer automatically possesses the means of sorting and hierarchizing provided by the properties of the diatonic collection. Each member of an aggregate has exactly the same catalog of intervals between it and all the other members. With no differentiation of elements, there can be no differentiation of scale degrees. Such a situation calls for a radical reinterpretation of the significance of virtually all our basic musical perceptions, from our way of construing difference and similarity among intervals to the metaphors we use to describe music. In twelve-tone music we cannot depend on the same sorts of collectional properties that form the very basis of our sense of tonal music.

As collections of pitch classes, aggregates are indistinguishable. What makes them distinguishable from one another, and what can perform the basis of comparison among them, is the interior distribution of their constituent elements, the twelve pitch classes. The distribution of pitch classes encompasses a variety of musical means and dimensions, including time, register, instrumentation, articulation, and dynamics. All may serve individually and in conjunction to group the pitch classes in various ways. Such groupings, to various degrees, constitute orderings of the elements of the aggregate. Composing in the total chromatic using concatenated aggregates entails controlling the order of their constituent elements. Babbitt's music suggests that this is the fundamental lesson he learned from his early contact with Schoenberg's scores.[8]

How did aggregate music come about? A comprehensive examination of this question is beyond the scope of this volume, and Schoenberg's practice was firmly established by the time Babbitt decided to adopt and extend it for his own. Nevertheless, the question is fundamental to a proper understanding of how twelve-tone music works, and how we might best go about listening to it.[9] The great chromatic enrichment of composition in the latter half of the nineteenth century helped to break down the very distinctions it sought to enrich. By overwhelming the diatonic collection, composers obscured its crucial properties, gradually obliterating the different degrees of distance and direction it provided within and among keys. Syntactical problems arose through the increased use of ambiguity in the interpretations of intervals, and the increased stabilization of certain sorts of dissonance. While the period produced a wonderful variety of music, more and more composers were forced to find unique compositional solutions. Schoenberg's emancipation of the dissonance was merely the logical extension of what he heard around him, and it led, as one might expect, to a complete breakdown of tonal syntax. Each new composition required its own syntax, and the extreme difficulty of composing extended works based on contextual associations is reflected in the works of Schoenberg's middle period by their brevity or their dependence on a text for structure.[10] As the vestiges of tonal voice leading recede in the music of Schoenberg's middle period, the ways collections may be partitioned into smaller ones or assembled into larger ones become increasingly evident as the motivating structural strategy.[11] The maximal size for larger collections is the aggregate, and eventually it took on a significance of its own. Schoenberg, faced with the compositional problem of dealing with large collections sliced into smaller ones, or small ones compounded into larger collections, sought ways of controlling them that led to the twelve-tone system. The important point to realize is that the twelve-tone system emerged as the *solution* to a compositional problem and did not spring from nowhere into Schoenberg's mind. The understanding of the significance of twelve-tone composition, however, depends on our ability to understand what it means to hear music in terms of aggregates.

Can we hear aggregates—and if so, how? Chromatic enrichment of the diatonic scale not only clogs the distinctions among pitch classes within the collection but also reduces the vividness of pitch classes not included in the collection. What does remain vivid is the recognition of pitch class membership in a highly chromatic context. Thus, given a collection of a large number of different pitch classes, each represented once, we *can* recognize—although we are not able vividly to determine what pitch classes we have not yet heard—whether or not any additional note represents a new pitch class. By interpreting the recurrence of a pitch class as a signal that we have crossed a boundary, we can parse a highly chromatic undifferentiated musical surface into a discrete series of large bundles of pitch classes that we might call *perceptual aggregates*. Perceptual aggregates may or may not contain all twelve pitch classes, but because of their size this will not be a particularly vivid aspect of our hearing. Their pitch class content is not vivid, but our awareness of their boundaries will be. The maximum size of a perceptual aggregate is twelve pitch classes. By choosing to use twelve consistently, Schoenberg in the twelve-tone system used the maximal size of perceptual aggregate, analogous to tonal music's use of the maximal collection size serving its purposes, the diatonic collection.

The preceding is predicated on our recognition of pitch class repetition and its use to indicate boundaries between aggregates. In most twelve-tone music there are extensive examples of pitch class repetition within aggregates, so that it is necessary to distinguish those repetitions within from those between aggregates. Both Schoenberg and Babbitt distinguish among the different kinds of repetition articulated in different musical dimensions, and in both composers' music repetition has the effect even within aggregates of indicating boundaries of some kind. While the potential for ambiguity is frequently employed to good effect, context generally makes clear the function of repetition in both their work.

Aggregate hearing marks a profound reinterpretation of musical information, a fundamental shift in the construal of what we hear. It is crucial to note, however, that it does not mark a change in the perception of such fundamental musical entities as pitch class and interval but signifies a radical reinterpretation of their significance in ways that affect every aspect of our hearing. For example, octaves and unison repetitions will, in various manners, suggest boundaries between their constituent elements. Pitch classes will no longer assume hierarchical differences based on scale degrees. This is *not* to say that all pitch classes will have the same significance, but their differentiation will be based on their placement within aggregates. Functional identities between intervals of different absolute sizes implied by the terms *major* and *minor* will no longer obtain. New associations of intervals and of collections of different sizes and types will arise from similarities in their ways of fitting into the aggregate. The metaphor of moving voices can no longer be invoked, due to its dependence on the differentiation of scale degrees. The techniques of aggregate hearing need not imply that our sense of the music be static, but the metaphor of motion in twelve-tone music must be based on different criteria from those used in tonal music.[12]

Both tonal hearing and aggregate hearing depend on two interrelated ways of indexing pitch class events: by content and by order. It is important for both kinds of hearing to be able to recognize not only the recurrence of pitch classes themselves but the patterns of intervals among them as well. Our ability to recognize both pitch classes and

Example 1.1.   Four aggregate sketches

intervals as well as follow their shifting associations underlies our ability to recognize change of chord and key in tonal music and plays similarly fundamental roles in our hearing of twelve-tone music. Order in tonal music manifests itself in various dimensions. The functional distinction between a root-position tonic chord and a cadential $^6_4$ chord is based on a difference of order manifested in register, while the difference between a progression from I to V and one from V to I is dependent on order in time. The dual nature of our musical perceptual strategies in tonal music allows us to recognize the preservation of functional relationships, based on interval patterns, at different transposition levels, while hearing the degree of nearness or farness of a transposition, based on pitch class intersection.

Similarly, we can recognize changes of intervallic order and pitch class content and their interactions among aggregates. Example 1.1 provides some simple illustrations using four aggregate sketches. These sketches, labeled A, B, C, and D, are not fully composed in terms of instrumentation, dynamics, rhythmic detail, or articulation but consist of registrally distinct lines combined to produce simple chords. The first three, A, B, and C, contain three lines yielding four chords, while the last, D, uses four lines in a slightly more elaborate way. Sketches A and B share the pitch class content of each of their three lines as well as their sequences of intervals (to within octave displacement). However, both the content and the kinds of chords formed between the lines have been altered. Between sketches B and C, the contents of the highest and lowest lines have been exchanged, associating the different interval patterns of the outer voices with each other's collectional contents. While the contents of the resulting chords differs, the combinations of pairs of chords in B and C yield the same pair of collections. The four lines of sketch D unfold the contents of A's chords in time, in the order found registrally in A. Although it is obvious that a simple note-against-note counterpoint of these four lines would result in four-note chords whose contents would equal the contents of A's three lines, a little compositional fiddling allows the production of *transpositions* of those three collections to unfold in time.[13]

As may be seen, different degrees of association between and among compositional aggregates can be brought about by invoking both collectional and intervallic criteria. Our sketches exhibited only a bare minimum of composition; more fully realized aggregates will permit a variety of simultaneous interpretations based on additional ways of associating events in the musical surface. Because of this, an aggregate may participate in a variety of different local and long-range trajectories in a composition.

Composing with aggregates entails the control of the sorts of relationships shown above, based on the interactions of patterns of intervals and pitch class collections. Schoenberg's solution to composing with aggregates was the twelve-tone system as he practiced it, which is the use of a particular ordering of intervals that will generate an aggregate, conjoined with a set of transformations that will alter and combine the resulting intervallic and collectional configurations in certain simple and predictable ways.[14] The transformations yield in classical practice forty-eight ordered strings of twelve pitch classes, the rows. Twelve-tone rows may be thought of in two complementary ways—as strings of intervals or as strings of pitch classes. Both aspects of row structure are important in our hearing of twelve-tone music and reflect the duality discussed above.[15]

A twelve-tone row, whether thought of as a particular ordering of the twelve pitch classes or as a chain of intervals, is an abstraction, because the dimension in which the order is manifested is not defined, nor is the order of other dimensions determined. It is fundamentally important to realize that any compositional representation of a row contains a great deal more musical structure than is specified by the row itself: musical realities are aggregates, with their identifying distributions of pitch classes; rows are compositional tools used to control the structure of aggregates. The fact that the abstract ordering, the row, is manifested in only one musical dimension at a time, for the most part, allows its compositional realization to possess differentiations articulated in counterpoint against its recurring intervallic and collectional patterns. These differentiations can create linkages with other aggregates here and there in the composition, based in various ways upon the structure of the rows. Twelve-tone composition involves marshaling these various connections into strategies both local and long range to create the dramatic accretion that is a piece of music; to a large extent, the study of twelve-tone music is the study of the myriad ways this is done.[16]

This is the compositional situation that Babbitt decided to take on as his own, to explore and extend in as many ways as he possibly could. That this is a vital and dynamic task can be seen from the variety of works he has produced in the past forty years. Babbitt's thinking about the ways notes work in twelve-tone composition has affected every dimension of his music, including instrumentation, dynamics, rhythm, and articulation, but he has always been particularly aware of the perceptual differences among the various musical dimensions. Babbitt's extension of principles derived from twelve-tone composition into other domains is not a simple translation of numerical values without regard to consequences. His music reflects his sensitivity to the different properties of dynamics and timbre, pitch and time.[17]

A Word about Notation, and Some Definitions

Before examining the various ways Babbitt has extended twelve-tone thought in his compositions, we shall make a few remarks about terminology and notation. As we stated above, twelve-tone rows are abstractions, orderings of pitch classes in a single dimension. For that reason, any notation of rows using *pitches* must be accompanied by a disclaimer that the registers specified do not necessarily obtain in the actual composition. Staff notation, therefore, is not the best notation for rows. Twelve-tone theory has gained a certain notoriety for its use of numbers to represent pitch classes, but numbers are easily the most useful names for pitch classes in twelve-tone music. As I suggested above, tonality and its admittedly familiar terms carry a great freight of assumption and association not necessarily appropriate to aggregate hearing; the very names of pitch classes—C, C♯, D♭, and so forth—derive from the diatonic collection and its chromatic inflections. Just as diatonic pitch class names are particularly suited to illuminating relations in tonality, so numbers are most effective for dealing with aggregate music. However, since their use as musical terminology may be unfamiliar to some readers, I shall use staff notation for most of the examples (with the understanding that registers are *not* specified), and informally use the familiar tonal names in contexts where they are unambiguous.

This is also a good place to define more formally a few terms that we have used, as well as a few that will arise in the following discussion. As may readily be inferred from the foregoing, a *pitch class* is the class of all pitches related by octave transposition, and in twelve-tone theory, enharmonically equivalent notes are considered to be members of the same pitch class. The twelve pitch classes are notated in numbers as C=0, C♯ and D♭=1, and so forth. For convenience we shall notate 10 as t and 11 as e. We shall define a *collection* as an unordered batch of pitch classes, notated in curly braces: {0, 1, 2, 3, 4, 5}, for example, representing C, C♯, D, D♯, E, and F, in any order and register. A *collection class* is all the collections that are equivalent under transposition or inversion. Collection classes are notated in square brackets: [0, 1, 2, 3, 4, 5], for example, representing a general type of collection akin to that just mentioned. Transposition and inversion of unordered pitch class collections do not have anything to do with order, so that we must forget any lurking implications of preserved melodic contour that may still adhere to these terms. They are defined as operations upon the pitch class numbers as follows: transposition is $T_x \{a, b\} = \{a+x, b+x\}$ and inversion is $I_y\{a, b\} = \{y-a, y-b\}$; addition and subtraction, mod 12. (A second method of notating inversion is also found in the literature, $T_z I$, which may be defined as follows: $T_z I \{a, b\} = T_z\{0-a, 0-b\} = \{(0-a)+z, (0-b)+z\} = \{z-a, z-b\}$. z, the reader will infer, will have the same value as y.) x, in the preceding, is called the *constant of transposition*, while y is called the *index number of inversion*. In real musical situations, the constant of transposition can manifest itself as the fixed or compound intervallic distance between two transpositionally related notes; the constant of inversion, the index number, is a little more abstract, but each index number associates pairs of pitch classes in clear and predictable ways.[18]

It is important to remember that unordered pitch class collections are just as much abstractions as are twelve-tone rows; an actual bunch of notes in a composition will have several additional attributes. As with a number of the terms here defined, the abstractions of unordered collection and collection class membership permit our association of different chunks of music based on particular criteria. For ease of reading I shall frequently use more informal alternate terms for collection and collection class, such as *trichord, hexachord, trichord type*, and so on; any additional implications will be clear in context.

A useful concept for dealing with the ways collections fit into aggregates is the *mosaic*.[19] A mosaic may be defined as an unordered collection of discrete unordered pitch class collections dividing up the aggregate. The concept of the mosaic is a tool for describing the ways the totality of the aggregate may be sliced up into smaller discrete

Mosaic Classification

Classification	Example

Mosaic   W1

Trichord types: [0, 1, 2]   [0, 1, 5]   [0, 1, 4]   [0, 1, 3]

Mosaic class   All $T_x W_1$ and $I_y W_1$

Mosaic classes with shared constituent collection classes   W2

Trichord types: [0, 1, 2]   [0, 1, 5]   [0, 1, 4]   [0, 1, 3]

W_1 and W_2 are not members of the same mosaic class but share constituent collection classes.

Mosaic classes with shared aggregate partition types   W3

Trichord types: [0, 1, 6]   [0, 4, 8]   [0, 2, 6]   [0, 1, 5]

W_1 and W_3 both contain four trichords, but they do not belong to the same set of collection classes.

Mosaic classes in general   W4

W1 and W4 have different types of partitions.

Example 1.2.   Mosaic classification

collections. A *mosaic class* is all the mosaics equivalent to one another under transposition or inversion. The study of mosaics is fascinating. In addition to class membership, mosaics may be associated into larger bunches by shared classes of constituent collections, and more generally by shared partitions of the aggregate. This is illustrated in Example 1.2.

A twelve-tone row, as suggested above, may be defined as a particular ordering of the twelve pitch classes. One way of doing this, originated by Babbitt himself, is to associate each pitch class with an *order number*.[20] Doing so has interesting consequences for twelve-tone theory. Following the pattern used above, we may define a *row class* as all the rows that may be transformed into one another under a certain set of operations. In classical twelve-tone theory these would include transposition and inversion applied to the pitch classes, conjoined with retrogression. As retrogression can be seen to be the same concept as inversion using index number eleven (Ie) applied to a row's

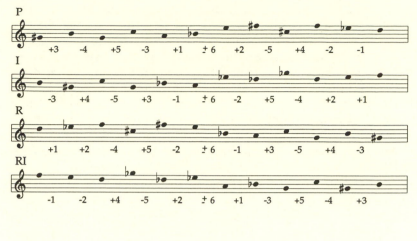

Example 1.3.   Ordered interval patterns

order numbers, we can see that twelve-tone row operations in effect are applied in two dimensions.

A twelve-tone row may also be defined as an interval pattern, more formally a sequence of single-dimensionally ordered interval classes. This will be notated as a string of italicized numbers from *1* to *6*, with plus or minus signs to indicate their order in one dimension. The classical transformations of twelve-tone theory change the sign or the order of the numbers as follows: transposition has no effect; inversion changes the sign of the numbers, retrogression reverses the order of the numbers and changes the sign, and retrograde inversion reverses the order of the numbers while maintaining their signs. We shall similarly use shorter strings of intervals when discussing ordered collections with fewer than twelve elements. Interval patterns of various sorts are illustrated in Example 1.3.[21]

The preceding distinctions give us tools to examine the various ways aggregates are shaped and transformed to provide a wide variety of different connections in twelve-tone music.

Maximal Diversity

A fundamental principle Babbitt derives from the very nature of the twelve-tone system is the idea of *maximal diversity*. A given aggregate achieves its nature from the interior disposition of pitch classes, using

the maximum number of available pitch classes, and different configurations will yield aggregates of different natures. A row class contains the maximum number of different ways to transform a given
ordering under a certain set of constraints. Babbitt has extended this
idea to virtually every conceivable dimension in myriad ways
throughout his compositional career. All sorts of aspects of Babbitt's
music involve the disposition of all possible ways of doing something
within certain constraints. Just as the particular disposition of pitch
classes in an aggregate will give the aggregate its particular character,
so the disposition of elements in another domain can give that aspect
of a composition its own character. Babbitt further composes his music so that these various domains interact: as we shall see later, he
applies analogous configurations to various dimensions over a full
range of time spans, in ways that create associations and resonance
throughout a composition. Developing an awareness of this principle
in all its manifestations is central to the study of Babbitt's music.[22]

Babbitt's Pitch Structures

Principal among the various dimensions of Babbitt's music is pitch
structure. As has been suggested, a constant running throughout
Babbitt's work is the functional presence of the aggregate, whose internal distribution, in terms both of collections and of their interval
patterns, forms the basis for structure in twelve-tone music. As Babbitt has noted, his treatment of the aggregate derives both from
Schoenberg's practice and from certain characteristics of Webern's
music.[23] Each Viennese composer in his own way used rows as a
means of controlling the internal dispositions of aggregates and thus
the relations among aggregates.

Schoenberg's practice of *inversional hexachordal combinatoriality* allowed rows to exert their influence over more than one aggregate at a
time. Example 1.4 contains a pair of aggregates from Schoenberg's
Violin Concerto, op. 36, and a representation of the two rows underlying them. As will no doubt be familiar, the two rows are inversionally related to each other, and their combination yields a pair of
aggregates unfolded over time as well as the pair of aggregates represented by the rows themselves. Such abstract combinations of rows
into horizontals and columns of aggregates can be generalized to an
enormous extent. The resulting compositionally uninterpreted structures are usually called *arrays*,[24] and their horizontals, before they are
interpreted musically, are called *lynes*.[25] More extended arrays may be
formed by concatenating *blocks*, which consist of arrays, like that in

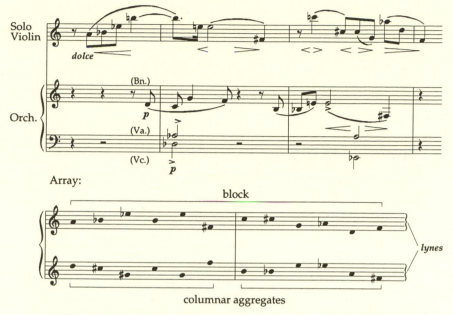

Example 1.4.   Violin Concerto, op. 36, by Arnold Schoenberg.
Reprinted by permission of G. Schirmer, Inc. (ASCAP)

Example 1.4, in which each lyne contains a single row. Babbitt's practice generally involves such arrays, although arrays need not be so constructed.[26]

Schoenberg's practice has several consequences, each of which Babbitt has generalized and extended. First, in Example 1.4 we can see pairs of aggregates musically projected over two different sorts of time spans, the first in successive time spans and the second simultaneously over the span of the passage, distinguished in the musical surface by their modes of projection, in this case the soloist and the orchestra. These various aggregates all represent the same hexachordal mosaic; that is to say, each aggregate may be parsed into the same pair of hexachordal collections, and each constituent collection manifests some segment of the row class's interval pattern. Second, and more generally, we can see from the underlying array of the passage that the intervals between pitch classes at the same order numbers of the two inversionally related rows yield predictable patterns, which themselves may be used to create associations among aggregates.[27] (Although the import of this may not be immediately apparent from the passage excerpted, it plays a significant role elsewhere in Schoenberg's work, both in general and in the concerto in particular.) Third,

Example 1.5.   Row relations, Schoenberg Violin Concerto, op. 36

by using hexachords that are members of the same collection class for both halves of a row, Schoenberg increases the number of interval patterns that a fixed collection of six pitch classes may project as part of the row class. These points are all illustrated in Example 1.5.

Babbitt has expanded upon all these features in various ways. The fundamental slicing of a row into two segmental hexachords has remained a feature of Babbitt's compositional practice throughout his work, with few exceptions. At the heart of virtually all of his compositions is Schoenberg's hexachordal combinatoriality. Babbitt has generalized this considerably, however. For most of his career, he has employed a very special selection of hexachordal collection classes, the *all-combinatorial* hexachord types, illustrated in Example 1.6. Of the six, Babbitt has tended to limit himself to the first five, the whole-tone scale collection striking him as too redundant for compositional use.[28]

The all-combinatorial hexachords extend Schoenberg's practice in two ways. First, as they all may be inverted onto themselves and both transposed and inverted onto their complements, a given all-combinatorial collection of six pitch classes may represent all the possible classical transformations of the interval patterns of both discrete hexachords of a row. This means that a given hexachordal mosaic may be maintained through a greater number of intervallic dispositions,

Example 1.6.   All-combinatorial hexachords

all reflecting interval patterns of the row class. The three hexachord types labeled D, E, and F extend this possibility in that they may be tranposed onto themselves at at least one nonzero interval and thus inverted onto themselves or their complements at more than one index number, and transposed onto their complements at more than one interval. Thus the same absolute string of intervals may be projected in more than one way through a fixed hexachordal mosaic, distinguished by the distribution of pitch classes within hexachords.

Second, because of the all-combinatorial hexachords' flexibility with regard to complementation, Schoenberg's hexachordal combinatoriality based on inversion may be extended to pairs of rows in all possible transformational relations to each other, with multiples of each relation in the case of the higher-order hexachords, D, E, and F. Each of the resulting intervals found at fixed order numbers between pairs of combinatorial rows will form predictable patterns, some dependent on the ordering of a row, some not.[29] These may be used to create relations among aggregates, as illustrated in Example 1.7.[30]

Example 1.7 is derived from the opening section of the first of Babbitt's *Three Compositions for Piano*, his earliest published work. As may be seen, the principle of maximal diversity is in operation here at a variety of levels. By restricting himself to one hexachordal mosaic throughout, Babbitt achieves the maximal variety of orderings of individual hexachordal collections. He has also used all possible combina-

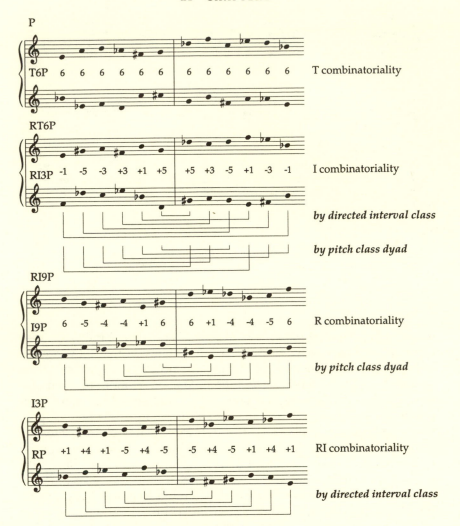

Example 1.7. *Three Compositions for Piano*, no. 1:
hexachordal combinatorial relations

torial combinations of pairs of rows. Furthermore, the rows themselves have been ordered so that each successive interval between adjacent elements is different, meaning that any possible interval formed in any way in the composition may cross-reference some adjacency in some four members of the row class. So-called *all-interval* rows are found in many of Babbitt's compositions;[31] a more recent development is the *all-trichord* row, in which each of the ten segmental trichords of a row is a member of a different collection class.[32] Such rows will be discussed at greater length in chapter 3.

One more feature of many of Babbitt's rows also derives from the structure of the all-combinatorial hexachords. Since each of these hexachordal types has the capability of being transposed onto its complement, each must therefore exclude at least one type of interval from its makeup. The three first-order hexachords, A, B, and C, each contain all the intervals except the tritone. D excludes the minor third; E excludes the major second and the tritone; and F, the whole-tone collection, excludes all intervals containing an odd number of half-steps. (There is one additional hexachord type that excludes an interval, but it can *only* be transposed onto its complement. It is [0, 1, 3, 4, 5, 8].) In rows built from segmentally discrete pairs of all-combinatorial hexachords (or [0, 1, 3, 4, 5, 8]), excluded intervals are only available *between* discrete segmental hexachords and therefore can function to signal boundaries between complementary hexachords within aggregates, in a manner analogous to octaves and unisons signaling boundaries between aggregates themselves. Thus, the selection of a hexachord type for the construction of a row can have an immediate effect upon the different functional roles to be played by the different types of intervals.

TRICHORDAL ARRAYS

While hexachordal combinatoriality underlies most of Babbitt's music, a particular generalization from it yields a structure that informs much of the work of his first period, the *trichordal array*.[33] This, combined with a technique derived from Webern, will be seen to have far-ranging consequences, not merely for Babbitt's first period, but throughout his career. By combining two pairs of hexachordally combinatorial rows, it is possible, given certain restrictions, to construct an array in which aggregates may be found over three different kinds of time spans: those representing the rows themselves, those representing the paired hexachords of hexachordally combinatorial rows, and those representing the columns formed by the four discrete segmental trichords. As is the case with hexachordal arrays, each level of

Example 1.8.   Aggregates in a trichordal array

aggregate in a trichordal array is shaped in ways that variously reflect the interval pattern of the underlying row class, and the resulting intervals between rows still form predictable patterns. This is illustrated in Example 1.8.

One can see that the columnar aggregates are shaped by still shorter segments of rows than those found in hexachordal arrays, each aggregate allowing a closer scrutiny of the manifestations of smaller portions of the row class's interval pattern. The more atomic nature of columnar aggregates in trichordal arrays invites a different kind of attention. It is here that we find Webern's influence. As has been noted many places, Webern found he could represent the transformational features of the twelve-tone system in microcosm by constructing his rows from four members of a single trichordal collection class, ordered to embody the four classical twelve-tone operations.[34] The trichord is, in fact, the smallest musical entity that can do so unambiguously. Babbitt wished the various aggregate spans in his trichordal arrays to exhibit the same sorts of transformations, and an abstract structure that would allow him to do so is illustrated in Example 1.9.[35] Such a structure imposes considerable constraints on the ways transformations of trichords may be distributed so that the resulting lynes might all be members of the same row class. For example, if the upper left corner is a given trichord, P, the upper right corner must be I(P). However, Babbitt, employing the all-combinatorial hexachords, also wished to be able to signal the hexachordal boundary in his lynes with the hexachord's excluded interval, and this was not possible if all four lynes were members of the same row class.

Babbitt's solution to the problem was to create so-called *derived rows*

A	B	C	D
C	D	A	B
B	A	D	C
D	C	B	A

A, B, C, D represent the four classical transformations of a trichord forming an aggregate.

Example 1.9.   Trichordal transformations
in a trichordal array

of differing orderings so that the constituent rows of a given array would not be all members of the same row class. Generally, Babbitt employs the same row class for both members of a hexachordally combinatorial pair of lynes, related by inversion. Many of his trichordal arrays consist of two blocks, the second the retrograde of the first, so that the entire array will contain the four classical transformations of the interval patterns of the two derived row classes.[36] This is illustrated in Example 1.10.

A significant consequence of Babbitt's decision was to push the fundamental interval pattern of a composition farther into the background, with successive arrays generated from various combinations of segments of the fundamental rows. Such a consequence, however, is itself a generalization of the principles that underlie Schoenberg's hexachordal combinatoriality: each successive aggregate of a Schoenberg array is generated from transformations of a segment of the fundamental interval pattern, drawn from two members of the row class.

One of the interesting possibilities of using trichordal segments to generate arrays involves the different ways trichords can generate hexachords. With the exception of the whole-tone scale collections, each all-combinatorial hexachord type can be generated by four different types of trichords, sometimes at more than one trichordal transposition level. With the exception of [0, 3, 6], which cannot generate any all-combinatorial hexachord type, and [0, 1, 6] and [0, 2, 6], which can only generate one all-combinatorial hexachord type each, all trichord types can generate at least two all-combinatorial hexachord types. Just as no two all-combinatorial hexachord types have the same catalog of trichordal generators, no two trichord types will generate the same catalog of all-combinatorial hexachords. All-combinatorial hexachords can also be partitioned into two trichords of different types, one, both, or neither of which might be a trichordal generator of the hexachord type in question, depending on the hexachord type. Example 1.11 is a chart of the relationships among the twelve trichord types and the six all-combinatorial hexachords.[37]

The various combinations of trichords into different types of hexa-

Example 1.10.   Trichordally derived trichordal array

chords allows the construction of pathways within and among various collection classes in the different aggregate interpretations of a trichordal array. Hexachords found segmentally in lynes of one array might later appear as the combination of trichords in hexachordally combinatorial lyne pairs, or they may appear generated from another type of trichord. For example, a chromatic ([0, 1, 2, 3, 4, 5]) hexachord generated from two [0, 1, 4] trichords might initially appear as a segment of a lyne, later appear as the combination of initial [0, 1, 4] trichords of two lynes generated from a pair of E-type ([0, 1, 4, 5, 8, 9]) hexachords, and still later appear as a lyne segment generated by two [0, 1, 3] trichords. Different compositional strategies can be assembled using various ways of tracing paths of relationships from the basic interval pattern of the fundamental row class into trichordal arrays, through a variety of different hexachord and trichord types. Much of Babbitt's first period of composition was spent exploring the possibilities inherent in the trichordal array and its simple extensions.[38] We shall examine their consequences in more detail in the next chapter.

In a trichordal array generated from a single trichord type, such as that found in Example 1.10, every aggregate may consist of a simple redistribution of four ordered collections. Except for the reassignment of the four collections to whatever articulative means are used to distinguish lynes of the array, the structure of the aggregates provides no mode of telling aggregates apart. Distinction among such aggregates is created by the composition of their details, the generation of significant collections and intervallic patterns from the counterpoint of lynes.[39]

Hexachords	Trichordal generators				Trichordal pairs
A [0, 1, 2, 3, 4, 5]	[0, 1, 2]	[0, 1, 3]	[0, 1, 4]	[0, 2, 4]	[0, 1, 2] + [0, 1, 5]
					[0, 1, 3] + [0, 1, 4]
					[0, 1, 3] + [0, 2, 5]
B [0, 2, 3, 4, 5, 7]	[0, 1, 3]	[0, 2, 5]	[0, 1, 5]	[0, 2, 4]	[0, 1, 2] + [0, 2, 7]
					[0, 1, 3] + [0, 3, 7]
					[0, 1, 4] + [0, 2, 5]
C [0, 2, 4, 5, 7, 9]	[0, 2, 5]	[0, 2, 7]	[0, 3, 7]	[0, 2, 4]	[0, 2, 7] + [0, 1, 5]
					[0, 2, 5] + [0, 3, 7]
					[0, 1, 3] + [0, 2, 5]
D [0, 1, 2, 6, 7, 8]	[0, 1, 2]	[0, 1, 5]	[0, 2, 7]	[0, 1, 6]	[0, 1, 6] + [0, 2, 6]
E [0, 1, 4, 5, 8, 9]	[0, 1, 4]	[0, 1, 5]	[0, 3, 7]	[0, 4, 8]	
F [0, 2, 4, 6, 8, t]	[0, 2, 4]	[0, 4, 8]	[0, 2, 6]		

Trichords and the all-combinatorial hexachords they generate

[0, 1, 2] : A, D
[0, 1, 3] : A, B
[0, 1, 4] : A, E
[0, 1, 5] : B, D, E
[0, 1, 6] : D
[0, 2, 4] : A, B, C, F
[0, 2, 5] : B, C
[0, 2, 6] : F
[0, 2, 7] : C, D
[0, 3, 6] : —
[0, 3, 7] : C, E
[0, 4, 8] : E, F

Example 1.11.   The all-combinatorial hexachords
and their trichordal generators

In Babbitt's practice, pitch classes in an aggregate of an array are abstractly ordered with regard only to their own lyne, and not to members of other lynes. This provides him with a great deal of flexibility for the composition of details. Decisions about the internal disposition of pitch classes in an aggregate beyond the partial order determined by the lynes are central to the compositional process and vary strategically from piece to piece. The differences in strategies for composing and assembling details, affected by the choice of hexachordal and trichordal pathways through the arrays, are the greatest source of variety in Babbitt's early music.

One consequence of Babbitt's practice illustrates the function of pitch class repetition within his aggregates. In Babbitt's compositions,

```
A│   B│C        D│  B│A          D│C
  C│D      A│B  D│  C            B│A
  B│  A│D      C│  A│  ·      B│C    D
D│  C│  B      A│C          D│    A│B
```

Example 1.12. The partitions of four distinct
elements into two or fewer parts
in a trichordal array

the elements of lynes of the arrays are ordered in time. Although pitch classes in an aggregate are generally fixed in register, a pitch class from one lyne is not ordered with regard to pitch classes from any of the other lynes and so may through repetition occur both before and after a pitch class from another lyne. This sort of repetition, although occurring within an aggregate, can still signify a boundary —in this case between the two aggregates of the two lynes in question.

Subsets and Partitions of Four Elements

While various pieces exhibit different strategies in the composition of their aggregates, one recurring pattern is worth noting as another example of Babbitt's maximal diversity principle. This pattern, applied variously to a wealth of different musical dimensions, can be found in critical roles throughout his career. Trichordal arrays naturally divide their aggregates each into four parts. There are fifteen subsets of a set of four elements (sixteen if the null set is counted), and these can be combined into eight partitions of a set of four distinct elements. Many of Babbitt's compositions contain some presentation of the fifteen subsets of four, frequently projected as the eight partitions of four distinct elements into two or fewer parts. Eight partitions can readily be accommodated by the eight aggregates of two blocks of a trichordal array, but Babbitt does not restrict himself to arrays alone. We shall see examples of combinations of trichord types in successive arrays, sections of whole arrays, dispositions of instruments, registers, and ensembles of instruments all presented in various dispositions of the subsets of four, articulated over a variety of time spans. Example 1.12 illustrates an example of the partitional list applied to the abstract structure of a two-block trichordal array, equivalent to that found in Example 1.9 plus its retrograde. As may be seen, the example actually contains two representations of the list of partitions of four, in terms both of the lynes of the array and of the array's trichordal elements. This is not a trivial consequence, as either representation could be maintained without the other, simply by swapping the positions of the (3+1) partitions.[40]

(dotted lines indicate underlying trichordal array)

53^21 53^21 43^22 43^22

Example 1.13. New partitions generated by swapping

ALL-PARTITION ARRAYS

Another technique that provides variety among aggregates of an array marks the major change between Babbitt's first and second periods. With few exceptions, the trichordal array dominated the music of Babbitt's first period. Despite the variety of ways that trichords could be fitted into an aggregate, and the variety of ways aggregates could be projected, the basic partition of the aggregate into lyne segments remained the same. In some of the first-period compositions Babbitt added a new twist: the generation of new aggregate partitions by swapping pitch classes across aggregate boundaries. This produced aggregates whose partition by lyne segment differed from trichordal aggregates. In addition to all the previously mentioned means of distinguishing aggregates, the resulting aggregates' very basic shape lent them a certain identity. This is illustrated in Example 1.13.[41]

During Babbitt's second period there emerged a number of compositions that generalized upon the partitional experiments of the first period. The new works employed a new kind of array whose distinguishing feature is its use of all possible partitions of an aggregate into a given number of parts, or fewer. These new arrays have come to be known as *all-partition arrays*.[42] As in Babbitt's earlier practice, each array is made up of hexachordally combinatorial lyne pairs, but unlike most trichordal arrays, all the lyne pairs employ members of a given row class. Like his earlier practice, Babbitt has restricted himself to the all-combinatorial hexachords in constructing his row classes.

The number of lyne pairs present in Babbitt's all-partition arrays is,

Partitions of 12

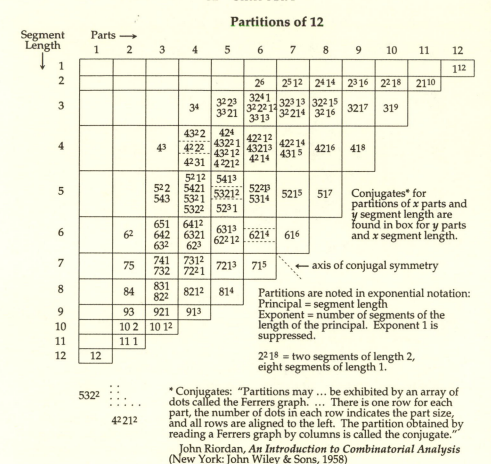

Segment Length ↓ \ Parts →	1	2	3	4	5	6	7	8	9	10	11	12
1												1^{12}
2						2^6	$2^5 1^2$	$2^4 1^4$	$2^3 1^6$	$2^2 1^8$	$2\,1^{10}$	
3				3^4	$3^2 2^3$; $3^3 2\,1$	$3\,2^4 1$; $3^2 2^2 1^2$; $3^3 1^3$	$3\,2^3 1^3$; $3^2 2\,1^4$	$3\,2^2 1^5$; $3^2 1^6$	$3\,2\,1^7$	$3\,1^9$		
4			4^3	$4\,3^2 2$; $4^2 2^2$; $4^2 3\,1$	$4\,2^4$; $4\,3\,2^2 1$; $4\,3^2 1^2$; $4^2 2\,1^2$	$4^2 1^4$; $4\,3\,2\,1^3$; $4\,2^3 1^2$	$4\,2^2 1^4$; $4\,3\,1^5$	$4\,2\,1^6$	$4\,1^8$			
5			$5^2 2$; $5\,4\,3$	$5^2 1^2$; $5\,4\,2\,1$; $5\,3^2 1$; $5\,3\,2^2$	$5\,4\,1^3$; $5\,3\,2\,1^2$; $5\,2^3 1$	$5\,2^2 1^3$; $5\,3\,1^4$	$5\,2\,1^5$	$5\,1^7$	*(see conjugates note)*			
6		6^2	$6\,5\,1$; $6\,4\,2$; $6\,3^2$	$6\,4\,1^2$; $6\,3\,2\,1$; $6\,2^3$	$6\,3\,1^3$; $6\,2^2 1^2$	$6\,2\,1^4$	$6\,1^6$					
7		$7\,5$	$7\,4\,1$; $7\,3\,2$	$7\,3\,1^2$; $7\,2^2 1$	$7\,2\,1^3$	$7\,1^5$						
8		$8\,4$	$8\,3\,1$; $8\,2^2$	$8\,2\,1^2$	$8\,1^4$							
9		$9\,3$	$9\,2\,1$	$9\,1^3$								
10		$10\,2$	$10\,1^2$									
11		$11\,1$										
12	12											

Conjugates* for partitions of x parts and y segment length are found in box for y parts and x segment length.

← axis of conjugal symmetry

Partitions are noted in exponential notation:
Principal = segment length
Exponent = number of segments of the length of the principal. Exponent 1 is suppressed.

$2^2 1^8$ = two segments of length 2, eight segments of length 1.

$5^2 3$ ⁚ ⁚ · · · · · $4^2 21^2$

* Conjugates: "Partitions may … be exhibited by an array of dots called the Ferrers graph. … There is one row for each part, the number of dots in each row indicates the part size, and all rows are aligned to the left. The partition obtained by reading a Ferrers graph by columns is called the conjugate."

John Riordan, *An Introduction to Combinatorial Analysis* (New York: John Wiley & Sons, 1958)

Example 1.14.   The seventy-seven partitions of twelve into twelve or fewer parts

with a couple of exceptions, determined by the number of distinct members of the underlying hexachord's mosaic class.[43] Thus Babbitt has constructed for himself arrays containing two lyne pairs (four parts) from the E hexachord type, three lyne pairs (six parts) from the D hexachord type, and six lyne pairs (twelve parts) from the A, B, and C hexachord types. An all-partition array will contain as many aggregates as there are different ways of slicing the number twelve into the number of parts present, or fewer. Thus, four-part arrays contain thirty-four aggregates, six-part arrays contain fifty-eight, and twelve-part arrays (usually) contain seventy-seven aggregates. Example 1.14 contains a list of the seventy-seven partitions of twelve into twelve or fewer parts.[44]

Example 1.15.   A block of an all-partition array

Example 1.14 displays the partitions symmetrically arrayed around the conjugal axis. Every partition is paired with another, or itself, by conjugation, which is defined and illustrated in the example.[45] Babbitt has occasionally restricted the length of segments in his all-partition arrays, and it is easy to see from the symmetrical display why both six-part arrays with segments of twelve or fewer elements and twelve-part arrays with segments of six or fewer elements should each have fifty-eight aggregates. A short portion of a typical all-partition array is found in Example 1.15. A number of complete arrays, notated in pitch class numbers, are found at the back of this volume.[46]

Because arrays may be interpreted in a wide variety of ways, and because they are not the easiest things in the world to construct, Babbitt has tended to reuse the same rather small bunch of all-partition arrays in a number of works, varying them under certain types of operations. We shall refer to different arrays within and between pieces related by various transformations as the same array type.

We shall examine the specific properties of some of these arrays and look at their various interpretations in chapter 3. Nevertheless, there are certain general properties of all-partition arrays that may be profitably discussed here. First, they are clearly another manifestation of

Babbitt's maximal diversity principle. Each aggregate, in addition to its unique constraints of partial ordering, is uniquely identified by its own partitional shape. Second, as with the trichordal arrays, the aggregates of all-partition arrays only partly determine the disposition of their constituent elements, so that all-partition arrays may manifest a number of compositional strategies in their musical realization. Third, because all-partition arrays are built out of hexachordally combinatorial lyne pairs, they have at their heart the Schoenbergian principle that has been present in Babbitt's music from the start. Because the hexachordal boundaries of lyne pairs are usually respected, particularly in those arrays using segments of at most six elements, the all-partition arrays will also have aggregates unfolding over several different time spans, articulated by different criteria.

In Babbitt's practice all-partition arrays are built up of blocks of rows consisting of one lyne pair from each of the distinct mosaics of the discrete segmental hexachord type. Thus each block will contain as many rows as there are lynes, and each lyne will unfold the same number of rows over the span of the array.

Because the number of partitions for a given number of lynes does not, in the cases mentioned, equal a simple multiple of the number of lynes, all-partition arrays must contain more aggregates than rows. The additional aggregates are made by repeating elements of rows in subsequent aggregates without violating order within lynes. Thus a four-part thirty-four-partition array will be made of eight blocks and contain thirty-two rows, and a twelve-part seventy-seven-partition array might contain seventy-two rows in six blocks, clearly with some repetitions of members of the underlying row class in addition to the repetition of row elements. While the fifty-eight-partition arrays of six parts might be built of fifty-four rows in nine blocks, those of twelve parts must be built of forty-eight rows in four blocks. This suggestive number, the number of rows in a row class, has motivated Babbitt to construct both his six-part arrays and those twelve-part arrays containing segments of at most six elements so that each member of a row class appears just once. Arrays of this sort may be considered *hyperaggregates*, or row class aggregates, unique presentations of all the members of the row class, just as aggregates are unique presentations of all twelve pitch classes. Such arrays exhibit one more manifestation of the principle of maximal diversity.

Before discussing how all-partition arrays are transformed, it is worth making a few remarks on their perceptual implications. At first blush it might seem that using all partitions in an array is an intellectual conceit, that no listener could be expected to count up a list of partitions, recognizing what has yet to be heard. Indeed, this is not the point of the all-partition array, just as counting to twelve is not the point of hearing aggregates. The desired goal is the construction of a long string of aggregates, each with a different partitional shape. All-partition arrays maximize this end. Repetition would entail different kinds of compositional responsibility. A different kind of difference would obtain between two aggregates of like partition and would invite an added layer of compositional solutions. This is not to say that such repetition is a priori an undesirable end, merely that it is not part of Babbitt's choices within this particular set of restrictions. Babbitt does repeat partitions within compositions, but he does so by presenting transformations of whole arrays.

Array transformation, within and between compositions, is slightly more complex than the analogous transformations of rows. It is easy to see that the retrogression of an entire array along with its partitions will maintain columnar aggregates while exchanging the sequential order of hexachords within lyne pairs. A simple transposition of the array by the interval that maps each hexachord onto its complement restores the order of hexachords within lyne pairs. Things get a little more complex under inversion, however. We can invert an entire array at a single index number, thus preserving columnar aggregates, but doing so scrambles the various positions of the hexachordal mosaics among lyne pairs, with regard to their participation in the array's partitions. This is because each lyne pair represents a different transposition of the hexachordal mosaic and thus would require its own index number to map onto itself. If we invert each lyne pair at its own appropriate index number, we can do so to retain the proper hexachordal content of lyne pairs for either inversion or retrograde inversion, but except for special cases, we will no longer wind up with aggregates in the partitional columns of the original array. Babbitt has used such transformations, and the term that has come to refer to such partitions is *weighted aggregates*.[47] Weighted aggregates have all sorts of interesting characteristics based on the kinds of collections that result within partitions.

Needless to say, weighted aggregates will yield a conspicuously different musical surface from classical aggregates, given the repetitions of pitch classes in different lynes. When listening to music composed with weighted aggregates we can still use twelve-tone listening strategies to good effect, however. In such passages, classical aggregates unfold over longer spans, by hexachordally combinatorial lyne pair and by individual row. The octaves and unisons found within weighted aggregates themselves serve a dual function, articulating collections in the surface, while indicating the contrapuntal independence of their disparate lyne sources. This will be discussed further in chapter 3.

Babbitt uses two other transformational techniques when reemploying an array in several compositions. In addition to the transformations discussed above, Babbitt uses the *circle-of-fifths transformation*, which maps the chromatic scale onto the circle of fifths and vice versa. This operation maintains aggregates within the partitions while changing the underlying row's interval pattern in predictable ways.[48] The other transformational technique is to change the order of blocks in an array. This can only be done, however, to those arrays whose blocks are self-contained and do not exhibit any swapping across block boundaries to form desired partitions.

It must not be thought that Babbitt's use of a given array and its transformations in various pieces implies that the pieces will be simple recompositions of one another. On the contrary, every array can be viewed from a variety of perspectives, including both the manner in which its lynes are projected and in the way that its aggregates are composed. This lends distinct strategies and qualities to each piece of a group using transformations of the same array. On the other hand, it must not be thought that an array is so remote from our experience of a composition that it is there only as a tool for the composer. Indeed, those compositions based on the same array type frequently share characteristics akin to a family resemblance, largely in part to their sharing of a particularly powerful kind of musical gene.

As the rows of Babbitt's music are spread over increasingly larger time spans, he has found it necessary to become very clear in his techniques for projecting rows on the musical surface. As most aggregates in his all-partition pieces are built of segments from more than one row, his music can contain very fanciful mixes of instruments and registers—but over the long span we can hear that they result from combinations of much more regular presentations of rows in individual instruments or registers. Babbitt's compositions use a variety of ways of projecting lynes, and the change of lyne articulation through the span of a piece frequently is one of its shaping aspects, but these changes are generally coordinated with the completion of blocks of the array.

Instrumentation, articulation, and register have all been used in various combinations to project lynes of an array, as has syllabic structure in some of Babbitt's vocal compositions.[49] While many works separate lynes of a combinatorial pair by some means, in other works the two lynes are not distinguishable in the musical surface. The partial orderings derivable from Schoenberg's hexachordal combinatoriality form a layer of relations in Babbitt's music that lies between relations determined by the array and those determined by the rows themselves. Changing the degree to which one may distinguish combinatorial lyne pairs over the span of a piece frequently generates the long-range dramatic structure in Babbitt's compositions. We shall detail a number of related compositional strategies in the following chapters.

Babbitt's third and most recent period is marked by his use of *superarrays*, consisting of all-partition or trichordal arrays assembled into larger contrapuntal networks. Superarrays have taken several forms, combining two, three, and four different transformations of an array type in various ways. Superarrays are adumbrated in the very structure of Babbitt's arrays themselves. Each array, as noted above, is the combination of Schoenbergian combinatorial pairs, so that each array is itself a superarray of hexachordal arrays, carefully constructed to yield aggregates over the shortest time spans.[50]

One of the most interesting aspects of Babbitt's construction of superarrays is found in those using four strata of constituent arrays. Several four-part superarrays present a sequence of all fifteen different ways of putting together sections of their constituent arrays, the same sort of list we discussed earlier in conjunction with the trichordal arrays. In some of these superarrays, the underlying array type may be broken into four blocks, and Babbitt has managed in certain situations to superimpose a presentation of all possible combinations of from one to four block types on his presentation of the fifteen combinations of the constituent arrays. Thus the four solo array segments contain together all the partitions of the underlying array type. The solo sections of such superarrays provide a window to the structure of their constituent arrays, just as the various partitions in an array provide us with insights into the structure of its underlying row class. This is illustrated in Example 1.16.

Some of the most recent works show even more elaborate underlying structures. In certain concerted works, the superarray is itself an accompaniment to a solo part based on still another structure. Solo parts have themselves been built of simple and circle-of-fifths transformations of the accompaniment's array type, superarrays, and trichordal arrays generated from the successive trichords of the composition's fundamental ordering.

In many ways Babbitt's most current compositional practices show a reemergence of some of his earliest techniques, applied to much more complex structures. Once again we find lists of the subsets of four elements, but now applied to ensembles and arrays and combined in double interlocked patterns. We also find trichordal arrays structuring significant portions of compositions. An additional tech-

Array 1	I	II		III		IV	IV				III	II	I	
Array 2		IV	III		II	I		I		II	III	IV		
Array 3			I			II		III	IV		IV		III	II	I
Array 4				IV			III	II		I	I	II		III	IV

I, II, III, IV represent the four distinct block types to within the four
classical transformations.

Example 1.16.   The superarray structure
of *Ars Combinatoria*

nique delves even further into the past: in one piece, Babbitt actually
de-composes the arrays of a superarray, pulling them apart variously by
lyne and lyne pair, frequently revealing the Schoenbergian hexachordal combinatoriality that underlies all of his structural developments.
Paradoxically, as Babbitt's structures grow more elaborate, they more
readily reveal the accreted layers of his compositional thinking over
the past forty years.

Babbitt's Rhythmic Structures

Just as he had worked through the implications of the twelve-tone
system with regard to pitch structure, so Babbitt rethought the issue
of rhythm from first principles as he developed his compositional
practices. Although Schoenberg had employed traditional rhythmic
patterns in his twelve-tone music, Babbitt was quick to notice that he
had done so to project certain kinds of twelve-tone relationships.[51]
But since much traditional rhythmic practice is inevitably tied to tonal
syntax, Babbitt sought ways to create rhythmic structures that
stemmed directly from twelve-tone pitch relations rather than simply
adapt practices from earlier music for his particular ends.[52] This has
caused Babbitt throughout his career to readdress fundamental notions about many rhythmic issues, such as the nature of beats, measures, and meters. Babbitt's rhythmic practice has been considerably
more varied than his pitch practice, and it is possible to identify several different rhythmic techniques conjoined in myriad ways in his
output.

DURATION ROWS

During his first period Babbitt experimented with various rhythmic
approaches, but one technique that emerges in a number of composi-

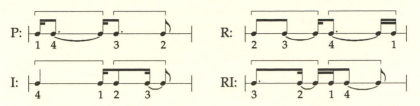

Example 1.17. *Composition for Four Instruments*: rhythmic derivation

tions is the *duration row*.[53] In his earliest published works, Babbitt
used series of four durations, compounded in various ways. As we
shall see in the following chapter, the *Composition for Four Instruments*
uses a pattern of four durations—1 4 3 2—which is transformed in
two distinct manners.[54] For the moment we shall be concerned only
with the one that most clearly mimics the classical pitch class operations. There are four forms of the series, including the series itself.
Retrogression is the simple reversal of the duration string. Inversion
is formed by subtracting the four durations from the value five. Retrograde inversion combines the operations. It is important to note that
Babbitt has picked his duration string so that the two discrete pairs
sum to five. This has several implications. Any manifestation of the
duration pattern is divisible into equal halves, and the various transformations preserve the two orderings of the durational pairs in different orderings relative to each other. This is illustrated in Example
1.17.

In later works of the first period, Babbitt expanded the idea of the
duration row to orderings of twelve durations of increasing incremen-
tal size from one to twelve durational units. The ordering of the durations in these works are simple numerical translations of the pitch
class orderings of the works' rows. By assigning numbers to each
pitch class, from one to twelve, Babbitt simply created orderings of
the resulting durations. A particularly clear example may be found in
the String Quartet no. 2, at that moment where the work's underlying
interval pattern first emerges in its most concentrated form. If we
read B♭ as one, we can see that the row found in the instruments
translates directly into the durational scheme of the musical surface.
This passage is found in Example 1.18.

Babbitt did not always simply present his duration rows as sustained tones. A duration frequently is initiated by a short note followed by rests or is subdivided into equal-length pulses. As the
pulses themselves often correspond with the unit of the durational
row, or with a multiple thereof, change of row duration is indicated

Example 1.18. String Quartet no. 2: duration row. Copyright © 1967 by Associated Music Publishers, Inc. (BMI). International copyright secured. All rights reserved. Reprinted by permission

by a change of subdivision. The passage in the String Quartet no. 2 immediately following that in Example 1.18 illustrates the principle. It is found in Example 1.19.

As we shall see in the following chapter, Babbitt applied many of his pitch-structural techniques to his duration rows, including trichordal derivation, combinatoriality, and combination by means of the partitions of four. These operations have a variety of consequences, particularly when combined with his subdivisional technique.

The use of duration rows has a number of interesting consequences. First of all, any row of the twelve durations of one through twelve will of necessity be seventy-eight durational units long. Different metrical interpretations will group a duration row into different numbers of beats, depending on the durational unit. Using the sextuplet as a unit yields thirteen beats per duration row, but Babbitt frequently uses the sixteenth-note or the thirty-second–note as the unit. The former will cause the durational row to be nineteen and one-half beats long, whereas the latter will be nine and three-quarters beats long. The placement of such durational rows with regard to the metrical beat will cycle, either every two or every four recurrences.

One might suppose that Babbitt's metrical notation is purely for convenience, and so the placement of durational rows with regard to the beat is immaterial, but two things suggest otherwise. First, when Babbitt uses different metrical interpretations of his durational rows, he frequently does so in ways that use the completion of a cycle to mark a significant articulation point in the pitch structure. For example, the final portion of the String Quartet no. 2 divides into three

Example 1.19.   String Quartet no. 2: even note value strings. Copyright © 1967 by Associated Music Publishers, Inc. (BMI). International copyright secured. All rights reserved. Reprinted by permission

large sections, each initiated (with the partial exception of the last) by a composition of one of the rows of the underlying row class, followed by more complex combinatorial arrays. The first two sections are each four duration rows long, and the unit is the thirty-second–note. This guarantees that the initiation of each major section of the finale coincides with a notated downbeat, as illustrated in Example 1.20.

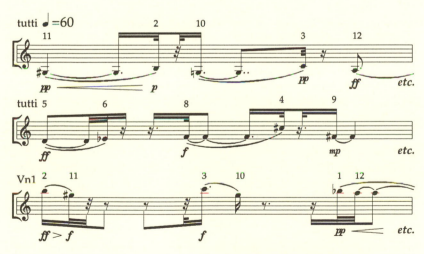

Example 1.20.   String Quartet no. 2: Initiations of major sections, part 4. Copyright © 1967 by Associated Music Publishers, Inc. (BMI). International copyright secured. All rights reserved. Reprinted by permission

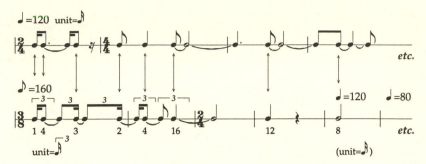

Example 1.21. *Composition for Four Instruments*: compensatory tempo and durational unit changes

Second, Babbitt sometimes changes the metrical interpretation of a set of duration rows by altering the tempo, while simultaneously changing the unit in a compensatory fashion, so that the absolute duration of the unit, and thus the rows, in real time does not change. The resulting changes of tempo are vivid in one's hearing of the music, articulating sections of the pitch structure of the composition. Such a tempo change is illustrated in Example 1.21.

The preceding suggests that one of the roles of tempo and beat in this music is to establish a grid against which to hear the rhythmic play. The interplay created by the change of this grid forms one of the compositional resources of Babbitt's early music.

The particular translation of pitch structures to the temporal domain that Babbitt used to create duration rows raises a number of serious problems. The analogy between pitch class and duration does not stand up well to scrutiny. We do not hear duration classes in the same way that we recognize pitch classes, and of course there is no reason to limit durations to twelve. More important, rows of pitch classes are in effect rows of *locations*, the distances between which form intervals. Transposition of a pitch class row changes the pitch class location associated with each order number, but one of the most powerful aspects of twelve-tone relations is that transposition of pitch class rows preserves the pitch class intervals between order numbers. More immediately, when we transpose a melody, we can instantly recognize it as the same melody, no matter how the pitch classes change.

Duration rows, on the other hand, are not orderings of locations but are already orderings of temporal spans, or time intervals. Transposition of a duration row relocates the elements, but as the elements

Example 1.22. Duration row transposition

are themselves intervals, the result is a scrambling of the perceived temporal intervals. This is illustrated in Example 1.22.

What is the equivalent of pitch class intervals in a durational row? It is the *difference* between successive durations, a very different sense of interval from that in the pitch domain. Thus the interval between durations of one and two units is the same as the durational interval between seven and eight units—a difference in each case of a single unit, but hardly equivalent in our hearing. The problem is compounded, of course, by the fact that as we continue to ascend incrementally, we shall eventually have to move from twelve units to one again, producing a supposed intervallic equivalence between a difference of one and a difference of minus eleven.

The analogy between pitch class rows and duration rows also breaks down as soon as one starts to investigate the effects of the classical operations. While the resulting sets of permutations of the durations themselves have definable and consistent kinds of relationships, they are not the same as those found among the same sets of permutations of the pitch class rows.[55] Nevertheless, Babbitt was able to manipulate his durational rows in ways that yielded significant kinds of relationships in themselves. First of all, retrogression of duration rows produces a clearly audible transformation by simply reversing the order of durations. Additional interesting results can be obtained from a careful use of inversion.

We shall suggest some of the relational possibilities of duration rows by examining the transformations Babbitt used in his String Quartet no. 2. The particular duration row found in Example 1.18 was selected so that the sum of the durations for each hexachord is the same. In the quartet, Babbitt limited himself to transposition by T_6, combined with retrogression, and inversion, which in this case entails subtracting every element from the value thirteen. The effects of these limited operations are considerable. Alone or in combination,

Example 1.23.   String Quartet no. 2: duration row transformations

they will either maintain or exchange the contents of the two discrete hexachords, simply reordering the two collections of durations within the fixed total durations of the hexachords themselves. This is illustrated in Example 1.23.

The row has an additional property with significant consequences under inversion. The discrete dyads of one of its ordered hexachords map onto themselves under the form of inversion that maps the contents of hexachords onto themselves. Obviously, this will be of great use in the pitch domain, but it can also be meaningfully interpreted with the duration rows. In the hexachords in question, the elements of each pair—the durations—will simply change places under the proper inversion. Since all three dyads map onto themselves at a fixed index number, the sums of the three pairs of durations must be equal, and therefore, the hexachord must consist of three equal larger durations. This has a considerable effect on the surface of the music, creating larger equal pulses of unequal pairs of pulses. Thus duration rows provide a palpable manifestation of the usually abstract concept, the index number of inversion. This is illustrated in Example 1.24.

The preceding does not exhaust either the possibilities or the problems of duration rows, but these will be further explored in the following chapter.[56] Babbitt was aware of these problems and found a solution to them in what became his most consistent and comprehensive rhythmic practice: the time point system.[57]

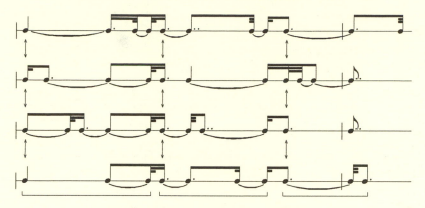

Example 1.24.   Preserved composite durations

TIME POINT ROWS

In the time point system, Babbitt sought to find a more profound analogy between the properties of twelve-tone pitch structure and his rhythmic structures. Admittedly, the temporal domain is profoundly different from the pitch domain, and so any translation of pitch structures to rhythmic structures will raise many questions. Nevertheless, the time point system's richer set of analogies to the properties he employed for pitches allowed him to highlight even more the perceptual differences between the two domains.

The mechanics of the time point system are as follows. The role of the octave in the pitch domain is taken over in the rhythmic domain by a fixed time span called the *modulus*. The modulus is itself subdivided into twelve units of equal length, representing the twelve time point classes. This is illustrated in Example 1.25.

Moduli are strung together to provide a regular grid against which time point rows are projected. A time point row consists of a specific ordering of the twelve time points and extends across as many concatenated spans of modular length as necessary. As in the pitch domain, the operations are fully defined as operations upon the elements—in

Example 1.25.   Time
point modulus

P: 0 9 1 8 5 4 2 6 7 3 t e
RI9(P): 1 2 9 5 6 t 8 7 4 e 3 0
I0(P): 0 3 e 4 7 8 t 6 5 9 2 1
R(P): e t 3 7 6 2 4 5 8 1 9 0

Example 1.26.   Time point rows: the four classical transformations

this case time points, or their order numbers. Examples of all four transformations are found in Example 1.26.

Babbitt allows himself to repeat a given element at a given order number in a row before proceeding to the next, so time point rows have no maximum length. However, time point rows do have minimal durations, consisting of the sums of the time intervals between adjacent elements of the row.

The contrast between time point rows and duration rows is considerable. The elements of time point rows are themselves not durations but locations within the modulus. Therefore, the resulting pattern of durations is a set of intervals between locations, just like the interval pattern of a pitch class row. The consequences of this are significant. Unlike duration rows, time point rows maintain the same sorts of relationships under the various twelve-tone operations as pitch class rows. Transposition preserves the duration pattern of a time point row, while shifting it against the modular grid. In duration rows, transposition scrambles the order of durations. Retrograding a duration row reverses the order of its elements, the twelve time intervals, but the same musical effect, the reversal of an ordered string of intervals, is associated with retrograde *inversion* in both pitch class rows and time point rows.[58] Furthermore, with time point rows combinatoriality becomes meaningful in ways that simply do not apply in the

RT6(P): 438
RI0(P): 1 2 9 5
I7(P):   7 t 6 e
P: 0

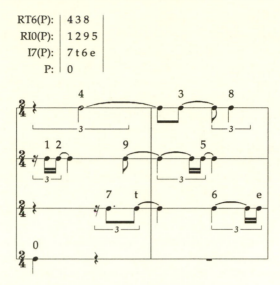

Example 1.27. A time point aggregate

case of duration rows. Relations among intervals between elements of different rows, a crucial aspect of combinatoriality in the pitch domain, are present in an analogous manner in the time point domain.[59] This is illustrated in Example 1.27.

Time point rows, as opposed to duration rows, provide a far greater potential for analogous structuring between the pitch and the temporal domains. Nevertheless, there are significant perceptual differences between the two musical dimensions that make it worthwhile considering the compositional consequences of the translation. One difference is the fact that time point rows represent the ordering of elements of a given musical dimension within their own dimension, but this can be duplicated in the pitch domain by ordering pitch classes in register as opposed to time.[60] More critically, our ways of cataloging intervals in the temporal domain are fundamentally different from those we use in the pitch domain. For example, we can easily register both diminution and augmentation of rhythmic patterns over all sorts of different time spans in ways that do not translate back into the pitch class domain. Furthermore, the quality of a temporal interval can change in *character* depending on its placement within the measure. Perhaps the most fundamental question, however, concerns the choice of twelve elements for the time point rows. Babbitt himself has pointed out that there is nothing inherent in the temporal domain that invites the use of twelve, and the profound perceptual differences between the two domains makes any simple translation seem at first blush more an act of numerology than composition.[61]

The significance of the translation of pitch class row structure to the temporal domain arises from Babbitt's longtime predilection for manifesting similar sorts of distributions of events in different domains over different spans of time. Babbitt's mature use of the time point system coincided with his first uses of the all-partition array. Those pieces whose rhythms are based on the time point system employ the same all-partition array type in both domains. Time point arrays and pitch class arrays generally do not unfold at the same rate in a composition and are not correlated in consistent ways. However, the analogy between the two domains arises from the distribution of the various partitions through each array. Just as Babbitt is extremely careful to ensure that the projections of lynes in a pitch class array remain consistent over prolonged stretches, so is he careful to maintain the differentiation among time point lines over analogous stretches. This allows the listener to follow analogous distributions of qualitatively differentiated material in the two domains.

Babbitt frequently reinforces this impression in the ways he distinguishes pitch class lynes and time point lynes in the musical surface. As suggested above, pitch class lynes or lyne pairs are frequently distributed registrally within an instrument. Similarly, time point lynes or lyne pairs are usually carried by dynamic levels.[62] Pitch class lynes projected by registers from low to high often have their counterparts in the temporal domain carried by dynamics ranging from soft to loud. The results of these dispositions are analogous contours within the registral and dynamic dimensions of a composition, frequently unfolding at different rates.

The varying structures of aggregates within an array, whether it be in the pitch or the temporal domain, permit various ways of creating relationships based on their interior composition. How these are accomplished varies from piece to piece, or from section to section within a composition. We shall examine some of these in the following chapters, but it is clear that the abstract structure of the array itself controls the distribution of such relationships, and thus their distributions in both the pitch and the temporal domains.

In short, the most powerful aspect of the analogy between the pitch and the temporal domain arises from the ways events of different sorts may be distributed in like manners. These, in turn, are dependent on the structure of the array, and the structure of the array is fundamentally dependent on the structure of its underlying row class. Using the same abstract interval pattern for both time point and pitch class rows provides Babbitt with the necessary tools for pursuing his desired compositional ends.

One of the most interesting aspects of the time point system is the way it interacts with meter in Babbitt's music. The primary structuring element of the time point system, the modulus, does not occur as a musical a priori in the same way that the octave does in the pitch domain. It must be established and maintained for the listener to be able to perceive many of the relationships created by time point rows. The music provides enough cues to the listener to be able to hear a regular grid against which to measure different time spans. Babbitt accomplishes this by having his time-point rows unfold against a regular metrical background.[63]

In most time point pieces, the modular length coincides with either the beat or the bar. This has a variety of consequences. First, meter is more intimately involved in the projection of time point rows than in the projection of duration rows. The latter cycle against a regular meter in ways mentioned above, but it is the meter itself that allows one to place and recognize transformations of time point rows. Second, the coincidence of modular length and meter creates qualitatively different beat classes, distinguished by their placement with regard to the beat. An event heard on the beat has a subtly different character from an event heard just before, just after, or between beats, and different beats in a measure will themselves have different qualities. Babbitt is highly attuned to these differences, and good performances of his music make them vivid. Time intervals acquire additional qualities depending on the nature of the beat classes forming their end points. A given time interval might arise from two very different pairings of beat classes, just as two time intervals of different length might reflect a similar pairing of beat classes. The potential for additional kinds of relationship is considerable. This is illustrated in Example 1.28.

Metrical beat classes coincide with the elements of time point rows in many compositions, but in passages of some works they do not. When the element is one fifth or one seventh of a beat, large-scale polyrhythms are formed, cycling the modulus against the meter. In these passages Babbitt is still at pains to keep the sense of the meter alive, while maintaining a vivid sense of the modulus.

The time-point system is very flexible, and Babbitt has used a number of different ways to enrich it. Changes of tempi can be brought about in two ways, each with its own significance. One way is to change the unit of the modulus, and thus the meter, while maintaining a basic pulse. Another is to change the actual underlying pulse of the meter. Each strategy, while sounding very different, creates the

Qualitative similarities of different
temporal intervals:

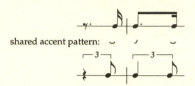

Different qualities of a fixed
temporal interval:

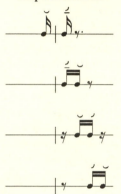

Example 1.28.   Temporal
interval qualities

opportunity for embedding some absolute set of durations in different tempi. Babbitt's music is full of augmentations and diminutions of various rhythmic patterns constructed from different sets of time-point intervals. In this and other ways Babbitt exploits the particular qualities of the rhythmic domain within the constraints of the time-point system. His works contain an enormous variety of combinations of such strategies to create a wide spectrum of rhythmic character.

One feature Babbitt has carried over from his duration row practice is the use of subdivisions to fill time spans, such as the intervals created by time point rows and their combinations. However, with time point row subdivisions, unlike duration row subdivisions, Babbitt avoids using those subdivisions that would articulate elements of the modulus. The subtler interaction of meter and combinations of rows in time point arrays encourages a stricter differentiation between attacks that arise as row elements and those that arise within subdivi-

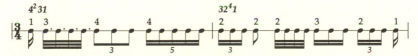

Example 1.29. *Semi-Simple Variations*: the subsets of four distinct items

sions. Because of the distinction, Babbitt need not use complete
strings of equal note values in his subdivisions and so can create various sorts of cross-reference by means of incomplete strands. We shall
observe several examples in later chapters.

ADDITIONAL RHYTHMIC PRACTICES

Babbitt's rhythmic practice has not been limited to duration rows or
the time point system and their extensions. Several compositions
from throughout his career have used still different ways to slice up
the musical surface. Some works use a steady pulse that is subdivided
according to different sorts of strategies. *Semi-Simple Variations* of
1956, for example, uses the sixteen subsets of four distinct elements
(the fifteen discussed above plus the null set) to shape its beats.[64] This
is illustrated in Example 1.29.

Other pieces use other schemes to break up measures containing
twelve elements into partitions of different sorts, which are further
subdivided using one or more strategies. Example 1.30 is derived
from two compositions, *Playing for Time* and *My Complements to Roger*,
piano pieces of the 1970s, each of which contains one pitch class aggregate per bar. In the first piece, the partitions of the twelve

Example 1.30.   Additional rhythmic strategies

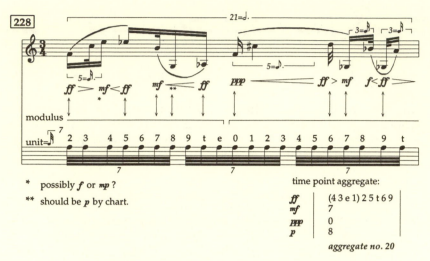

Example 1.31. *My Ends Are My Beginnings*. Reprinted by permission of C. F. Peters Corporation

sixteenth-notes of each bar are the same as those found in the aggregate of the pitch class array present. The segments of each partition are marked by changing subdivision, in the manner employed with duration rows. In the second piece, the rhythmic partition of each bar is determined by the *conjugate* of the partition of the pitch class array aggregate present. The resulting segments are then subdivided with equal note value strings that may or may not be complete, depending on issues of pitch class detail. Like those associated with the time point system, the subdivisions of the segments are usually formed of durations different from the elements used to determine the partition of the bar, to avoid ambiguity.

In addition to controlling surface rhythms, Babbitt has also used time point rows to control the duration of pitch class aggregates. In those pieces employing controlled aggregate durations, a concatenation of single time point rows, usually using the beat as the unit, determines the durations for pitch class aggregates, which are themselves rhythmically shaped in one or more ways. Some compositions use steady pulses that are further subdivided, but other works are more complex. In *My Ends Are My Beginnings*, for solo clarinet player doubling on B♭ and bass clarinets, the duration of pitch class aggregates is determined by a string of time point rows using the beat as the unit, the aggregates are shaped by a time point array unfolding at the rate of three pitch class aggregates per time point aggregate, and the modulus changes as often as once per pitch class aggregate.

The time spans created by the time point array are further subdivided to create an intricate web of rhythms interacting over the whole span of the piece. Each layer is distinguished by means of dynamics and rhythmic subdivisions, but there is ample opportunity for cross reference, and much of the play in the music arises from the multiple interpretation of rhythmic patterns in different portions of the composition. A brief portion of the piece is found in Example 1.31.

The foregoing is but a quick overview of some of the compositional practices found in Milton Babbitt's music of the past four decades. In the next three chapters we shall look at the wide variety of ways they have been combined in his compositions. While Babbitt has established for himself a clear set of established practices, each new piece is a unique exploration of their interactions, providing fresh, new perspectives on his musical world. A study of Babbitt's music celebrates the individuality of his compositions within their encompassing communality.

2

MAPPING TRICHORDAL PATHWAYS

(1947–1960)

MILTON BABBITT'S first published compositions reveal the degree to which he had assimilated and expanded upon Arnold Schoenberg's and Anton Webern's developments of twelve-tone compositional thought. The *Three Compositions for Piano* and the *Composition for Four Instruments* are fully realized works, the latter foreshadowing many of Babbitt's later techniques. These two are not his first essays in composition, however, and his list of works contains several pieces withdrawn or unfinished from this time and earlier. Nevertheless, it is extraordinary how fully Babbitt had realized the potential of twelve-tone composition at the very beginning of his artistic journey. These works obviously manifest a great deal of compositional and aesthetic thought and can in no way be considered experimental or tentative. Much of Babbitt's growth as a composer occurred during the years of World War II, when he was too encumbered with other responsibilities to write music.[1] This enforced period of compositional introspection produced a maturation of the ideas that blossomed forth in a string of works reflecting a wealth of approaches to composing within a certain set of structural constraints.

Most of the compositions from the late 1940s through the early 1960s are based on Babbitt's synthesis of Schoenbergian and Webernian practices, the trichordal array. Trichordal arrays have been discussed in the previous chapter as abstract structures; here we shall examine a number of compositions that employ them to understand the many different ways they can be used to create a vivid piece of music. Although all the works we shall discuss employ trichordal arrays, no two compositions operate in quite the same manner. Each has its own collection of compositional strategies, and each unfolds in fresh, individual ways. As I suggested above, Babbitt's works represent a constant recombination of a certain limited number of ideas, yet each achieves its own identity through the ways these ideas are combined and unfolded. Developing an appreciation for the interaction of a composition's individuality in light of its communality with a body of work goes a long way toward enriching our enjoyment not only of the composition itself but of the body of work from which it springs. This is as true of Mozart as it is of Babbitt, but we are more accustomed to dealing with the myriad works of the common practice period than we are to appreciating the variety of growth flourishing in the fertile soil of Schoenberg's garden. Babbitt himself has pointed out that twelve-tone compositions have fewer shared characteristics than tonal works, so that a listener has less to bring to a hearing of a twelve-tone piece.[2] Nevertheless, Babbitt's own body of work, through its repertoire of shared characteristics, begins to show us ways to develop more educated listening strategies that may extend to other composers' work as well.

In the following pages we shall examine a series of compositions using trichordal arrays that exhibit certain similar formal strategies. We shall follow with some examples of other works of Babbitt's first compositional period that use trichordal arrays to articulate quite different large-scale formal patterns. Crucial to all of the following discussion is the trichordal mosaic, discussed briefly in the preceding chapter and illustrated in Example 1.2. Trichordal mosaics fit into trichordal arrays in several ways, all of them important to our understanding of the music. They are found in both the columns and the lynes of the array as well as between hexachords of the array's combinatorial lyne pairs. Each of these three mosaic locations plays its own compositional role, and the variety of different mosaics and mosaic classes they may represent depends on the nature of their constituent trichords and the orientation of the resultant hexachords within trichordal arrays. Much of the play in this music involves mosaics changing location and orientation throughout a trichordal array. See Example 2.1.

An additional compositional resource involving trichordal mosaics is the fact that mosaics from different classes can contain the same multiplicity of trichord types. Such mosaics frequently have one generated hexachordal mosaic in common, so that they may be compared and contrasted under similar array circumstances.[3] One such pair is illustrated in Example 2.2.

A Wellspring of Possibilities:
The *Composition for Four Instruments*

Babbitt's first published ensemble work is a watershed of twelve-tone compositional practice. The *Composition for Four Instruments* is fully formed in its use of Babbitt's extensions to twelve-tone technique and in its multidimensional use of purely self-referential structures. We shall take a very close look at this piece, as it illuminates a wide vari-

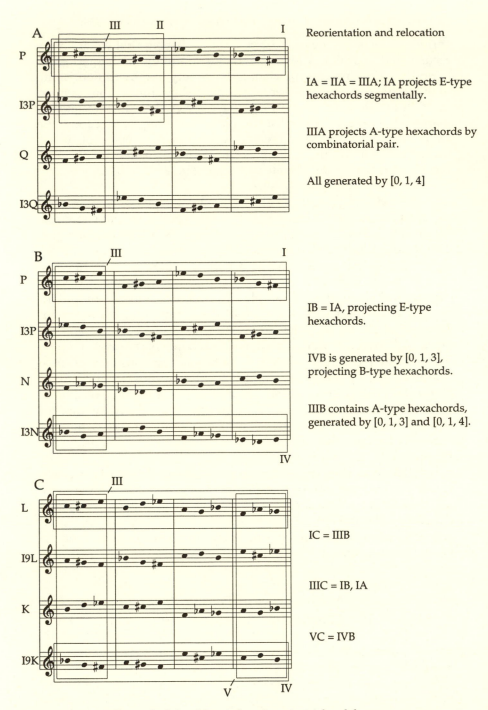

Example 2.1.   Mosaic locations in trichordal arrays

W1 and W2 both contain two [0, 1, 4]'s and two [0, 1, 3]'s, and both can project A-type hexachords, but W1 is not in the same mosaic class as W2.

Example 2.2.   Two mosaics

ety of Babbitt's compositional practices and dramatically demonstrates their effect on our hearing of twelve-tone music.[4]

The piece is written for two winds and two strings: flute, clarinet, violin, and cello. This fundamental division of the ensemble into two pairs of similar but distinct members is replicated in various dimensions throughout the work. It is apparent to the most casual hearing that the piece is divided into sections, each articulated by a different subset of the whole ensemble, which is itself reserved for the concluding section. A closer listening reveals that sections are grouped in pairs, by complementary instrumental subsets, so that in fact the whole ensemble is used every two sections.[5] As we might expect, the composition unfolds a succession of all the possible partitions of four distinct things into two or fewer parts. Such a pattern forms a list of all the subsets of the collection of four elements, each appearing once. Example 2.3 is a chart of the sections of the work. The abstract pattern found in Example 2.3, variously interpreted, informs every dimension of the *Composition for Four Instruments*, over a variety of temporal spans.

Example 2.4 reproduces the opening clarinet solo. At first glance, there does not appear to be much of a relationship between the solo in Example 2.4 and the unfolding ensemble partitions found in Example 2.3, but let us look more closely. The first aggregate, up through bar 6, is distributed between the high and low registers of the instrument. The first three notes, separated from the remaining notes by a rest, form the interval pattern +4 −3. We can hear this same pattern, simply transformed, in the lower register of what follows. When we separate the remaining dyads into strands articulated by both register and time we can hear the same intervallic pattern in two further transformations. The four transformations, +4 −3 and −4 +3 in the lower

Violin		—		—	—			—		—	—			—	—	
Cello		—	—			—	—			—		—			—		—	
Flute		—		—	—			—			—			—	—		—	
Clarinet	—		—		—			—	—			—			—	—	

Example 2.3. *Composition for Four Instruments*:
distribution of ensembles

register and *+3 −4*, *−3 +4* in the upper, represent the four classical transformations of the twelve-tone system.[6]

Continuing through the second aggregate, we hear the opening three notes of the piece, in the same order, transposed up an octave. This ordered collection is conjoined with another of the ordered collections we have already heard. The latter, we may retrospectively realize, was perhaps the trickiest to extract from the preceding aggregate, being not only mixed up temporally with two others but registrally buried as well. Here in the second aggregate, nevertheless, it is clearly presented in its own register, in counterpoint with the clearest of the preceding aggregate's ordered collections. Similarly, we may hear the remainder of the aggregate divided between registers playing the two remaining ordered collections from the first aggregate.

The third aggregate initially seems to cloud the increased clarity created in the second aggregate, but the upper edge of its initial burst reveals once again the ordered collection found in the low register at the outset of the second aggregate, and we may retrospectively realize that the lower bunch of notes not only reproduces the same six-note collection heard in the same registral position in the first aggregate but may also be separated into the same pair of ordered collections as before. The third aggregate closes with the remaining ordered collection in the highest register, articulated by rests at each end, forming the most unambiguous presentation of any of the ordered collections since the opening gesture of the composition. Examination of the following aggregates reveals similar combinations of a small repertoire of ordered collections, all articulating transformations of the same interval pattern. In the fifth and following aggregates, the interior order of each of the four collections is retrograded, but their content is maintained.

The preceding has been but one pass over the span of music, and we shall return to this passage shortly, but our discussion begins to illuminate a way to parse the music's highly variegated surface into a more regular underlying pattern. As must be evident by now, the

Example 2.4. *Composition for Four Instruments*: opening solo.
Copyright © 1949 by Merion Music, Inc. Used by permission

Example 2.5. *Composition for Four Instruments*:
opening solo trichordal array

clarinet solo is constructed from a trichordal array derived from a single trichord type ordered by a single interval pattern. A quick glance suggests that because there are eight aggregates in the passage, the array must contain two blocks of four lynes. Because of the ordering constraints mentioned in the previous chapters, the rows of the lynes cannot all be members of the same row class if each aggregate is to contain all four classical transformations of the trichords. Example 2.5 is the array of the opening solo.

The array chart suggests some analogies with the ensemble itself. Just as the ensemble is divided into two pairs of similar but distinct instruments, so the four ordered trichords can be divided into two pairs of transpositionally related collections, made distinct by their content. The lynes of the array form a similar pair of pairs. Each lyne pair represents a different row class, while both row classes are generated from the same ordered trichord type.

The lynes conjoined by register employ classical transformations of given rows, so that the four rows in each lyne pair represent the four classical transformations. Because each of the two row classes is degenerate, their retrograde forms are equivalent to transpositions at the tritone. As previously discussed, the four pitch class collections of the array are themselves preserved throughout but are retrograded at the array's midpoint. Not surprisingly, all the aggregate locations in the array employ the same trichordal mosaic, with A-type hexachords found discretely in the lynes, and E-type hexachords found between combinatorial lyne pairs in the columns.

We can say a bit more about the disposition of trichords within aggregates in the passage. One feature of our hearing was the changing

	1 + 3	2 + 2	3 + 1	2 + 2	3 + 1		2 + 2	1 + 3	4 + 0
High	R	I	RI		P	T6RI	T6P		T6R	T6I
	RI	P		R	I	T6R	T6I		T6RI	T6P
Low	I		R	P		RI	T6P		T6RI	T6I	T6R
	P		RI		I		R	T6I		T6R	T6P	T6RI

P: +4 -3

Example 2.6.   Distribution of trichords

degrees of clarity of the different ordered collections from aggregate to aggregate. The collection most obscure in the first aggregate was more clearly revealed in the second and became instrumental in the clarification of our interpretation of the third aggregate, while the clearest collection of the first aggregate was gradually submerged in the subsequent passages. The fact that all collections maintain their order identity through the first block of the array allows us to hear this particular progression, but the nature of the progression arises from the way trichords are conjoined within aggregates. The first aggregate presented one trichord alone, followed by the remaining three overlapped. The second presented trichords overlapped two at a time, while the third reversed the pattern of the first aggregate, presenting three overlapped trichords followed by one alone. If this seems familiar, it should. As Example 2.6 illustrates, the layout of trichords in each aggregate represents the possible partitions of the four trichords into two or fewer batches, the same scheme as that used to divide the work into instrumental sections. Furthermore, the order of partitions and their relative distributions of constituent elements within the array exactly duplicates the pattern of the instumental disposition of the whole work. Last, the four solo statements of trichords in the array represent the four different collections as well as the four different transformations of the interval pattern found in the array.

The pattern of unfolding instruments of the entire composition is replicated in the unfolding of trichords in the initial solo! How is this borne out in the rest of the piece? Let us examine the arrays of the remaining solo sections of the composition. Example 2.7 contains the arrays and brief sections from the cello, violin, and flute solos.

Several features spring to view. First, all four solos represent the same disposition of partitions of constituent trichords within the arrays, to within retrogression and registral redistribution. Second, while each instrument unfolds its array similarly, the constituent trichords are not the same. In the case of the flute, the collections are

Example 2.7. *Composition for Four Instruments*: the other solos.
Copyright © 1949 by Merion Music, Inc. Used by permission

identical to those in the clarinet, but their interval pattern is different. The strings use two interval patterns imposed on an entirely different bunch of collections, all members of collection class [0, 1, 3]. This distribution of collections and intervallic patterns echoes and reinforces the pairs of instruments in the basic ensemble: both winds employ distinct orderings of [0, 1, 4] while both strings use different orderings of [0, 1, 3].

While each solo is characterized by its own ordered collection type, we can see what unites the solos by inspecting the trichordal mosaics in their arrays. The flute array contains the same trichordal mosaic as the clarinet solo array. It has been reoriented in its manifestations to yield E-type hexachords in the individual lynes of the array and A-type hexachords between lyne pairs. The two string solos are in a similar relationship, using two different orientations of the trichordal mosaic generated from the [0, 1, 3] collections. Uniting both mosaics, and thus both sets of arrays, is the A-type all-combinatorial hexachord, the only all-combinatorial hexachord type that can be generated by each of the two trichord types present, [0, 1, 4] and [0, 1, 3]. As we shall see later, these two trichords have an even more exclusive relationship with the chromatic hexachord.

Having briefly inspected the solo passages, we are now equipped to consider the ensemble sections of the *Composition*. Example 2.8 reproduces the beginning of the first section following the opening clarinet solo, and a portion of its array.

It is immediately apparent that once again the trichords of the array are distributed in the same manner as the sections discussed above. However, the array is no longer generated by a single ordered trichord type. Not only does the passage employ the remaining instruments but they in turn are projecting the remaining three ordered trichords types. As a result, the mosaics found in the various aggregate locations of the array must belong to different classes and must be oriented in ways to yield combinatoriality within the columns. Consequently, not only do the resulting lynes of the array carry members of two different row classes but these row classes employ different types of all-combinatorial hexachords as well. Those lynes based on [0, 1, 3] contain B hexachords segmentally, while those based on [0, 1, 4] contain E hexachords. The A hexachord arises between both sets of combinatorial lyne pairs to ensure their conjunction in the array.

What is true for the first pair of sections will be found for the subsequent pairs as well. Thus just as the instruments are deployed by partition through the composition, and just as the individual trichordal members of the arrays are deployed by partition through each

Example 2.8. *Composition for Four Instruments*: the first trio.
Copyright © 1949 by Merion Music, Inc. Used by permission

section, so too is the totality of ordered trichordal collections partitioned among the sections of the work. The deployment of ordered
trichords among instruments through the composition is illustrated
in Example 2.9.

We can note a couple of features of the overall structure of the piece
in Example 2.9. In the trio sections, the instrument not conjoined
with the other instrument of its pair has two lynes, while the remaining instruments each have a single lyne. The featured instrument also
employs the same ordered trichord type as the one in its solo section.
At the midpoint of the list of sectional partitions the order of trichord
partitions in every section is a retrograde of that found in the first
half, duplicating in the large the pattern of retrogression found in the
second block of each sectional array.

Two points become abundantly clear from the preceding. First, the
final section of the piece is climactic on several levels. It is the only
section of the work in which all instruments are playing, and it is the
only section of the work in which all the aggregates contain one of
each of the four different kinds of ordered trichords. The final section
also reproduces a reversed version of the entire composition in miniature, as each instrument follows the trichordal lyne analogous to its
own path through the composition. The final passage opens with the
unique aggregate in the work intermingling attacks from all four instruments and closes with a final trichord in the clarinet, mimicking
the opening gesture of the piece.

The second point alluded to brings us to the question of the composition's twelve-tone row. No passage is entirely composed with members of a single row class, and there is no row among any of the lynes
that contains all four of the ordered trichord types found throughout
the piece. Babbitt has suggested that the work's row is never literally
heard at the surface but serves as the structural influence and guide to
the progress of the composition. Indeed, Example 2.10 contains the
members of a row class that can serve as a catalog of the ordered
trichords of the piece, as well as of the principal hexachords, members of the A all-combinatorial hexachordal collection class, but these
rows never appear on the surface of the piece.[7]

The foregoing simply emphasizes a critical point about twelve-tone
music: twelve-tone rows are abstractions that determine the nature of
relationships found within a composition over a wide variety of time
spans. They do not necessarily have to be fully embodied within the
surface aggregates of a composition in order to exert a strong influence over their structure and progression.

Still another dimension of the *Composition for Four Instruments* reflects the pattern of partitions of four distinct items discussed above.

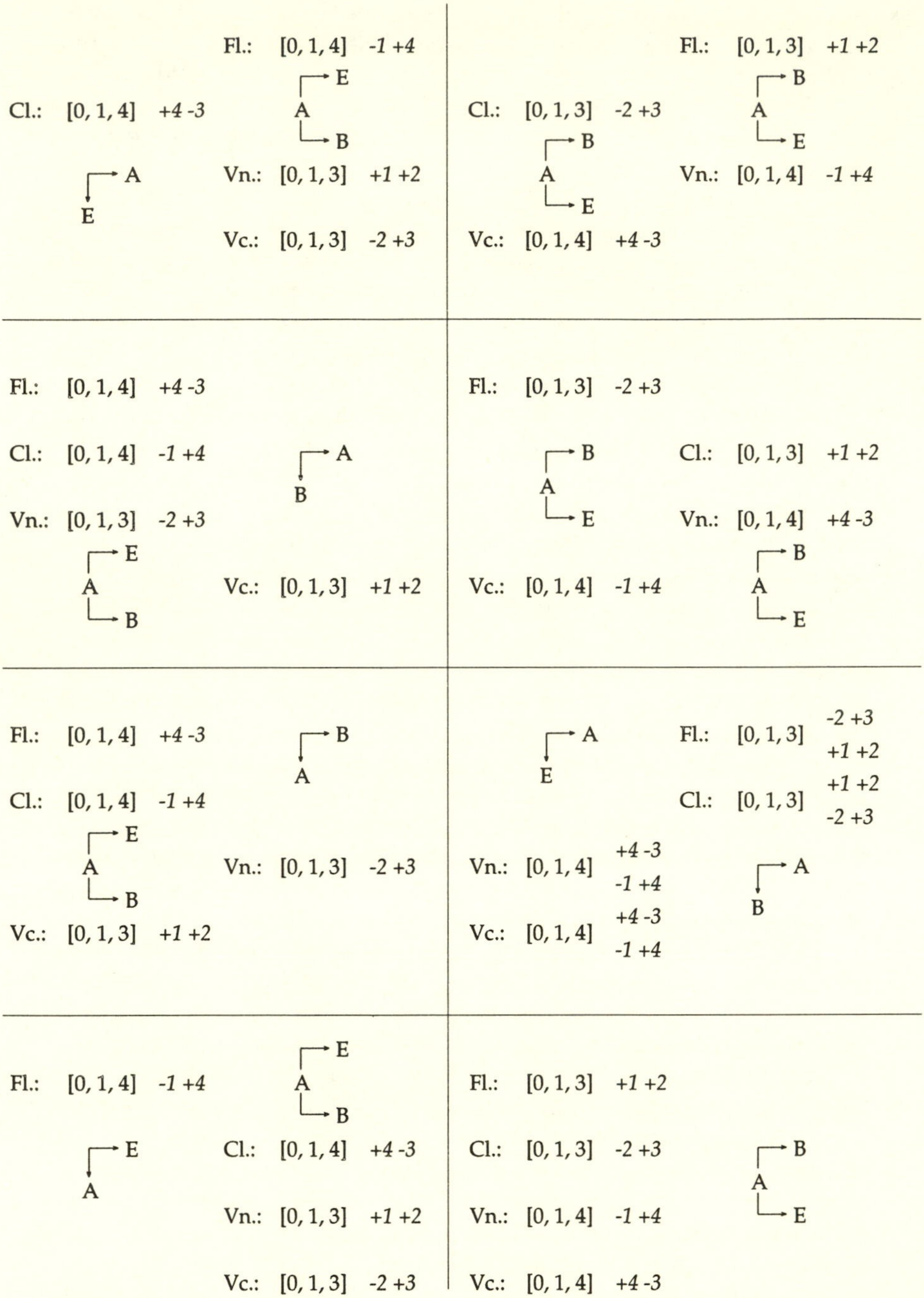

Fl.:   [0, 1, 4]   *-1 +4*
                    ┌─► E
Cl.:   [0, 1, 4]   +4 -3   A
                             └─► B
        ┌─► A   Vn.:   [0, 1, 3]   *+1 +2*
     E
                  Vc.:   [0, 1, 3]   *-2 +3*

Fl.:   [0, 1, 3]   *+1 +2*
                    ┌─► B
Cl.:   [0, 1, 3]   *-2 +3*   A
                             └─► E
        ┌─► B   Vn.:   [0, 1, 4]   *-1 +4*
     A
        └─► E
Vc.:   [0, 1, 4]   +4 -3

Fl.:   [0, 1, 4]   +4 -3

Cl.:   [0, 1, 4]   *-1 +4*   ┌─► A
                            B
Vn.:   [0, 1, 3]   *-2 +3*
        ┌─► E
     A   Vc.:   [0, 1, 3]   *+1 +2*
        └─► B

Fl.:   [0, 1, 3]   *-2 +3*

        ┌─► B   Cl.:   [0, 1, 3]   *+1 +2*
     A
        └─► E   Vn.:   [0, 1, 4]   +4 -3
Vc.:   [0, 1, 4]   *-1 +4*   ┌─► B
                            A
                               └─► E

Fl.:   [0, 1, 4]   +4 -3   ┌─► B
                          A
Cl.:   [0, 1, 4]   *-1 +4*
        ┌─► E
     A   Vn.:   [0, 1, 3]   *-2 +3*
        └─► B
Vc.:   [0, 1, 3]   *+1 +2*

        ┌─► A   *-2 +3*
     E   Fl.:   [0, 1, 3]   *+1 +2*
                                     +1 +2
Vn.:   [0, 1, 4]   +4 -3   Cl.:   [0, 1, 3]   *-2 +3*
                   -1 +4
                                        ┌─► A
Vc.:   [0, 1, 4]   +4 -3   B
                   -1 +4

           ┌─► E
        A
           └─► B
Fl.:   [0, 1, 4]   *-1 +4*

        ┌─► E   Cl.:   [0, 1, 4]   +4 -3
     A
                  Vn.:   [0, 1, 3]   *+1 +2*

                  Vc.:   [0, 1, 3]   *-2 +3*

Fl.:   [0, 1, 3]   *+1 +2*

Cl.:   [0, 1, 3]   *-2 +3*   ┌─► B
                            A
Vn.:   [0, 1, 4]   *-1 +4*   └─► E

Vc.:   [0, 1, 4]   +4 -3

Example 2.9.   *Composition for Four Instruments*: trichordal distributions

Example 2.10. *Composition for Four Instruments*: underlying rows

As we mentioned in the previous chapter, Babbitt eschewed any superficial borrowing from tonal practice in his pursuit of the implications of the twelve-tone system, seeking to turn every musical dimension to the ends of bodying forth the structural ramifications of a composition's premises. In the process, he sought to compose the temporal domain of his music in ways that would stem from the same first principles as those underlying his pitch structures. For the *Composition for Four Instruments*, Babbitt used a sequence of four durations to create his rhythms. We described in the previous chapter his techniques for creating four transformations of the basic duration pattern, 1 4 3 2. In addition, these four duration patterns are each expanded into longer duration patterns by multiplying each member of a given pattern by its own four successive members.[8] Thus an expanded pattern consists of a long statement of the generating pattern, each member of which represents a different-length version of the generating pattern. For example, 1 4 3 2 generates 1 4 3 2, 4 16 12 8, 3 12 9 6, and 2 8 6 4; and the others follow suit. The four resulting extended rhythmic patterns are combined in exactly the same way as the trichords within arrays, ordered trichords among sections, and instruments among sections of the entire piece. Once again, Babbitt has been able to find a way of manifesting the partitions for four distinct items.[9] The combinations of rhythmic patterns unfold at a different rate from the pitch patterns. The initial two partitions of combinations can be heard over the span of the opening clarinet solo. The first can be seen in Example 2.11.

An interesting feature revealed by the return of the partitions of the rhythmic pattern is its metrical reinterpretation. Babbitt changes the tempo at this point while changing the unit of the duration in such a way that its real-time length stays the same. This strongly suggests

Example 2.11. *Composition for Four Instruments*: rhythmic patterns

that Babbitt is very much attuned to the differences that can arise from metrical reinterpretations, based on the qualitative differences of attacks with regard to beat and bar. This is illustrated in Example 2.12.

The preceding has given only the gross characteristics of the underlying structures of the *Composition for Four Instruments*. The work is much more however, as the details of each section's realization articulate different aspects latent in the underlying structure and create a network of relationships across the span of the composition. Let us return to the opening clarinet solo to examine some of these details. Whereas we concentrated in our first pass on those aspects that aggregates held in common, we shall concentrate now on their differences. Our sense of progression in this music depends on our awareness of the dialectic between the individuality of aggregates changing against their commonality. As suggested above, differences among aggregates based on the same assembly of ordered trichords must arise from the ways the trichords are placed within the aggregate. The presence of the ubiquitous partition scheme determines certain sorts of differentiations, but a great deal of flexibility still remains.

Heard simply as a succession of notes, the first aggregate can be construed as an all-interval ordering of the twelve pitch classes.[10] Although the resulting twelve-tone row's interval pattern does not generate the row class of the composition, it does play an important role

Example 2.12. *Composition for Four Instruments*:
compensatory tempo and durational unit changes.
Copyright © 1949 by Merion Music, Inc. Used by permission

in the rest of the opening solo. A quick examination of the remaining
(3 + 1) partitions of the first array reveals that they represent the three
classical transformations of the first aggregate's interval pattern. But
the initial aggregate has still more influence over the first section: all
the slurred notes for the remainder of the passage are found as adjacencies in the first aggregate.[11] Some of these dyads are themselves of
critical interest for the work as a whole. The piece is constructed entirely from only two sets of four different unordered trichordal collections, four [0, 1, 4] trichords and four [0, 1, 3] trichords. The trichords
of each set can be mapped onto each other by only a few operations.
They are T_0, T_6, and inversion at index numbers one and seven, for
both sets of trichords. Each index number produces its own set of
dyadic mappings, which may be used either to reflect relations between collections or to generate the collections themselves. The
A-type hexachords in the arrays above, for example, map onto themselves at index number one and onto each other at index number
seven. Dyads from the index number seven cycle are found as adjacencies in the upper register of the opening aggregate. This is illustrated in Example 2.13.

Turning to the aggregates formed by pairs of trichords, we can see
immediately that they will collectively provide a catalog of the possible hexachords that may be generated within the trichordal mosaic

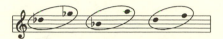

Example 2.13.   Intervals generated
by index number seven

found in the array's columns. It is to be remembered that this particular array contains a single trichordal mosaic at all aggregate locations.
In the case of the clarinet solo, the hexachords generated by pairs of
the mosaic's trichords include A hexachords, E hexachords, and the
only inversionally combinatorial hexachord type that may be mapped
onto its complement at more than one index number, [0, 1, 3, 6, 7, 9].
We shall refer to this as the H hexachord for the sake of simplicity.
These three hexachord types are interesting in themselves, since they
all play special roles in the composition as a whole. The A hexachord
is the focal hexachord type of the piece, being the only all-
combinatorial hexachord that is generated by both the work's trichord
types. The E hexachord appears in the lynes of the flute solo as well as
in lynes of [0, 1, 4] trichords in those arrays using both trichord types,
due to the necessity of using chromatic hexachords as those found in
pairs of like trichords in columnar aggregates. It also appears between
combinatorial pairs in those arrays employing the [0, 1, 4] trichord to
generate A hexachords in all the lynes. The H hexachord type can also
be generated by pairs of [0, 1, 3] trichords related by T_6 and so will
appear in those arrays based solely on either of the trichord types,
that is to say, the remaining solos and the pair of duos consisting of
the flute with the clarinet and the violin with the cello. This is illustrated in Example 2.14.

The second aggregate of the passage is that set of trichord pairs that
produces A hexachords. This is the primary hexachord type of the
composition, and the two hexachords in the second aggregate have
been ordered in a very special way. By alternating between lynes Babbitt has been able to unfold in time the four [0, 1, 3] collections that
will be used in the remainder of the *Composition*, embodying the two
distinct interval patterns associated with all the ordered [0, 1, 3] collections in the entire piece! In the first two aggregates Babbitt has

The H hexachord as it might arise as pairs of trichords related by T6.

Example 2.14.   [0, 1, 3, 6, 7, 9] (H) hexachord type

Example 2.15. *Composition for Four Instruments*: proleptic details.
Copyright © 1949 by Merion Music, Inc. Used by permission

adumbrated the materials and procedures of all that is to follow. This is illustrated in Example 2.15.

We have hardly exhausted the opening solo. For example, both the remaining aggregates based on pairs of trichords can be generated from the same unordered collection type, [0, 3, 7]. This trichord type is prepared in the first aggregate in conjunction with the upper register's material. Parsed as we did when discussing Example 2.4, this instance of an E hexachord yields two [0, 1, 4] collections, but parsed in time it can be heard as two [0, 3, 7] collections. But even more important for the progession of the entire work is the composition of the last aggregate, the first to use all trichords simultaneously. As may be seen in Example 2.15, the aggregate is composed of two B-type hexachords, in fact—those two collections that are generated by the [0, 1, 3] collections found in the composition!

In short, we can trace a number of different features of the composition, both local and long-range, to the detailed composition of the opening solo. The four transformations of the opening all-interval succession echo the constant recycling of the four transformations of the interval pattern of the generating trichords. The composition of the remaining aggregates is finessed to project the actual hexachordal collections that will occur later in the composition both in individual lynes and between combinatorial lyne pairs. The interior order of the A hexachords, in particular, is fashioned to reveal the trichords and interval patterns that generate later portions of the work. Detailed hearing will create a series of echoes and associations in the listener's mind that will resonate to the farthest reaches of the piece. We shall pursue a few of them.[12]

A number of features connect the ensuing trio to the opening solo. Much, of course, is new here. The remaining instruments are intro-

Example 2.16.   *Composition for Four Instruments*: details projected by
articulation. Copyright © 1949 by Merion Music, Inc. Used by permission

duced, and the passage is the first in which more than one instrument
plays. The array contains the remaining ordered trichords of the
piece, including a new ordering of the initial trichord type as well as
two orderings of an entirely new trichord type. The array therefore
contains new hexachord types, in a variety of different mosaics. Nevertheless, much can be heard that is familiar. The partitions of trichords within aggregates repeat the pattern of partitions found in the
opening solo. The first trichord of the first aggregate is in a new order
but is one of the collections we have heard before; in fact, it is the last
of the trichordal collections that we heard isolated in the initial solo,
during the last (3 + 1) partitioned aggregate. The trichord is also
played on the flute, the other wind instrument. The flute, being the
only unique member of an instrumental pair present, plays two lynes
of the array, both made of inversionally related combinatorial rows
whose discrete hexachords are of type E. The lynes are distinguished
by register. It will be remembered that the initial clarinet solo employed register to separate lyne pairs rather than lynes. Because of
this, the opening solo also projected E hexachords by register, arising
from the combination of trichords from the two lynes. Thus both
wind instruments project the same collections in the same ways in the
two passages, although their derivation is different.

Babbitt has also unfolded his rhythmic structures in such a way that
the initiation of the trio coincides with the beginning of one of the
rhythmic sections. The rhythmic section that starts at this point contains the duration pattern used at the opening of the work combined
with two others that allow the work's opening rhythm to be heard
unobscured. Thus the initial woodwind trichord of the trio section is
in the same rhythm as the trichord at the opening of the clarinet solo.

The beginning of the second section contains another interesting
feature: the overlay of articulational differentiations. The repeated

Example 2.17. *Composition for Four Instruments*: first duet.
Copyright © 1949 by Merion Music, Inc. Used by permission

and staccato notes in the first few bars of the trio taken together form B-type hexachords. This kind of hexachord, prefigured in the ordering of the last aggregate of the clarinet solo, is active in the lynes of the strings in the trio. This is illustrated in Example 2.16.

The remainder of the *Composition for Four Instruments* contains a wealth of additional detail creating a wide variety of degrees of connection and distinction among its constituent parts. We shall have to content ourselves here with a few brief observations as hints to the reader of routes deeper and deeper into the world of the work.

The arrival of the first duo, clarinet and cello, marks a number of significant points in the piece. It is the first return of any instrument in the composition, but it is also the first appearance of a wind instrument playing [0, 1, 3] trichords as its constituent trichord type. The passage is also the first duo and is marked by the first pizzicato in the composition. In this duo, while the clarinet continues to employ register to distinguish its lynes, the cello uses arco and pizzicato for that purpose, freeing up register for other tasks. Note that the first appearance of pizzicato, however, is associated with the very trichordal collection that opens the composition. The passage is illustrated in Example 2.17.

The changing use of criteria to project lynes or lyne pairs throughout the composition enables Babbitt to create multiple references. In the second duo, for example, the violin part employs arco and pizzicato to distinguish lynes, while register is used to create a collectional partition that duplicates the mosaics of the flute part. This is illustrated in Example 2.18.[13]

A brief survey of details from the various solos reveals interesting connections and aspects of the materials of the piece. The cello solo features a number of examples of a hexachord not found so far, the C-type all-combinatorial hexachord, which is closely allied with the A-

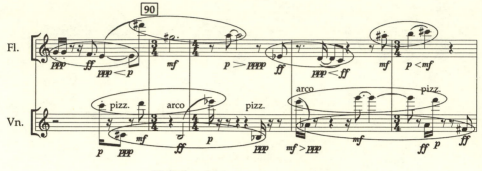

Violin by register: 023 475
                                   1et 896
Violin by articulation: pizz. 12t 956
                          arco 0e3 487

Example 2.18. *Composition for Four Instruments*: second duet.
Copyright © 1949 by Merion Music, Inc. Used by permission

and B-type hexachords, examples of which also appear in the passage. These three hexachord types also appear in the violin solo, derived in a number of ways from the lynes of the underlying array. The final solo, for flute, contains some lovely details connecting it with those passages we have already discussed. Its final trichord is the same ordered collection found at the flute's first entrance in the first trio. The first aggregate, composed of all four lyne trichords' attacks intermingled, projects E-type hexachords, the type found so often both in lynes and between combinatorial lynes in previous arrays. But perhaps the most telling moment in the passage, and a striking moment in the composition as well, comes near the end of the flute solo. Bar 340 marks another return of the opening durational patterns of the piece, and embedded in it is a revelation about the trichord types of the composition: not only can they be used individually to generate A-type hexachords, the fundamental hexachord-type of the composition, but the two together may generate it as well! This unifying aspect of the composition's trichord and hexachord types arises here as a result of the counterpoint of lynes. Lest the point be missed, Babbitt repeats the partitioning not only in the last aggregate of the flute solo but also in the first aggregate of the following penultimate trio and in the last aggregate of the final quartet, to mention but a few examples. The passages are illustrated in Example 2.19. As we shall see, Babbitt in later compositions undertakes to explore the ramifications of the dual possibilities of trichords to generate hexachords individually and in pairs.

Example 2.19.   *Composition for Four Instruments*: late details.
Copyright © 1949 by Merion Music, Inc. Used by permission

The preceding discussion just scratches the surface of the *Composition for Four Instruments*, but in addition to suggesting pathways into the individual work for the listener it hints at some of the basic procedures and ideas that preoccupied Babbitt for the next fifteen years and have informed his work to the present day. These include the submersion of the basic ordering beneath the immediate surface of a composition; the use of trichordal arrays derived in various ways from one or more trichord types, themselves ordered in one or more ways; the use of the different partitions of four distinct elements to create a flexible diversity among aggregates or ensembles; and the use of different instrumental distributions and modes of projection to produce multiple interpretations of aggregates.

Clear in the music of the *Composition for Four Instruments* is the dual importance of interval patterns and mosaic identity. Much of the play in the work arises from the recurrence of fixed hexachordal collections sliced into different trichords and fixed trichordal collections ordered variously, or conjoined variously into different types of hexachords. All these strategies are controlled by ways the aggregate can be partitioned into collections and the ways these collections can be ordered. The work's twelve-tone row class, viewed both as a set of transformations of ordered pitch classes and as a set of interval patterns, provides the perspective on the total chromatic that allows the composition both the diversity of its parts and the compelling unity of its totality.

Realizing the Implications of the *Composition for Four Instruments*

The next few compositions we shall examine expand and extend a number of the features we have seen in the *Composition for Four Instruments* in various ways. Each of them takes up one or more of the ideas or materials of the preceding work and conjoins it with features of its own to create new musical situations. These works' individuality arises from the new and different ways Babbitt combines his compositional genes, but their originality is only thrown into its highest relief by our familiarity with their common roots.

COMPOSITION FOR VIOLA AND PIANO

The *Composition for Viola and Piano* was composed a few years after the *Composition for Four Instruments*. It is contemporary with his setting of *The Widow's Lament in Springtime* and follows the *Composition for Twelve*

Instruments.[14] In the latter work, Babbitt turned to the problem of composing with twelve-part arrays, an issue to which he returned in full force in his second period. With the vocal setting and the viola work, he resumed the use of four-part trichordal arrays, which underlie most of his first-period compositions.

The *Composition for Viola and Piano* and the *Composition for Four Instruments* have much in common. Both use rows whose hexachords are generated by two pairs of different trichord types, each member of each pair identified by its own interval pattern. Like the earlier piece, much of the viola work involves the composition of arrays based on various combinations of different orderings of these two trichord types. However, there are many differences. Although both works depend on the same trio of hexachord types—A, B, and E—each piece employs a different pair of trichord types. While the *Composition for Four Instruments* is based on [0, 1, 3] and [0, 1, 4], the viola work uses [0, 1, 4] and [0, 1, 5] as its row's discrete trichord types. The change of trichord pairs effects a change of focal hexachord. In the earlier work, the A hexachord was the sole type generated by both trichord types and thus emerged as the row class's discrete segmental hexachord type. In the viola piece, it is the E-type hexachord that is generated by both trichord types.

The change of focal hexachord has numerous consequences as well as interesting implications. Although all three hexachord types will once again be found throughout the arrays of the work, their relative importance, position, and orientation will be shifted from what we found in the *Composition for Four Instruments*. This would also be true had the B-type hexachord been made the focal hexachord of the trio, as it could with the selection of [0, 1, 3] and [0, 1, 5] as the generating trichord types. It is worth noting, in fact, that this is precisely what happens in a later composition—*Two Sonnets*, on poems by Gerard Manley Hopkins, for baritone voice, clarinet, viola, and cello. In a very real sense the pitch language of this last work was inevitable, given the existence of the *Composition for Four Instruments* and the *Composition for Viola*.

Of particular consequence for the viola piece in contrast to the earlier or later works mentioned is the choice of the E hexachord as the focus. This alone makes a tremendous difference because unlike any of the three first-order all-combinatorial hexachords, A, B or C, the E-type hexachord can be partitioned in several ways into pairs of generating trichords of a given type. (In fact, unlike the A, B, or C hexachords, the E hexachord can *only* be partitioned into pairs of trichords of a given type.) Thus not only will a given hexachord yield more than one trichordal partition by a given trichord type, the resulting combi-

Example 2.20.   [0, 1, 4] trichordal mosaics

nations of partitions of pairs of hexachords into trichordal mosaics will yield different mosaic classes generated from a single trichord type. This fact has a considerable impact on the kinds of hexachords that will be generated by trichordal pairs in aggregates of the array, and as the work uses the same four-part partitional apparatus as the *Composition for Four Instruments* to compose its aggregates, the resulting hexachord types appear frequently in the musical surface.[15] This is illustrated in Example 2.20.

The E hexachord is a slippery creature, open to multiple interpretation, and this very notion informs the work from the outset. Example 2.21 contains the first aggregate of the *Composition for Viola and Piano*. The viola part may be sliced two different ways, by temporal succession and by registral line. Each slicing yields a pair of [0, 1, 4] trichords forming the E hexachord. Each pair manifests transformations of a different interval pattern; by register, *+1 +3* related by inversion; and in time, *−3 +4* related by retrograde inversion. The piano is also open to dual-order interpretation, based on a combination of time and register. The two collectional interpretations of the viola part, conjoined with a single collectional interpretation of the piano part, yield examples of the two different mosaic classes that may be generated from the single trichord type, [0, 1, 4]. The first aggregate presages much that will follow in the *Composition*.

The *Composition for Viola and Piano*, however, is much more than a translation of the procedures of the *Composition for Four Instruments* to another pair of trichords. Nor is it simply the exploitation of the differences between A and E hexachords that alone makes up the distinctions between the two pieces. The viola work projects its row structure in considerably different ways from those used in the earlier piece, yielding in the process not only a very different surface but a different dramatic path through its structure.

The *Composition for Viola and Piano* falls into seven sections distinguished by duration, playing style, tempo, ensemble, and muting. These are found in Example 2.22.[16] Each section uses materials from

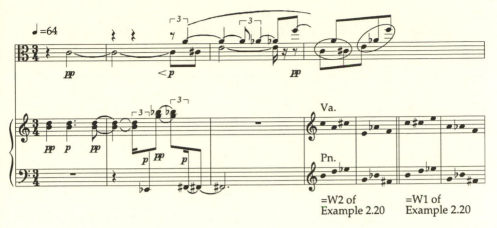

Example 2.21. *Composition for Viola and Piano*: opening aggregate.
Reprinted by permission of C. F. Peters Corporation

the row class in different ways. Example 2.23 illustrates a member of the row class and its constituent trichords and their orderings.

The ordering of the row of this work is itself another example of Babbitt's maximal diversity principle. While the E hexachord cannot be partitioned into trichords from more than one class at a time and does not contain a large enough variety of interval classes to yield an all-interval row, Babbitt has seen to it that each occurence of a trichord type is ordered differently and that the ordering of the two trichords that cross the hexachordal boundary themselves are ordered so that they might exhibit the four basic twelve-tone transformations. This latter is not trivial in either case, as both the trans-hexachordal trichords are inversionally symmetrical. The characteristics of this row are found in some of Babbitt's later uses of E hexachords in his rows.

The structure of the entire composition echoes certain aspects of the structure of the row itself. The main body of the work is contained

Section:	1	2	3	4	5	6	7
Tempo:	♩=64	♩=96	♩=64	♩=96	♩=64	♩=96	♩=64
	Viola con sord.	senza sord.			solo		con sord.
				tutti		tutti	
	Piano una corda	tutte le corde	solo				una corda
Bars:	1–20	21–117	118–35	136–57	158–79	180–258	259–275

Example 2.22. *Composition for Viola and Piano*: major sections

[0, 1, 4]	+3	+1		+3	-4			-1	+4		
[0, 1, 5]		+1	+4				+5	-1			+5	-4
[0, 3, 7]			+4	+3					+4	+5
[0, 2, 4]					-4	+2
[0, 2, 7]						+2	+5

Example 2.23. *Composition for Viola and Piano*: ordered trichords

in the two lengthy ensemble sections surrounding the central triptych. Each is an exploration of the segmental trichords of the row's
discrete hexachords. Not only are the discrete trichords used, as in
the *Composition for Four Instruments,* but so are the two other trichords
found as adjacencies within the ordered hexachords. Both extended
sections are made of ten subsections, each of which in turn is made of
trichordal arrays containing two blocks. The resulting eight aggregates are themselves composed to project the eight possible partitions
of four different things into two or fewer batches, ordered variously
through the composition. The ten subsections are made up of the four
arrays built on the individual ordered trichords and the six arrays
built on possible pairs of ordered trichords within a hexachord. Each
large section of the composition unfolding the materials of a hexachord does so in the same pattern. This is illustrated in Example 2.24.

Because all three trichord types found within the hexachords are

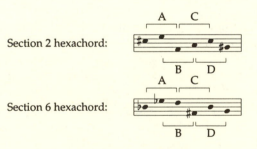

Section 2 hexachord:

Section 6 hexachord:

Pattern of trichordal combinations in sections 2 and 6.

A^2 B^2 AB C^2 AC   BC D^2 AD   BD   CD

Example 2.24.   *Composition for Viola and Piano*:
trichordal structure

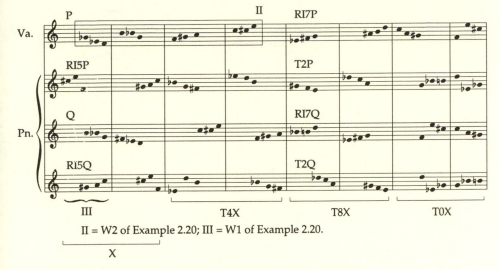

Example 2.25.   *Composition for Viola and Piano*: array structure

(and must be) generators of the E hexachord, the E hexachord dominates all these arrays, either by lyne or by combinatorial lyne pair. Unlike the first-order hexachords, the E hexachord can remain fixed in content while its constituent trichord pairs are transposed. This allows Babbitt to create variety in his arrays that he could not in the *Composition for Four Instruments*. This is illustrated in Example 2.25.

As may be seen, each successive block of hexachords is transposed by T_4 so that the trichordal collections of the last block match those of the first, in retrograde order. The consequence of these transpositions is to yield different types of mosaics in the columns from those in the lynes, despite the fact that both sets of mosaics are built from [0, 1, 4] trichords. Babbitt was to explore the ramifications of such structures even further in subsequent works.

While each subsection is distinguished by its constituent trichords, the subsections are further articulated by changes of mode of projection in various combinations between the two instruments. In some passages all three notes of a trichord are unfolded in time; in others, dyads and single notes alternate, or the trichord is played as a simultaneity. Still other passages connect notes of temporally projected trichords in separate registral strands to create secondary trichordal interpretations of the hexachord. Both registral ordering and temporal ordering function in the composition, and since the row contains all possible orderings of the two principal segmental trichordal types, this provides a wealth of cross-reference among arrays from all over

By time: [0, 3, 7] +4 +3; +3 +4
By line: [0, 1, 4] -1 +4; +3 +1

Example 2.26. *Composition for Viola and Piano*: trichordal articulation.
Reprinted by permission of C. F. Peters Corporation

the piece. The different modes of projection are illustrated in Example 2.26.

The individual composition of the aggregates also creates cross-references. Those aggregates containing pairs of lyne duos are a catalog of hexachords in the various columnar mosaics, and many of the different mosaics share hexachord types in their trichord pairs. Those aggregates that represent both the (1 +3) partition and the (0 +4) partition of trichords are also composed to project hexachord types found elsewhere in the composition in or between lynes. This is illustrated in Example 2.27.

The middle of the *Composition for Viola and Piano* consists of three parts. The first, for solo piano, is based on the hexachordal ordering unfolded over the span of the first extended section. The last, for solo viola, is based on the hexachordal ordering that is used for the following extended section. In both sections hexachords are distinguished from one another by articulation, including those that are strings of single notes, those that are dyads and single notes in varous pairings, those that are played as pairs of three-note chords, and those that are polyphonized into two parts. Dyads and trichords played as simultaneities are ordered sometimes from top to bottom and sometimes the other way around. The arrays of the two sections are not simple Schoenbergian hexachordal arrays, moving by pairs of hexachords, however. Babbitt has once again contrived to project the eight partitions of four distinct items, in this case hexachords, both in register (in the piano section, at least) and in articulation. The viola section reverses the order of partitions found in the piano section. As Example 2.28 illustrates, Babbitt has arranged his hexachords in much the same sort of way as he does with his trichords, maximizing the variety of ways he can project his material.

The central section of the composition joins the two instruments once again in trichordal arrays. This middle section is special in a number of ways. In it the viola and piano have equal amounts of material, like the opening and closing sections of the work, but unlike

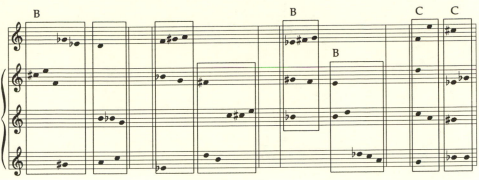

[0, 1, 2, 3, 5, 7]

May appear in trichordal mosaic made from [0, 1, 5]'s generating
E-type hexachords:

$$\frac{e\,0\,4\ \ |\ \ 3\,7\,8}{6\,2\,1\ \ |\ \ t\,9\,5}\ \ \longrightarrow\ E$$

[0, 1, 2, 3, 5, 7]

Example 2.27.   *Composition for Viola and Piano*: generated hexachords

them, the material in the central passage is based on trichordal arrays.
Unlike the more extended sections based on trichordal arrays, however, each instrument has a lyne pair. Most important, however, are
the trichords used. These belong to the [0, 2, 4] and [0, 2, 7] types, the
two trichord types found across the hexachordal boundary in the center of the row. Thus, just as the two main sections of the piece reflect
the two hexachords of the row, so does the central section compose
out the central portion of the row.

The central section represents the farthest remove from the rest of
the work due to the fact that its constituent trichords cannot generate
or even appear in the work's focal E hexachord type. Nevertheless, a
number of the hexachords that do arise belong to types that arise in
many of the arrays of the more extended sections. This is illustrated
in Example 2.29.

The introductory and closing sections of the *Composition for Viola
and Piano* are built of row statements in one instrument combined
with aggregates derived from each of the four segmental trichords of
the row in the other instrument. The piano contains the row statements in the opening section, while the viola plays multiply interpretable aggregates based on trichords. The piano's row statements,
however, are projected both as combinations of dyads and as single
notes, and polyphonized into lines so that they are open to multiple
construal. This is illustrated in Example 2.30.

Example 2.28.   *Composition for Viola and Piano*: piano solo array

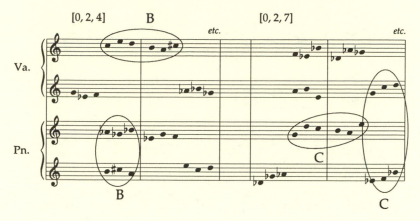

Example 2.29. *Composition for Viola and Piano*: central section trichords

It is only with the final section that we hear fully unambiguous projections of the composition's interval pattern. The viola's flowing lines are simple concatenated row statements, accompanied by trichordally generated combinatorial aggregates in the piano. The piano's trichords are the [0, 1, 4] and [0, 1, 5] types found discretely in the row class, ordered in register. The entire composition closes with a trichordal array combining the four transformations of the four discrete trichordal interval patterns of the composition, as illustrated in Example 2.31.

The *Composition for Viola and Piano* represents a considerable expansion of the twelve-tone techniques found in the *Composition for Four Instruments*. Similarly, the later work's rhythmic structure represents a maturation of Babbitt's duration row technique, found in embryo in the earlier piece. With the *Composition for Twelve Instruments*, Babbitt

Example 2.30. *Composition for Viola and Piano*: row projection

Example 2.31. *Composition for Viola and Piano*: final array

began to employ translations of orderings of the twelve pitch classes
into rows of twelve durations as the basis for his rhythmic structures,
and the *Composition for Viola and Piano* is so composed.

The rhythmic structure of the viola piece has many interesting features. Although we will not offer a complete analysis here, we can
suggest some of the ways Babbitt has extended his techniques for
shaping the local and long-range rhythms in his early music. The
opening section of the composition contains a series of five rhythmic
sections, each thirteen beats long. Each section is built of one or more
duration rows superimposed to form the surface rhythms. The duration unit is the sextuplet, and the tempo is sixty-four quarter-notes
per minute. A quick look at the pattern of combinations suggests that
this represents the opening of a presentation of the partitions of four
distinct items—in this case, duration rows representing the four classic twelve-tone operations. The continuation is found not in the following section, however, but in the subsequent piano solo, which
resumes the tempo of the opening. A portion of the opening is illustrated in Example 2.32.

Although Babbitt has used hexachord-preserving and -exchanging
transformations for his duration rows, their superimposition cannot
really be considered combinatorial, in the sense used in the pitch domain, or later in the time-point system. Superimposition merely creates a series of shorter durations, each attack representing the initiation of one or more of the durations from the rows. All rows of a
thirteen-beat section start at the same time, and all finish at the same
time. Although Babbitt uses transformations that ensure that the
overall duration of the discrete hexachords of all rows remains the

P:	12	4	11	7	8	3	1	5	2	10	9	6
	(3 2 1 6)	(3 1)	(6 4 1)	(4 2 1)	(3 5)	(3)	(1)	(3 2)	(1 1)	(1 5 4)	(1 3 2 3)	(6)

RI9P:	3	12	11	7	4	8	6	1	2	10	5	9
	(3)	(2 1 6 3)	(1 6 4)	(1 4 2)	(1 3)	(5 3)	(1 3 2)	(1)	(1 1)	(5 4 1)	(3 2)	(3 6)

I5P:	5	1	6	10	9	2	4	12	3	7	8	11
	(3 2)	(1)	(6)	(3 1 6)	(4 1 4)	(2)	(1 3)	(5 3 1 3)	(2 1)	(1 1 5)	(4 1 3)	(2 3 6)

Example 2.32. *Composition for Viola and Piano*: composite duration rows.
Reprinted by permission of C. F. Peters Corporation

Example 2.33. *Composition for Viola and Piano*: duration subdivisions

same, the relations among duration rows do not correspond to those among pitch class rows of the same transformations. Nevertheless, Babbitt's ways of creating relations among duration rows do have some interesting musical consequences.

A particularly dramatic and far-reaching example of Babbitt's use of duration row transformations determines the relationship between the rhythmic structure of the first section and the following section. The second section of the composition contains changes in both duration unit and tempo. The duration unit is expanded from the sextuplet to the sixteenth-note, while the tempo is increased to ninety-six quarter-notes a minute from sixty-four. The combined changes cancel each other out, so that the absolute durations of the duration rows are exactly the same in both tempi; what *is* changed is the metrical interpretation of their elements. Babbitt has been careful to demonstrate this in his choice of duration rows to open each section. The work opens with a duration row beginning with a duration of six units, equivalent to the beat of the section. The second section opens with a statement of T_2 of the initial duration row, producing an initial duration of eight units. This latter duration represents two beats in the new tempo, or a bar in the predominant meter of $\frac{2}{4}$. Thus the choice of transposition itself articulates the difference between the two tempi of the work.

The faster sections of the *Composition for Viola* also unfold different combinations of the four distinct duration row transformations, but they are further differentiated from the opening section by an additional technique. In the faster sections, and later in the slower sections, Babbitt fills in the durations of a row, or the durations produced by the superimposition of rows, with strings of equal note values. A change of duration is marked by a change of subdivision. The rhythms of the opening of the second section are illustrated in Example 2.33.

This technique allows Babbitt a great deal of flexibility in the composition of the rhythmic surface and also reinforces the sense of each tempo. In the viola composition, the subdivisions used are those that are readily available within a meter and tempo, so that the different tempi invite different kinds of subdivision. The subdivision that opens the second section, for example, would be difficult to achieve in the tempo of the opening section.

WOODWIND QUARTET

If the *Composition for Viola and Piano* depends on the ambiguity of multiple interpretations provided by the E-type hexachord, Babbitt's Woodwind Quartet exploits a multiplicity of interpretation of quite a different order. The quartet returns to the trichordal material of the *Composition for Four Instruments*, but with a difference.[17] As we shall see, the quartet starts where the *Composition* leaves off. To this is added not only the viola work's technique of using the inner segmental trichords of the row's hexachords and the two trans-hexachordal trichords but an entirely different way of slicing the row altogether. This variety of new techniques appears in a work that in some aspects seems like a step backward from other works of this period: the Woodwind Quartet contains a remarkable amount of almost literal recurrence, not just of unordered collections but of collections motivically shaped in recognizable contours and rhythms. The very use of traditional sectional headings suggests a concious effort to associate the music with past practice. There are even some subtle homages to Schoenberg's music that go beyond the inevitable commonalities between works written with shared assumptions. It is a bit of a surprise that this work, in many ways more accessible than most of Babbitt's works, at least in its use of familiar compositional devices, is as little known as it is.

The quartet is in six big sections titled *Introduction, Canons for Clarinet, Trios for Flute, Duets for Bassoon, Cadenza and Recitative for Oboe,* and *Finale.* Preceding the *Introduction,* between the *Canons* and the *Trios,* and the *Trios* and the *Duets,* and following the *Finale,* are four brief interpolated sections that foreshadow or echo material in the work.

Like the *Composition for Four Instruments,* the fundamental rows of the quartet contain two [0, 1, 3] trichords and two [0, 1, 4] trichords in a pair of A hexachords, but unlike in the earlier work, the trichords are not paired by type within each hexachord. The fact that each trichord type may itself additionally generate the A hexachord opens up the work to a wealth of compositional possibilities. Example 2.34 contains a member of the work's row class and derived hexachords based on the two trichord types.[18]

Like both the works so far discussed, the quartet contains passages

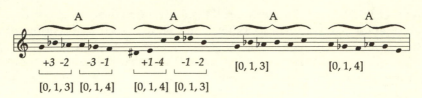

Example 2.34. Woodwind Quartet: row structure

composed of arrays generated from combinations of row segments, but unlike those works, Babbitt keeps alive in each section segments from the whole extent of the row's interval pattern instead of concentrating on one or two segments at a time. The row's interval pattern is only gradually disclosed in the course of the work, but unlike those previous pieces, it is as though it is continually folded upon itself in different ways rather than exposed a bit at a time. This is a markedly different strategy from those found in the earlier works.[19]

One of the results of this approach is the use in the composition of different classes of mosaics employing the two constituent trichords, and the dialectic created by fixing transposition levels of the underlying hexachordal mosaics created by the trichords. This is illustrated in Example 2.35.

Tracing the structure of the sections of the quartet reveals its similarities to and differences from the earlier compositions. As noted above, the quartet takes as its point of departure the structural climax

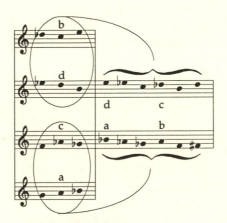

a, b, c, d = order patterns

Example 2.35. Woodwind Quartet:
trichordal derivation
of first aggregate

Example 2.36.   Woodwind Quartet, *Introduction*: first trichordal array

of the *Composition for Four Instruments*. The *Introduction* consists of four statements of transformations of a four-lyne, eight-aggregate trichordal array in the by now familiar presentation by trichordal partition. The lynes of the arrays are each generated by one of the four discrete segmental trichords of the work's row. This is illustrated in Example 2.36.

The *Introduction* is preceded by a three-bar passage, found in Example 2.37, that serves as a synopsis of much that follows. First, columnar aggregates of the opening passage represent the mosaics generated by each of the four discrete segmental trichords of the

Example 2.37.   Woodwind Quartet: opening bars. Reprinted by permission of Associated Music Publishers, Inc. (BMI)

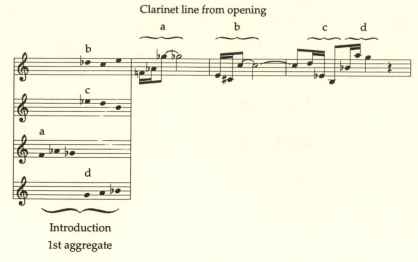

Example 2.38.   Woodwind Quartet: trichordal derivation.
Reprinted by permission of Associated Music Publishers, Inc. (BMI)

composition's fundamental row class. When read vertically, the aggregates of the opening are equivalent to the four mosaics found in the lynes of the ensuing arrays. Consequently, each instrumental part of the first three bars represents one of the columnar aggregates of the *Introduction*, by collectional content. This is illustrated in Example 2.38.

Second, while each individual instrumental part of the opening may be read as a derived row based on inversionally combinatorial hexachords, partitioning the music into instrumental pairs distinguished by tone production (double reeds for one pair, and flute and clarinet for the other) yields a pair of inversionally related lynes unfolding A-type hexachords at the transposition level that will dominate the work.

The synoptic aspect of the brief passage is further illustrated by the way the initial aggregate foreshadows the initiation of each new transformation of the array in the Introduction.[20] This is illustrated in Example 2.39.

Whereas the *Introduction* combines the four discrete trichords of the row, the *Canons* for clarinet combine variously the remaining trichords found within and between the hexachords of the row. It is worth noting that Babbitt has ensured in his ordering that all the trichord types found within the fundamental interval pattern can generate the A-type hexachord. This is one of the rare cases in which Bab-

Example 2.39.   Woodwind Quartet: trichordal recurrence. Reprinted by permission of Associated Music Publishers, Inc. (BMI)

bitt does not mark the hexachordal boundary of the row with the excluded interval. Of particular interest is the fact that the second hexachord of the row is itself that unique ordering of the chromatic hexachord that contains all its generators; the first hexachord duplicates one of the trichord types found discretely but provides its third possible ordering pattern.[21] All these features are exploited in the *Canons*. This is illustrated in Example 2.40.

This passage has interesting ensemble features. The clarinet has two lynes of the array, which are sometimes distinguished by register and other times distinguished by dynamic level.[22] At the outset of the passage, the clarinet's lynes are generated from [0, 1, 2] trichords, ordered in the way they are found segmentally in the fundamental interval pattern of the work's underlying row class. Later, the clarinet employs other ordered trichords, based on the remaining interior trichordal segments of the row. The flute part at the outset is based on [0, 1, 3] hexachords, ordered in the manner found inside the first hexachord of the fundamental interval pattern. The remaining two instruments combine to form a final [0, 1, 3] trichord per aggregate, joining with the [0, 1, 3] trichord of the flute to create the complementary A-type hexachord to that of the pair of [0, 1, 2] trichords in the clarinet part. The oboe and bassoon, however, are each carrying their own lynes generated from [0, 2, 4] trichords ordered in part according to the appropriate segment of the fundamental interval pattern. The two instrumental parts unfold twice as slowly as the flute part to form [0, 1, 3] trichords between them. As the section progresses, the as-

Fl.: +1 -3

Example 2.40.   Woodwind Quartet, *Canons for Clarinet*: trichordal array

signment of trichords to instruments and pairs of instruments changes, with the clarinet always carrying two lynes.

Having explored the generative possibilities of the trichords of the row, Babbitt turns to another property of the work's fundamental ordering in the *Trios for Flute*. The new approach is embodied in essence in the brief passage between the *Canons for Clarinet* and the following major section. Just as the opening brief passage included motivic material for what followed, so does the present passage prepare the next sections. This is illustrated in Example 2.41.

Here we find our first example of Babbitt's use of tetrachordal combinatoriality, in which the aggregate is generated by three members of a single all-combinatorial tetrachordal collection class.[23] A glance at a member of the composition's row class reveals that its members may be partitioned into three concatenated [0, 1, 2, 3] tetrachords, each projecting a different interval pattern. Both the brief passage and the following *Trios* are composed of arrays formed by combining three tetrachords of this type unfolding various interval patterns of different sorts, different transformations of a given sort, or some combination of the two. Such arrays fundamentally differ from trichordal arrays in that no aggregate based on an undegenerate interval pattern can completely express the totality of the classical twelve-tone transformations. Babbitt nevertheless achieves this end in the brief adumbrational passage by shifting the completion of a statement of order transformations across the aggregate boundaries. Nor does the passage completely abandon the material that has gone before. Phrasing and dynamics bring out certain significant trichord types and orderings, and the flute line itself is a member of the work's underlying row class.

Example 2.41.   Woodwind Quartet. interlude. Reprinted by
permission of Associated Music Publishers, Inc. (BMI)

The next brief passage, between the flute's *Trios* and the bassoon's
Duets, unfolds whole hexachords of the row, including rows within
individual instrumental parts. The passage foreshadows the following section, *Duets for Bassoon*, which employs different types of mosaics containing two [0, 1, 3] trichords and two [0, 1, 4] trichords, both
those found in the *Introduction* and those found in later arrays based
on members of the fundamental row class.

The *Cadenza for Oboe* is the culmination of the gradual presentation
of different foldings of the row. Here at last we have an aggregate that
represents a complete member of the row class unambiguously ordered in time. Nevertheless, much that has been heard before is embodied in the composition of this passage. The oboe's line is slurred to
bring out the sorts of tetrachords and dyads heard in earlier passages;
it is further registrally deployed to articulate trichordal mosaics based
on [0, 1, 4] heard at the outset. This is illustrated in Example 2.42.

The following *Recitative* consists of four row statements presented
in classical Schoenbergian fashion. Each trichord of each row in the
oboe is accompanied by the remaining instruments playing the remaining trichords of the row ordered in register. The trichords have
been divided up to yield aggregates in the lines of the accompanying

Example 2.42.   Woodwind Quartet, *Cadenza for Oboe*. Reprinted by permission of Associated Music Publishers, Inc. (BMI)

instruments, based on a variety of trichord and hexachord types. This passage is a salute to one of Babbitt's favorite compositions by Arnold Schoenberg, the Fourth String Quartet, op. 37. Schoenberg's work opens in much the same manner as the *Recitative*, with complete row statements in the first violin accompanied by their own trichords played as simultaneities in the remaining instruments. What clinches the resemblance, however, is the duplication of a significant detail in Schoenberg's work, the composition of its first aggregate. As Babbitt has noted, the combination of the two violin parts and the combination of the viola and cello parts in the opening aggregate of Schoenberg's work yields a transposition of the segmental hexachordal mosaic of the first violin's row, foreshadowing a later passage in the composition.[24] In Babbitt's own Woodwind Quartet, the analogous combination of the flute and oboe parts of the first aggregate of the *Recitative* yields a hexachord that is not only the same type as that found in the instrumental lines of the work's opening but the same type as Schoenberg used in his Fourth Quartet! This is illustrated in Example 2.43.

The *Finale* is composed of different passages exploiting the various combinatorial potentials of the work's fundamental row class. Several features are worth mentioning. The *Finale* contains all the possible duos and trios of the ensemble and features both tetrachordal and trichordal arrays. Some of the tetrachordal arrays are based on canons of complete row statements, as illustrated in Example 2.44. It is worth noting that the slurring of the passage emphasizes trichords.

Of particular interest are trichordal arrays based on the four ordered trichords of the row. Unlike the trichordal arrays found in the *Introduction*, the lynes of the arrays found in the *Finale* contain hexachords made of one of each of the trichord types, so that the resulting

Example 2.43. Schoenbergian echo. String Quartet no. 4, op. 37, by Arnold Schoenberg, copyright © 1939 (renewed) by G. Schirmer, Inc. (ASCAP); Woodwind Quartet by Milton Babbitt reprinted by permission of Associated Music Publishers, Inc. (BMI)

Example 2.44.   Woodwind Quartet: tetrachordal array. Reprinted by permission of Associated Music Publishers, Inc. (BMI)

trichordal mosaics are of different types from those found in the earlier passage. The contrast between the two passages is emblematic of the strategy of the composition.[25] This is illustrated in Example 2.45.

The work closes with a final synoptic passage, conjoining material from all over the composition. Some of the more literal of the multitude of echoes are illustrated in Example 2.46.

Central to the work, and implicit in the plurality of its various sectional titles is the notion of multiple interpretation, the simultaneous or successive reinterpretation of the composition's constituent materials. Much of the drama of the work involves the exploration of the mosaic-generating possibilities of its constituent trichords, and many passages afford the listener the chance to interpret aggregates in more than one way, depending on grouping criteria. The *Canons*, *Trios*, and *Duos* all contain several different interpretations of the surface, each reflecting a different mosaic configuration of the basic materials of the piece. The different combinations of configurations constitute the compound strategies of the composition, gradually revealing its underlying row structure. While all the myriad relations of the work are implicit in the structure of its fundamental row class, the strategies with which they are revealed are not. It is the composition of these strategies into a coherent, dramatic unfolding that is at the heart of

Example 2.45. *Woodwind Quartet*: contrasting trichordal arrays.
Reprinted by permission of Associated Music Publishers, Inc. (BMI)

making twelve-tone music, and following them through a work is central to our pleasure as listeners.

STRING QUARTET NO. 2

Milton Babbitt's Second String Quartet has received a fair amount of attention as well as a good number of performances, and it has become one of his better-known works.[26] We shall not spend too much time discussing this piece, except to show how it draws on a great deal of what we have already discussed and combines these by now familiar techniques and materials with some materials we have not looked at so far. These new materials have themselves been used in an earlier work, the song cycle *Du*, which we shall discuss later in the

Example 2.46.   Woodwind Quartet: final bars and cross-references.
Reprinted by permission of Associated Music Publishers, Inc. (BMI)

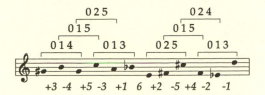

Example 2.47.   String Quartet no. 2:
row structure

chapter. The string quartet, however, marks the apotheosis of the strategic design of the three works we have already examined, while *Du* represents a different line of compositional strategy.

The string quartet shares a number of features with both the *Composition for Viola and Piano* and the Woodwind Quartet. It is in four large sections of varying length, distinguished by tempo, ensemble, muting, doublings, and so forth. The first and third sections are based for the most part on trichordal arrays, while the second section, for muted string trio dispensing with the second violin, is based on tetrachordal arrays. The final section is based on arrays with variable numbers of lynes and is marked by the most concentrated emergence of the work's fundamental interval pattern at the musical surface. In addition to the sorts of arrays that expand upon trichords, tetrachords, and hexachords of the underlying row class, the string quartet also contains passages generated from dyads.[27]

Like the other pieces we have examined, the string quartet is an intense examination of the properties of a fundamental twelve-tone interval pattern. The member of the work's fundamental row class that appears at the beginning of the fourth section is found in Example 2.47.

The row is the unique nondegenerate all-interval ordering of a pair of A-type hexachords, to within order-number transposition by six.[28] In the most general terms, the work as a whole progresses through the segments of the row much the way the *Composition for Viola and Piano* progresses through its fundamental ordering, but the string quartet is nowhere near so straightforward and symmetrical as the earlier work. Like the Woodwind Quartet, the Second String Quartet takes advantage of the all-combinatorial tetrachord found segmentally to generate the arrays of its second section. In addition to being all-interval, we can also see that the row does not represent the sort of mosaic of its discrete trichords familiar from the earlier pieces. This observation has many consequences in the way the piece unfolds.

As in the *Composition for Viola and Piano*, the two longest sections of

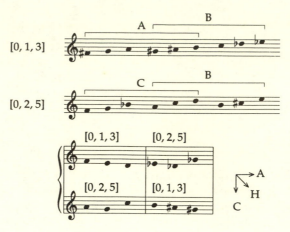

Example 2.48.   [0, 1, 3] and [0, 2, 5] trichords,
and generated hexachords

the string quartet compose out the trichords of the two hexachords in various combinations within arrays.[29] Here the resemblance ends, however. The two sections are not directly analogous, as in the viola work. In addition to the trichordal arrays, the sections are further interspersed with dyadic passages projecting the successive intervals of the row. The dyadic passages are distinguished in the musical surface by their use of octaves to project lynes. But even more striking in the overall progression of the string quartet is the fact that, unlike both the earlier works, not all the trichords within the hexachords are generators of the hexachord type in question, and each hexachord invokes a different world of trichord-hexachord mosaic relations. The first hexachord invokes the world of the compositions we have examined with its [0, 1, 4], [0, 1, 3], and [0, 1, 5] trichords; its [0, 2, 5] trichord is the only new addition to the family and can both itself generate B-type hexachords or be combined with a [0, 1, 4] trichord once again to generate a B hexachord.

The second hexachord, however, is a different world. Its discrete trichord types, [0, 1, 3] and [0, 2, 5], combine in mosaics variously to generate A-, B-, and C-type hexachords, in a manner subtly different from what we have seen before. This is illustrated in Example 2.48. As may be seen, each of the two trichord types may generate B-type hexachords, while [0, 1, 3] generates A-type hexachords and [0, 2, 5] generates C-type hexachords. So far, the situation is similar to that of the trio of A, B, and E hexachord types focused by selecting two of the three trichord types [0, 1, 3], [0, 1, 4,], and [0, 1, 5]. What is different

All B-type hexachords

Example 2.49.   String Quartet no. 2: B-type hexachords

about the trichord and hexachord family in question, however, is the fact that [0, 1, 3] and [0, 2, 5] can be combined with each other to produce both A hexachords *and* C hexachords and can do so simultaneously in the same mosaic! This property cannot be duplicated within the former family of trichords and hexachords; the only pair of different trichord types that combine to form an all-combinatorial hexachord within that family is [0, 1, 3] and [0, 1, 4], which we know yields the A-type hexachord, the same that this particular pair of trichords makes the focus of the trio of hexachords. The relational balance among the three hexachord types of the second family is considerably different, and this difference underlies the significantly different strategic qualities of the song cycle *Du*.[30] In the string quartet, the difference serves to underscore the contrast between the two major sections of the composition.

Still another set of features distinguishes the two large portions of the string quartet. While the trichordal arrays of the first section conjoin trichords in for the most part familiar configurations, the third section contains not only trichords from the second hexchord but those from the first hexachord, and complete instances of the first hexachord, as well. A special feature of the four segmental trichords of the second hexachord is that all of them can generate the B-type hexachord, and this is exploited in an extended passage for the two violins. This is illustrated in Example 2.49.

The unique feature of the [0, 2, 4] trichord type—that it can generate all three first-order, all-combinatorial hexachords—is also exploited in the third section, in passages where it is conjoined in various mosaics with itself or other trichord types, or with complete instances of the initial hexachord. An example is illustrated in Example 2.50. The effect over the span of the work is a constant accumulation of relations within and between the constituent parts of the composition's fundamental interval pattern.

We have dealt with the string quartet in only the most general terms to show its communality with the preceding pieces and to suggest

Example 2.50.   String Quartet no. 2: [0, 2, 4] trichords. Copyright © 1967 by
Associated Music Publishers, Inc. (BMI). International copyright secured.
All rights reserved. Reprinted by permission

certain ways it extends Babbitt's techniques. We have had to pass over
many interesting features, including the surface composition of aggregates, the use of different kinds of instrumental articulation to project various types of all-combinatorial hexachords in an overlying web
of additional relationships, the use of certain fixed transpositions of
the various hexachord types based on those two index numbers that
will map the hexachords of the row found at the beginning of the
fourth section onto themselves or each other, and the various ways
dyads are compounded to form aggregates in the dyadic passages.
These features have been covered elsewhere, and I hope the preceding has been sufficiently intriguing to invite the reader to explore the
work further.[31]

We shall make only one further point about the string quartet. As
we suggested in the previous chapter, Babbitt employs duration rows
to structure the rhythmic surface of the piece, taking advantage of the
consequences of the row's structures in its durational interpretation.
The majestic rocking of the dyads that sweep the work to its close is a
result of the inversional invariance previously discussed. The constant presence of hexachords of equal length is also a feature of the
transformations Babbitt has elected to use, as we mentioned before.

Unlike rhythmic structures we have examined in previous pieces,
however, Babbitt has additionally employed trichordally derived duration rows in the quartet. These have also been constructed to reflect
the sorts of transformational invariance found in the duration rows
based on the underlying pitch class row. Example 2.51 contains the
duration rows of portions of the composition. As may be seen, the
rhythms of the dyadic passages are based on duration interpretations
of the fundamental row, while the trichordal passages are based on
derived duration rows built with the same types of trichords as are

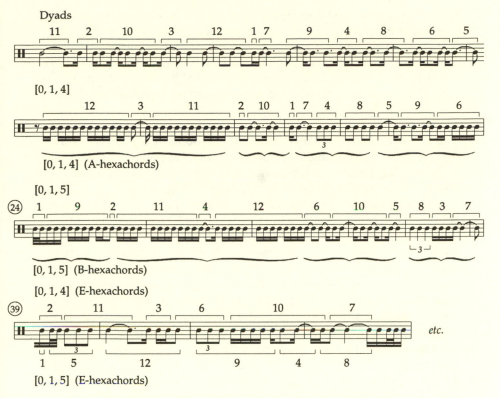

Example 2.51.   String Quartet no. 2: derived duration rows

found in the pitch class arrays. The pitch class array built on two trichord types employs pairs of trichordally derived duration rows superimposed, based on the two trichord types of the pitch array.

Additional Compositional Strategies

All the compositions we have examined so far have in various ways only gradually exposed the underlying orderings that govern their structures. In the *Composition for Four Instruments*, the fundamental interval pattern emerges through the progressive recombination of its discrete trichords. In the *Composition for Viola and Piano*, the discrete trichords continue to dominate the composition's progress, while the remaining segmental trichords, both within and between hexachords, take on important secondary roles. The particular qualities of the basic hexachord determine a further distinction between trichords within hexachords and trichords crossing the hexachordal boundary. The same properties of the hexachord also permit shifting transpositions of the generating trichords against fixed transpositions of the hexachord, creating a dialectic between collection and interval pattern among sections of the music. Longer interval patterns emerge in the use of ordered hexachords and complete rows in certain sections of the piece.

The two later pieces offer a dramatic contrast of approach within the context of gradual revelation. The Woodwind Quartet offers a new means of revealing its underlying interval pattern, as well as a new way of projecting differences of trichordal collections against fixed hexachordal collections. In the quartet, segments from throughout the row are always present, combined for the most part to project a fixed transposition level of the fundamental hexachord type.[32] From section to section, longer and longer stretches of the row are conjoined in the arrays. Much of the drama of this work arises from the fact that the two trichord types found discretely in the two hexachords can be assembled into different types of mosaic, all of which can project the same hexachord type. In contrast, the String Quartet no. 2 moves gradually through the structure of its row, examining every segment individually, and only eventually combining different stretches. The ordering of its hexachords are wildly dissimilar, and the composition accretes a wealth of different combinational strategies in its progress. While the Woodwind Quartet's materials always fold in on themselves to generate variously the same hexachordal collections, the Second String Quartet's materials reach out to sweep in a variety of collections of different types. Guiding this potentially overwhelming accumulation is a careful use of two fixed index numbers, one and seven, that map the hexachords of the row found at the outset of the last section onto either themselves or each other. Virtually all the other all-combinatorial hexachords used in the composition map onto themselves or their complements under these two index numbers, ensuring a constant recirculation of a fixed number of dyads and larger collections within and between the lynes of the myriad different arrays.

In both quartets, the underlying strategy is to reveal the controlling interval pattern of the work complete only by the end of the piece, but this is accomplished in radically different ways. The wind composition pulls ever-longer segments out of its sleeve, all dealing with the same hexachords, while in the string work we swirl through a wealth of different collectional material to the single pattern of intervals that can act as a crossroads for all the myriad collectional pathways in the music. The expressive natures of the two pieces arise from the ways their strategies for revealing their basic interval patterns interact with the collectional materials contained in those patterns. The earlier work's trenchant striving outward into increasingly longer segments of its interval pattern is always circumscribed by the constantly regenerated chromatic hexachord. In the string quartet, our quest for a single governing factor takes us through a wide and varied terrain. The underlying drama of each work depends on the dialectical opposition of its compositional strategy and the portion of the twelve-tone universe it occupies. The exchange of strategies and domains for the two pieces would produce two remarkably different compositions.

Although all the pieces we have discussed have been revelatory in various ways, it should not be assumed that gradual assembly or emergence are the only strategies Babbitt used to shape his compositions during his first period. Different materials and orientations suggest different musical unfoldings; we have merely traced one particularly vivid strand through Babbitt's oeuvre and will now turn to examples of a couple of contrasting approaches. Although the following pieces are for the most part based on the familiar trichordal arrays projecting the familiar partitions of four distinct items, each uses combinations of trichords and all-combinatorial hexachords that invite markedly different approaches from those we have seen so far.

Du

Du is a cycle of seven songs on poems by August Stramm, written for soprano voice and piano.[33] Between the first and second songs and between the last two songs are two piano interludes. *Du* distills a distinctly different compositional strategy from its material, compared to those works we have analyzed. As suggested above, its controlling structural premise is the relationships among the A, B, and C hexachords mediated by the two trichord types [0, 1, 3] and [0, 2, 5]. The underlying array structure of the opening two aggregates encapsulates these relationships and is illustrated in Example 2.52.

As may be seen, each lyne is made up of a [0, 1, 3]- and a [0, 2, 5]-type trichord, with the upper two parts—the voice and highest register of the piano—forming A-type hexachords and the lower two forming C-type hexachords. The resulting columnar aggregates are based on mosaics each generated from one of the two trichord types and containing A-, B-, C-, and H-type hexachords. Each columnar aggregate represents the four classical transformations of an ordered trichord. Much of the song cycle consists of a panoramic review of the possible orientations of these types of mosaics within the subsequent arrays. A quick glance at a segment of the array structure of the final

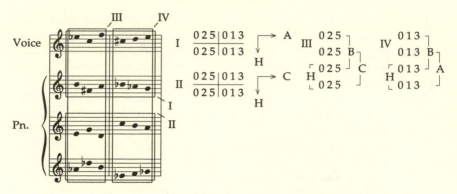

Example 2.52.   *Du.* first song, initial aggregates

song reveals the exchange of hexachord types within lynes, and one may find the columnar mosaic types appearing in various lynes of other songs. See Example 2.53.

But the structure of the song cycle is a bit more subtle than the simple shifting of mosaic distributions. A glance at both Examples 2.52 and 2.53 reveals that no two linear hexachords are ordered in the same way. What, then, controls the unfolding of the work? A clue may be garnered from the composition of the aggregates at the beginning of the opening song. This passage is reproduced in Example 2.54.[34]

Each of the four aggregates of the passage may be heard as generated from a different ordered trichord type, arising from the combination of notes from the different lynes of the array. Two of these are the ordered trichord types of the underlying array; the other two are

Example 2.53.   *Du:* last song, initial aggregates

Example 2.54. *Du*: first song, trichordal details. Copyright © 1957 by Boelke-Bomart, Inc., Hillsdale, N.Y. Reprinted by permission

II. Wankelmut

Mein _____ Su - chen sucht!

Example 2.55. *Du*: second song,
initial trichord. Copyright © 1957 by
Boelke-Bomart, Inc., Hillsdale, N.Y.
Reprinted by permission

found segmentally within the voice's opening hexachord. That the latter two trichord types will control much of the remainder of the composition is immediately apparent both in the piano interlude and in the beginning of the second song. As Example 2.55 illustrates, the second song begins with a trichord found segmentally within the voice's opening line.

What of the last song, with the C-type hexachords in the voice? We can see that the C-type hexachord cannot contain the [0, 1, 4] trichord type; therefore we must seek another path of reasoning to connect this particular orientation of the fundamental mosaics to the initial song. We can do this as follows: It will be remembered that [0, 1, 4] with [0, 1, 5] and [0, 1, 3] variously link the A-, B-, and E-type hexachords in arrays, as was found in all the previously discussed pieces. By analogy, [0, 3, 7] along with [0, 1, 5] and [0, 2, 5] form an identical grouping of the trio of hexachord types, C, B, and E. Babbitt has ordered his two constituent trichord types, [0, 2, 5] and [0, 1, 3], so that at the proper transposition and relative orientation, they may be conjoined in an ordered A-type hexachord containing [0, 1, 4]- and [0, 1, 5]-type trichords segmentally, and an ordered C-type hexachord containing [0, 3, 7]- and [0, 1, 5]-type trichords segmentally. These are the two ordered hexachords found in the voice in the first and last songs.

It is worth noting that the eight ordered hexachords found in the lynes of the opening pairs of aggregates from the first and last songs represent the eight possible ways of conjoining the interval patterns of the two generating trichord types within the A- and C-type hexachords. Only the two hexachords found in the vocal part at these two spots contain within themselves segmentally those trichords that will create the kinds of relationships among the work's constituent hexachords and the E-type hexachord that underlie the composition's array structures. The remaining hexachords either contain a duplicate trichord type or imply different chains of relationships with other hexachord types. The two vocal orderings are furthermore the only

Example 2.56.   *Du*: first interlude, array structure

two that can generate all-interval rows. The whole song cycle is symmetrically disposed to display the analogous array-generating properties of the two sets of hexachord trios containing E-type hexachords, all providing the motivations for the overall pattern of reorientations of the fundamental mosaics found in the opening two aggregates.

All of the above could have been explained with a different theoretical apparatus: the circle-of-fifths transformation, which transforms a musical structure by mapping the chromatic scale onto the circle of fifths.[35] Babbitt uses this transformation in his later period in ways we shall investigate in the next chapters, but I have chosen not to describe the workings of *Du* in this way in order to dramatize how the piece constantly reorients its fundamental mosaic materials, made of both trichords and hexachords, in its underlying arrays. Although I feel that the aural consequences of the circle-of-fifths transformation, based on the redistribution of intervals in consistent ways, can be a vivid part of hearing twelve-tone music, in *Du* the most immediate consequence of Babbitt's operations is the manipulation of the recognizable ordered trichords heard at the very opening.[36]

The same principle of reorientation is demonstrated in the first piano interlude. This passage also embodies another subtlety of the composition that has ramifications later in the cycle (as with most of our analyses, our brevity can only hint and entice, but then again that is the point of this volume). The interlude is made of a three-part tetrachordal array, but the lynes themselves contain trichordally generated rows. The first half of the array is built of trichord types [0, 1, 3], [0, 1, 4], and [0, 1, 5], and the second half is built of [0, 1, 3], [0, 1, 5], and [0, 2, 5] types. These are the four trichord types found in the initial vocal hexachord, and they are ordered by the interval patterns found therein.[37] This is illustrated in Example 2.56.

Example 2.57. *Du*: first interlude, trichordal details. Copyright © 1957 by Boelke-Bomart, Inc., Hillsdale, N.Y. Reprinted by permission

Not only do the lynes of the interlude themselves represent the relocation of the trichords found temporally in the opening aggregates but the interlude itself embodies trichordal reorientation in the composition of its aggregates. The second half of the interlude is composed so that the slurred and simultaneous trichords formed by the combination of lynes themselves represent the same kinds of ordered trichords as those found in the lynes of the preceding part of the interlude. This is not a consequence of the circle-of-fifths transformation but does represent the same sort of compositional strategies found throughout the work. The passage is illustrated in Example 2.57.

Du differs from the other pieces we have looked at in that it does not have a single twelve-tone ordering that controls the entire composition. What it does have is a central compositional idea, based on the mosaic-forming properties of two kinds of trichords and the all-combinatorial hexachords they may generate. The cyclical nature of the composition is reflected in the way its constituent mosaics are constantly reoriented, but a sense of forward, cumulative motion arises through the use of that special band of trichord types that appear segmentally in the controlling vocal part. This becomes particularly dramatic in the penultimate song, the first appearance in the vocal part of the [0, 3, 7] trichord type, the one type of the work's material that is not contained in the opening passage. What seems the most remote moment in the composition becomes integrated into the whole with the opening of the final song, where the [0, 3, 7] trichord appears in the context of the opening mosaics of the composition, the point of completion of several different long-range strategies.[38]

PARTITIONS

Still another set of strategies underlies Babbitt's work *Partitions*, a brief but dense composition for piano written in 1957. The work is based on an ordered B-type hexachord and contains seven sections. The piano is divided into seven registers, and each of the seven sections unfolds its four-lyne array in a different set of four registers drawn from the registral totality. Like most of the pieces we have looked at, *Partitions* is based on trichordal arrays derived from the segmental trichords of the work's underlying interval pattern, in this case generating an ordered all-combinatorial hexachord, rather than a complete twelve-tone row.[39] Unlike those other works, however, *Partitions* presents its fundamental interval pattern right at the start, in a four-part array projected over the widest possible separation, the unique subset of four noncontiguous registers. Each register contains a complete aggregate, formed by following an initial ordered hexachord with its retrograde transposed by a tritone. The remainder of the piece consists of six sections of trichordal arrays derived variously from the segmental trichords of the fundamental interval pattern. Each of the subsequent patterns is eight aggregates long and unfolds the by now seemingly inevitable partitions of four distinct items into two or fewer parts. A summary of the work's pitch structure is found in Example 2.58.

Several interesting points spring to view. First, the pitch class partitions of the array of the first section are not the same as those found in the remaining trichordal arrays. Obviously the new partitions have been created through the simple swapping of elements across aggregate boundaries of a straightforward trichordal array, but nevertheless they yield a remarkably different shape on the musical surface.[40] This is not the first appearance in Babbitt's compositions of irregularly partitioned aggregates; one need only consider the final synoptic passage of the Woodwind Quartet for an earlier example, but this technique is the harbinger of the music to follow in Babbitt's second and third compositional periods.

Second, we can see that with the exception of the final section, all the subsequent sections of the piece employ combinations of trichords in their derivations, consisting of two lynes each derived from a given trichord type. These five sections represent the five possible combinations of two trichord types drawn from the hexachord that can generate the same all-combinatorial hexachord type. The only combination that cannot, [0, 1, 4] and [0, 2, 5], are the two trichords found discretely in the fundamental ordering. The final section, in a

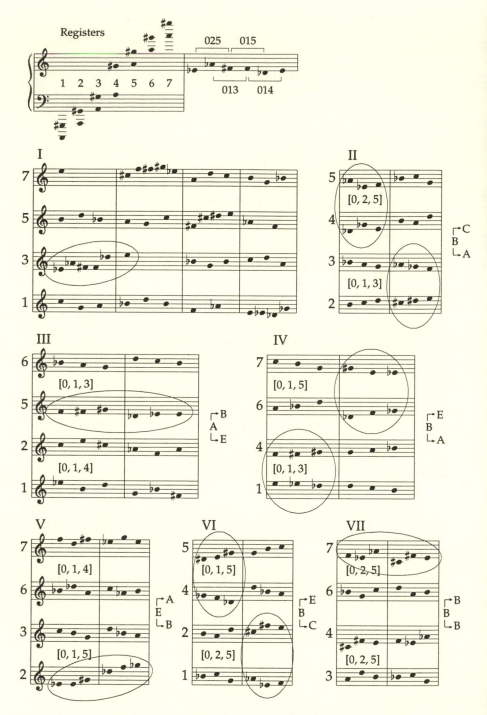

Example 2.58. *Partitions*: registral and trichordal structures

sense the punch line of the composition, is based on a single trichord type, [0, 2, 5].[41] This is the only one of the two discrete segmental trichords that will generate the same type of hexachord as is generated by the fundamental interval pattern.

A constant throughout the composition is the use of fixed transposition levels for the hexachord types found in the lynes and columns of the arrays. Thus, one can trace through the work the constant reshuffling and reorientation of a fixed number of A, B, C, and E hexachordal collections at various locations in the arrays. The B hexachord, the type of the fundamental interval pattern, is the only hexachord found in all the arrays in the piece and is the thread we follow through the progress of the piece.

We must pass over much of the richness of the composition's details, but we can gain a sense of them by inspecting the composition of the opening aggregate. As may be seen, all the simultaneities, as well as the slurred groups, represent trichords of the types found in the subsequent arrays, in their proper orderings.[42] This is illustrated in Example 2.59.

Later in the composition additional trichord types are introduced in the details, reflecting various cross-relations among the fundamental materials of the work.

Our principal concern with this rather brief look at a composition, which despite its actual length is anything but brief, is to observe the way its overall strategies differ from what we have already examined. *Partitions*, in a move that is the reverse of the revelatory compositions, seems downright confessional with its initial divulgence of the most concentrated versions of its compositional premises in the form of the registrally distinct ordered hexachords. The remaining sections tenaciously probe the implications of the opening passage, eventually rendering back to us the same hexachordal collections in the same relative registral orientation, but now normalized, in effect, both by the regularity of their partitions and by their generation from a single ordered trichord type.

The background progression of confession, scrutiny, and purification is counteracted by the composition of the surface details, however. During the opening section, the details of each aggregate dutifully manifest the various trichordal interval patterns of the fundamental ordering, articulated in both register and time. With the advent of the subsequent passages, new interval patterns associated with familiar trichord types as well as various orderings of new trichord types emerge, causing the surface to invoke more remote realms, just as the background is sorting out and simplifying its basic premise. This is dramatically apparent in the last aggregates of the

Example 2.59. *Partitions*: initial bars, trichordal details.
Reprinted by permission of Lawson-Gould Music Publishers, Inc.

work, in which, among other things, the fundamental B-type hexa-chordal collections of the composition arise out of the counterpoint generated by a new ordering of [0, 1, 5] trichords, and new trichord types [0, 1, 2], [0, 2, 7], and [0, 1, 6] are abundantly represented. These latter have been introduced in the composition of details in the preceding trichordal sections. The last bars of the work appear in Example 2.60.

One other feature of *Partitions* is worth mentioning, due to its implications for Babbitt's later work. An aspect of the rhythmic structure of the piece is another reflection of its title. The work appears to be an attempt to use all the fifty-eight partitions of twelve into six or fewer parts in the rhythmic domain. In the present case, bundles of twelve unit-durations are parsed into time spans that are in turn filled with equal rhythmic-value strings of various sorts. The unit-duration

Example 2.60. *Partitions*: final bars, trichordal details.
Reprinted by permission of Lawson-Gould Music Publishers, Inc.

changes between the sextuplet in the $\frac{4}{4}$ and $\frac{2}{4}$ bars, and the sixteenth note in the $\frac{3}{4}$ bars. Downbeats, whether articulated or not, initiate new partitioned spans. The rhythm of the opening bars is found in Example 2.61.

Because of ambiguities in the interpretation of certain sections, the scheme cannot be followed out completely; Babbitt has indicated that other compositional factors did not allow him to realize fully this particular aspect of the rhythmic structure in the composition,[43] but in later works he was able to employ similar strategies to shape his music. In comparison to the other works we have observed, *Partitions* represents a notably different technique in the rhythmic domain, but

Example 2.61. *Partitions*: rhythmic partitions

it has its precursor in *Semi-Simple Variations*. As I mentioned in the previous chapter, the surface rhythms of the earlier piece are based on the various subsets of four sixteenth-notes. We shall see a similar practice in the next work we shall examine, *All Set*.

ALL SET

With *All Set* and *Partitions*, Babbitt began giving his compositions epi-grammatic titles at once humorous and elliptically descriptive of their materials and procedures. His earlier title *Composition* is less self-effacing than one might think at first, however, when one remembers the use of the term in mathematics to refer to ordered partitions in combinatoric theory.[44] Babbitt's more recent titles carry multiple meanings suggestive of their works' attributes. *Partitions*, as we may infer from the preceding, is about partitions on many different levels: the aggregates themselves represent various partitions of twelve, as does the rhythmic structure, whereas the registral progression through the piece represents various partitions of musical space into active and inactive slices. Nor should we forget the partitions of four distinct items into two or fewer parts displayed by the trichordal lay-out of the aggregates, for that matter.

All Set is for a jazz ensemble consisting of alto and tenor sax-ophones, trumpet, trombone, vibraphone, drum set, string bass, and piano. Although the work is fully written out and is based on many of the structures we have already discussed, the piece is nevertheless imbued with qualities of jazz, particularly the more complex jazz of the late 1940s and early 1950s. It is to be played very fast, and despite its straight notation, it should swing.

The work is a reinterpretation of a number of jazz characteristics in Babbitt's own compositional world. It also represents a number of departures from or extensions to the practice he had developed over the previous dozen years. In *All Set* Babbitt generated his row class from the D-type all-combinatorial hexachord for the first time. This hexachord type is profoundly different from the other all-combinato-rial hexachord types Babbitt had been using for a number of reasons involving the abstract nature of the total chromatic; the composition ventures across a very different part of the twelve-tone topography from what we have already seen, and intersects with more familiar terrain in rather peculiar ways.

The most obvious difference, and one that colors the whole sound of the work, is that while the A-, B-, C-, and E-type hexachords all exclude the tritone, the D hexachord contains *three* tritones. This very particular musical color—in previous works relegated to marking the passage from one compositional unit to another, be it trichords, hexa-chords, or complete rows within lynes of an array—now occurs ob-sessively, insistently, at the center of the action. It would seem inevi-table that Babbitt at some time or another would want to explore the properties of the D all-combinatorial hexachord, but how appropriate to initiate that expansion of his technique with a work that reverber-ates with the evocations of a body of music so fundamentally engaged with its own exploration of extended functional uses of the tritone!

The work is in three big sections followed by a drum solo with the bass and a final brief coda. The body of the work consists of the sixty-three subsets of the six-member ensemble comprising the reeds, the brass, plus the vibraphone and the piano. The bass part does not participate in the array structure of the work but picks up notes from the ensemble to create row-related lines of its own. The sixty-three subsets are arranged into three sections of twenty-one subsets each. With the exception of the first subset, all three sections contain the same distribution of subset size throughout, although they are not isomorphic in terms of instrumental distributions. Example 2.62 is a chart of the instrumental sections of *All Set*.

For the most part, the music of the instrumental subsets within each section is composed of trichordal arrays derived from the various segmental trichords of the fundamental ordering. There are a variety of exceptions, including subsections that are simply statements of complete rows and arrays constructed from more than four lynes in some of the quintet sections. Example 2.63 offers a sample trichordal array along with a portion of one of the more unusual arrays of the piece.

Each of the three sections is initiated by the equivalent of a head in a jazz composition, and the work closes with a similar passage. At the outset, the head is played by the six primary instruments, without bass or drums. The two other sections are initiated by complementary three-member ensembles, drawing one instrument from each of the three timbral duos. The coda unites the entire octet for the first time. The heads are based on four-part arrays containing the four classical transformations of the work's interval pattern, combined not in a tri-chordal array but in an array composed of $4^2 2^2$ partitions. The nature of the work's hexachords and their orderings allows Babbitt to con-struct the arrays in two different ways. Example 2.64 illustrates the array found at the beginning of the work as well as the final eight-part array that is formed through the combination of the two four-part array types.

The unfolding of the subsets of the instrumental ensemble of *All Set* is a strategy familiar from Babbitt's earlier work, but it additionally

	Head	1	2	3	4	2	3	4	3	4	5	5	4	3	2	4	3	2	3	2	1
I Alto Sax.	—			—	—		—		—			—	—	—	—	—	—	—	—	—	—
Ten. Sax.	—		—	—	—			—			—	—								—	
Trpt.	—					—	—		—	—	—	—	—			—					
Tbn.	—						—		—	—	—					—			—		—
Vib.	—				—		—	—		—	—	—	—			—			—		
Pn.	—		—	—	—	—	—	—	—	—	—			—			—		—		
II Alto Sax.									—		—	—	—	—							
Ten. Sax.	—				—	—	—	—	—		—	—						—	—	—	
Trpt.	—			—	—	—					—	—	—						—		
Tbn.			—	—	—	—	—	—	—	—	—			—	—	—	—				
Vib.	—				—		—	—		—		—	—	—	—	—	—	—	—	—	—
Pn.				—				—			—	—	—	—			—	—		—	—
III Alto Sax.	—			—	—	—				—	—	—	—			—	—	—			
Ten. Sax.			—	—	—	—	—	—	—	—	—	—			—	—		—			
Trpt.				—	—	—	—	—			—	—	—	—	—	—	—	—	—	—	—
Tbn.	—					—	—	—	—	—	—	—	—			—		—			
Vib.					—					—	—								—	—	
Pn.	—					—	—		—	—	—					—		—			

Example 2.62. *All Set*: instrumental ensembles

echoes the improvised and composed solos and ensembles of jazz performance. This is further evoked by the variety of different ways the underlying arrays are composed, sometimes with individual instruments on a part and other times with octave or unison doublings. The fact that the basic shapes not only of the trichordal array but also of the ubiquitous trichordal distributions are present for most of the work also reflects jazz's formal structures, with their dialectic of an enormously varied surface elaborated over deeper fixed patterns of regularly recurring time spans. By opening each section of the work as well as closing the composition with arrays built of complete rows, Babbitt provides his music with the equivalent of a head, containing the raw materials for the subsequent elaborations just as the heads in jazz fix the harmonic landmarks for the ensuing improvisations.

Even the rhythmic structure reflects Babbitt's translation of jazz practice. The ensemble rhythm of the first eight bars, the head of the

Example 2.63. *All Set*: selected arrays

first section, presents the sixteen subsets of four eighth-notes in the sixteen half-notes of its duration. In the following sections, the rhythmic pattern is picked up and transformed extensively by the drums but for much of the opening section cycles around to a new transformation every eight bars. Later in the work this rhythmic pattern is augmented to sixteen bars, with the quarter-note as the unit, but its regular recycling throughout the composition sets up a pattern of recurring time spans against which the lengths of the instrumental sections flexibly vary. Like a lot of jazz, Babbitt's *All Set* creates a dialectic between the flexibility of its surface and the strict regularity of its underlying pitch and rhythmic structures.

All Set is not simply a pastiche of jazz gestures in a foreign syntax. Rather, Babbitt has perceived the strong analogies between his musi-

Initial Array

Final Array

Example 2.64. *All Set*: initial and final arrays

cal thinking and that of the jazz masters and has brought them most dramatically to the musical surface in this particular work. Although the composition is not jazz in the most immediate sense of the word, it nevertheless draws upon and reflects a wide range of jazz practices and attitudes that find resonance in Babbitt's musical world.

3

EXPANSION AND CONSOLIDATION

(1961–1980)

THE TEN YEARS following the completion of *All Set* saw an enormous expansion of Babbitt's compositional world. These years are marked by significant developments in all the areas of his music, from the underlying structures of both pitch and rhythm to the very way in which the sounding surface is produced. Most noticeable about the latter is the appearance during this period of Babbitt's first works for synthesizer, both alone and in combination with voice or instruments. These included the *Composition for Synthesizer*, *Ensembles* for synthesizer, and one of the first works to combine live and electronic music in a tightly controlled collaboration, *Vision and Prayer*. Not to be ignored, however, are his first published orchestral works, *Relata I* and *Relata II*, which also represent a tremendous change in the sound of Babbitt's music.

As striking as the use of an orchestra or a synthesizer may be, it is in the domains of the underlying pitch and rhythmic structures that Babbitt's musical developments of the 1960s are most profound. Even though these structural changes may have been engendered by the new performing resources available to him, Babbitt did not relinquish them in his subsequent compositions for solo instruments or small ensembles, the instrumental complements of his earlier works. Most of Babbitt's compositions throughout his career have been for such forces, and the thinking that underlies his earliest work formed the foundation for his subsequent developments. The synthesizer represented for him not so much a different musical world as an opportunity to hear his music accurately performed. While it changed the ultimate limitations on his music making from what could be managed by a performer to what could be taken in by a listener,[1] the synthesizer did not mark a break in Babbitt's compositional style so much as it represented an invitation to expand the sorts of ideas he had been compiling during the previous twenty years.

Babbitt's orchestral music was found to be extremely demanding, and his experiences with performances of both *Relata*s, as well as *Correspondences* for string orchestra and synthesized tape, were not happy ones.[2] With the exception of the still-unperformed *Concerti* for violin, small orchestra, and synthesized tape, Babbitt waited until 1981 to write another work for an ensemble anywhere near orchestral size. Technical difficulties with the Mark II RCA synthesizer and the demands of time have also limited Babbitt's synthesized compositions, and the most recent at the time of writing is *Images* for saxophonist and synthesized tape, of 1979. The new resources that provided the impetus for Babbitt's compositional developments of the 1960s have not proved an unmixed blessing; nevertheless, those developments at the structural level wrought profound changes in his music, the implications of which he is exploring to this day.

The structural hallmark of Babbitt's compositional practice in his second period is the all-partition array, described briefly in the first chapter. The all-partition array did not appear suddenly in his music, nor did it completely supplant the trichordal array. We have mentioned several works of the first period containing aggregates with various partitions other than the simple compounding of four trichords, and the notion of partitional exaustion is evoked in the rhythmic structure of *Partitions*. However, the experiments in portions of the arrays of *All Set* or the *Composition for Twelve Instruments* do not set out to deal comprehensively with the question of partitions of lynes into twelve or fewer parts.[3] Nor was *All Set* the last large-scale trichord piece: the *Composition for Tenor and Six Instruments* of 1960 is even vaster and, in its use of trichordal arrays, more complex.[4] Both *Vision and Prayer* and the *Composition for Synthesizer* also employ trichordal arrays to a great extent. Such arrays underlie the *Minute Waltz* (1977)[5] and the *Three Cultivated Choruses* (1987) and play very important roles in several superarray compositions, including the recent *Consortini* (1989), as we shall discuss in the next chapter.

The other major structural contribution of the second period was the development of the time point system in the rhythmic domain, supplanting the duration rows of Babbitt's earlier works. The time point system seems to have had its genesis in Babbitt's electronic composition, and his first description of it appears in the article "Twelve-Tone Rhythmic Structure and the Electronic Medium" (1962). While some of the ideas in that article would seem to suggest compositional interpretations best suited to electronic or mechanical performance, the system itself was sufficiently flexible and musically general to find useful compositional employment in his purely instrumental works.[6] We shall see a variety of applications of the time point system in the subsequent discussions.

The typical practice of Babbitt's second period, the use of all-partition arrays in the pitch domain frequently composed with translations of the array structure into the rhythmic domain by means of

Example 3.1.   *Philomel*: initial aggregates

the time point system, was preceded by a number of interesting experiments. Both *Sounds and Words* (1960) for voice and piano and *Philomel* (1964) for soprano, recorded soprano, and synthesized tape employ rows whose hexachords are not members of the all-combinatorial collection classes used ubiquitously elsewhere in Babbitt's oeuvre.[7] In the former work, Babbitt has used the pair of hexachord types [0, 1, 2, 4, 7, 8] and [0, 1, 2, 5, 6, 8], which are not combinatorial under any but the trivial retrograde. However, the first of the pair is that unique type of hexachord that contains all twelve different trichord types as subsets, in effect marking the hexachordal apotheosis of his first period's trichordal underpinnings.[8]

Babbitt claims that *Philomel*'s unusual row construction arose from a programmatic impulse, vividly composed out at the beginning of the work.[9] As Richard Swift has described, the opening of the composition unfolds a series of six rows related by transposition so that in each successive row a given pitch class, E, moves successively through the order positions.[10] Each row, up through the appearance of the recurring note, is sung in the recorded voice, and the reiterated note plus the remaining notes form an aggregate. This is illustrated in Example 3.1.

One consequence of this operation is the presence of embedded ordered row segments spanning the passage. But it also reflects a reinterpretation of the sorts of properties underlying Stravinsky's rotational arrays and suggests the more general reasoning behind Babbitt's programmatic impulse.[11] The constraints placed upon the structure of the row in order that the passage might be composed as it is are considerable and exclude the all-combinatorial hexachords.[12]

Experimentation through the 1960s eventually led to a more codified yet flexibly interpretable set of practices embodied in a series of pieces running through the 1970s, and still employed to this day in such works as *Homily* (1987) and *Play It Again, Sam* (1989). In all these works, a collection of materials and strategies is recombined in a variety of ways reflecting Babbitt's constantly imaginative approach to making music.

Babbitt's enriched technique acted as a stimulant. Not only are many of the works of his second period larger and more complex than his earlier pieces but there are more of them. For this reason we must take a somewhat different approach to our subject. Rather than proceed piece by piece, we shall look at some more general considerations, illustrated with examples drawn from compositions, and conclude with two more extended analyses.

Effects of All-Partition Arrays

A superficial interpretation of Babbitt's second period practice might lead one to suppose his compositional method so straitjacketed by the use of pitch and rhythmic arrays that there would be no flexibility, that the method would compose works "automatically" with little or no variety. The fact that many pieces share arrays to within certain limited transformations would, under such suppositions, render the music even more impoverished in content and spirit. Happily, this could not be farther from the truth. Although the all-partition array is a powerful tool for structuring a composition, it is enormously flexible in the ways it may be projected and composed out. In the following pages we shall consider some of the ways the uses of all-partition arrays affect a composition, in both the pitch and the rhythmic domains, to suggest the variety of interpretations Babbitt has employed over his career.

There are three interrelated areas to consider when thinking about music using all-partition arrays. They are the abstract structure of the array, how it is projected on the surface of the music, and how the partial orderings determined by its individual aggregates are composed out. Each area affects and is affected by the others, and each area provides the composer with varying degrees of compositional flexibility. The same abstract array can be used under a variety of different strategies of projection and composition and concatenated in various transformations to create wildly different compositions. Like a twelve-tone row and its transformations, arrays contain certain structural potentials that can be realized in a number of different strategic solutions. The individuality of a given compositional solution will shed light on the more general aspects of the array, just as the fundamental structural attributes of an array will illuminate the family resemblance of diverse compositions based upon its transformations.

Abstract Array Structure

The abstract structure of the array affects a composition in a number of ways. It is itself, not surprisingly, highly determined by the nature of its underlying row class. As we discussed in the first chapter, Babbitt determines the number of lynes in an array by the number of distinct transpositional areas of the row's segmental all-combinatorial hexachords, each represented by a combinatorial lyne pair in the blocks of the array. Exceptions to this are the eight-part arrays of the Third String Quartet, in which the duplication of one of the D-type hexachordal areas in two lyne pairs echoes the duplication of an instrumental type in the ensemble,[13] and the early experimental hexachordal arrays of *Sextets*[14] and *Post-Partitions*, discussed in more detail below.

How rows are combined in lyne pairs considerably affects the qualities of an array. One particularly dramatic example may be drawn from the array used both in *Reflections* and, under the circle-of-fifths transformation, in *A Solo Requiem*.[15] Example 3.2 contains a block of the array.

The reader will note that the rows of the array can be generated from the row class of the Second String Quartet by swapping the hexachords. As we observed in our discussion of that work, one of the hexachords of this ordering inverts onto itself in such a way that the discrete dyads are preserved. Because the hexachord maps onto itself at an odd index number of inversion, we can see that the dyads preserved under inversion must themselves arise between like order numbers of a different pair of rows, inversionally related by the same index number. The array is constructed of six combinatorial row pairs, representing the six hexachordal areas, and all the combinatorial pairs are related by inversion. This means two things: not only are all six odd index numbers of inversion represented within individual hexachords in the six transpositional areas but the same six index numbers are all represented relating combinatorial pairs of rows. Thus, the discrete hexachordal dyads of the appropriate hexachords

Example 3.2.   All-partition array block

of each row in the array are found elsewhere in the array between like order numbers of combinatorial row pairs.[16]

The preceding example was derived from inversional combinatoriality, but the principle may be extended to include the other sorts of interval formations found between rows related by the other traditional operations. While the row class of *More Phonemena* (1977), for mixed chorus, extends the property of *Reflections'* first hexchord to all the discrete segmental dyads, its array combines its members in a wider variety of combinatorial relations within the row pairs, yielding new sets of relations between row segments and the intervals and collections produced between row pairs. This is illustrated in Example 3.3.

Example 3.3 illustrates a second strategy Babbitt has used for distributing rows within twelve-part arrays. As may be seen, the block can be broken into three quartets of rows, each quartet containing two combinatorial pairs. The rows of each quartet represent the four classical twelve-tone operations. Each of the three quartets exhibits a different relationship between the rows of its combinatorial pairs, thus exhausting the ways the four transformations may be conjoined to form combinatorial pairs. Successive blocks of arrays constructed in this manner contain transformations of entire quartets, preserving hexachordal areas as well as distributions of row transformations and relationships. Like the various locations for trichordal and hexachordal mosaics in the trichordal arrays discussed in the last chapter, the different locations of particular structures in these and other sorts of all-partition arrays allow multivalent compositional interpretations.

Another significant way in which the abstract structure of an array may affect a composition is the distribution of its partitions. All else being equal, each partition will have a unique ensemble of musical participants, determined by the way lynes are being projected, and the number of elements in its constituent lyne segments. Aggregates with many lynes participating will differ qualitatively from those with longer, fewer lyne segments. Big contrasts can be heard between highly differentiated aggregates; compare, for example, the opening aggregate of *Post-Partitions*, based on six dyads, one in each lyne pair, and a central aggregate also based on six dyads, but all in one lyne pair (we shall discuss this work in greater detail below). This is found in Example 3.4.

The various ways partitions are distributed in different arrays creates a striking contrast in our sense of flow through the aggregates of compositions employing them. The placement of the aggregate derived from a single lyne can be particularly dramatic from this point of view. In *Post-Partitions*, for example, this moment comes near the cen-

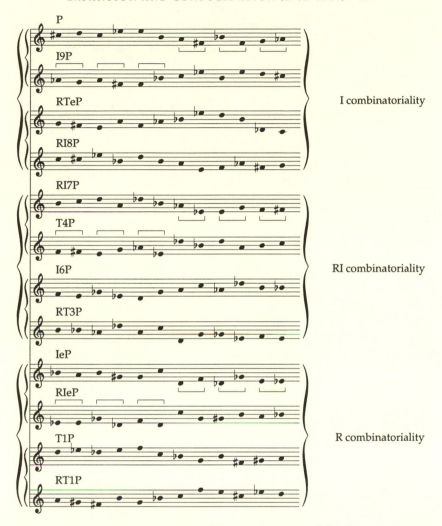

Example 3.3.   *More Phonemena*: preserved dyads

Example 3.4. *Post-Partitions*: contrasting aggregates.
Reprinted by permission of C. F. Peters Corporation

ter of the work, where the analogous moment in *My Complements to Roger* occurs near the end.[17] Both these works are brief piano pieces each using a single array transformation, but they are extraordinarily different, not only in their underlying array structures but in the way their details are composed out.

Different transformations of an array will preserve the distribution of its partitions to within retrogression, and this may be clearly heard in those pieces using concatenations of transformations of a given array. Various compositions that employ the same abstract array structure will tend to share the same sorts of distribution, the exception being those compositions employing an array whose constituent blocks contain no swapping across their boundaries. In such instances, the blocks of the array themselves may be redistributed, changing the flow of partitions. Such is the case with the array type shared by the Fourth String Quartet and *Phonemena* and that shared by *Sextets* and *Post-Partitions*.

Still another abstract structural feature of certain arrays has been mentioned in the first chapter: the use of each member of the array's row class exactly once. We have named these hyperaggregate or row class aggregate arrays to reflect their analogy with pitch class aggregates. This aspect of array structure has two immediate consequences. First, it guarantees each instance of the array's underlying interval pattern a specific distribution of the twelve pitch classes and provides any row invocation arising from some aggregate's partial ordering a specific point of reference in the underlying array. Second, it means that any transformation of the array that preserves its distinct hexachordal areas will simply be a reshuffling of the array's row contents, just as the classical transformations of a row reshuffle its pitch class contents. In both instances, the change of locations of constituent elements, whether pitch classes or entire rows, can provide the basis for creating musical structure.

The question of array transformation becomes particularly important in those works containing more than one instance of the array. As we shall see, Babbitt is especially attuned to the pathways of the various hexachordal areas through the partitions of successive arrays and so is concerned with the ways they are redistributed under various operations. Transformations involving transposition and retrogression, as we suggested in the opening chapter, are reasonably straightforward. In those arrays made with hexachords that may be transposed onto themselves at a given interval, such as the D- and E-type all-combinatorial hexachords, transposition of the entire array by that interval will preserve hexachordal areas in each lyne. This is the relationship between the arrays of the opening and closing sections of *Arie da Capo*.

Inversion invites two approaches, both of which Babbitt has used. Inverting the entire array by a single index number preserves the aggregates but shuffles the locations of the hexachordal areas in the array. In the case of the first-order all-combinatorial hexachords, for example, an odd index number will map one combinatorial pair of lynes onto themselves, map another pair a minor third away from the first pair onto each other, and exchange the remaining four by pair.[18] A clue to why this happens can be derived from the preceding discussion of the array of *Reflections*. An even index number scrambles all hexachordal locations by pairs. Babbitt uses such transformations in the Third String Quartet and *My Ends Are My Beginnings* (1978) for solo clarinetist, to mention a couple of examples.

The second approach is to invert each lyne pair by the index number that will invert the hexachordal contents of each lyne onto itself. This creates weighted aggregate arrays, and Babbitt has found such arrays to be very compositionally suggestive.[19] It should be noted that hyperaggregate arrays so inverted remain hyperaggregates, as all the hexachordal areas are preserved.

An interesting feature of arrays using rows whose hexachords can be inverted onto themselves or their complements at more than one index number is the fact that they may have their aggregates weighted in more than one way while still preserving the hexachordal areas of their lynes.[20] The different combinations of area-preserving index numbers for such arrays may change the nature of collections generated not only between lyne pairs but between lynes of combinatorial pairs themselves. Babbitt takes advantage of this property in *Arie da Capo*, which uses transformations of a fifty-eight-partition hyperaggregate array employing D-type hexachords.

Parenthetically, it should be noted that Babbitt has in at least one composition, *Four Play*, employed a different technique for weighting aggregates. In this work, for reasons that we shall explore in the next chapter, Babbitt has created weighted aggregates in part by retrograding the constituent rows of an array block without also reversing the order of the partitions.[21] This will also preserve hexachordal areas within lynes but will redistribute the pitch classes in ways that do not guarantee aggregates within the sequence of partitions.

Weighted aggregate arrays will, not surprisingly, create a very different sound on the surface of a composition, as different lynes project the same pitch class within the same time span. Just how these will arise on the surface will depend both on the manner of lyne projection and the composition of the array, but those portions of a composition using weighted aggregates will sound fundamentally different from those portions using classical aggregates. In compositions using a concatenation of array transformations, the placement of those using weighted aggregates will greatly affect our sense of the work. Three contrasting examples are provided by the String Quartet no. 4, *Arie da Capo*, and *An Elizabethan Sextette*. The earliest of these works, the quartet, contains four arrays arranged P, R, I, and RI, appropriately transformed to preserve pathways through the hexachordal areas. The second half of the piece is entirely composed of weighted aggregate arrays. Except for a few distinctive aggregates in which each collection within a lyne pair maps onto itself at the lyne pair's own index number, all of the second half is saturated with oc-

Example 3.5.   String Quartet no. 4: initiation
of weighted aggregates. Reprinted by permission of
C. F. Peters Corporation

taves arising from the weighted aggregates. This particular sonority is absent from the first half, and its emergence in the middle of the composition is a striking moment. This is illustrated in Example 3.5.

Arie da Capo is in five sections, the second and third of which are based on weighted aggregate arrays. Like the Fourth Quartet, this work's weighted aggregate passages are sonically distinguished by the use of octave doublings as well as of certain changes in the composition of their rhythms.[22] As hinted above, the arrays of the two sections are weighted in different ways, using two distinct sets of index numbers to preserve the hexachordal areas. The resulting collections formed between combinatorial rows are different in the two arrays, thus further distinguishing the two sections. Unlike the earlier work, *Arie da Capo* returns to the aggregate texture of its opening in the closing sections, framing the weighted aggregate passages with more normative twelve-tone music.

An Elizabethan Sextette in some ways is the strangest of all, opening with an array of weighted aggregates and arriving at its unweighted array only halfway through. The coyness with which this work reveals its underlying structures is reinforced in all aspects of its composition and echoes the nature of its texts.

The foregoing suggests some of the ways the abstract structure of an array can affect a composition. It also begins to intimate how different compositional decisions, even at an extremely abstract level, can set up markedly different musical strategies in works employing arrays. As we shall see in our discussions of lyne projection and surface composition, Babbitt has been able to keep alive the powerful compositional dialectics of his first period, in which the combination of different musical "genes" helps to create the individuality of a given piece in the larger context of a communal musical universe.

LYNE PROJECTION

Babbitt uses various means to project lynes of arrays in his music. In general, a given mode of projection is preserved for at least a complete row statement in a lyne, although there are exceptions.[23] Lynes are frequently projected by an instrument, or by a register of an instrument, as in his earlier music, but there are some additional techniques that are interesting. In *Relata I*, lynes of the array at the opening are projected by different ensembles of instruments, each of which has its own lyne to project over a longer span of the composition. At the initiation of the first array, following an introductory section, the two lyne segments of the first aggregate are projected by winds and strings, respectively, but each element of each lyne segment is played by a different instrument. This is found in Example 3.6.[24]

In *Phonemena*, the six lynes of its twelve-part array found in the voice are articulated by vowel sounds, freeing up register for different tasks. This work, like the *Composition for Tenor and Six Instruments*, *Sounds and Words*, and *More Phonemena*, does not set a text, but uses the voice to articulate a highly varied vocalise whose constantly changing syllables are projecting different structural strata.

In many compositions, a given lyne pair will be carried by the same mode of projection. Frequently, the two lynes will be distinguishable, by register or playing mode and articulation. In some works, however, lynes of combinatorial pairs are indistinguishable in the musical surface, suggesting that the partial orderings created by the combinatorial pairs of rows are of central interest. In other works, the degree to which one may distinguish lynes becomes part of the overall unfolding of the composition. In the piano work *My Complements to Roger* (1977), for example, the four lynes of the array, an all-partition array containing the thirty-four partitions of twelve into four or fewer parts, initially appear in two contiguous octaves in the middle of the keyboard. With the completion of aggregates formed by combinatorial pairs, the registers shift and gradually fan out, eventually separating the lynes into four distinct registers. These distinct registers collapse again, although not to the degree of compactness found at the opening. A climactic moment is achieved six aggregates before the

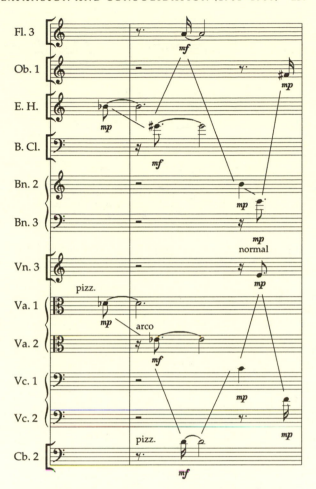

Example 3.6. *Relata 1*: 2⁶ partition aggregate.
Reprinted by permission of Associated Music
Publishers, Inc. (BMI)

(•)   Notes out of register
 o   Notes missing from registral aggregates
⌢   Direct continuation of incomplete registral aggregate
- - - -   Interrupted continuation of incomplete registral aggregate
 +   More than one lyne present in register

Example 3.7. *My Complements to Roger*: registral progression

Sextets, Part I

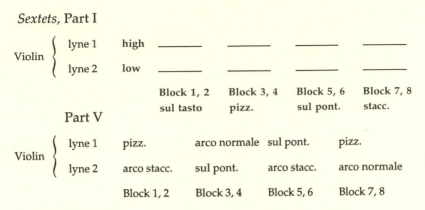

Example 3.8.   *Sextets*: row articulation in the violin

close with the appearance of the unique partition containing all twelve pitch classes in a single lyne. For this passage Babbitt has reserved the highest register of the instrument, not otherwise employed in the composition. A chart of the work's registral progression is found in Example 3.7.[25]

Motion through a composition, particularly one using several array transformations, is shaped and guided by the change of lyne projection. This frequently creates a vivid sonic progression that may be a good road into the heart of the music. Both *Sextets* (1966) for violin and piano and *Dual* (1980) for cello and piano articulate not only array transformations but blocks of their arrays with changes of numbers of lynes per instrument or modes of articulation. In *Sextets,* the five array transformations are differentiated by the number of lynes in the instruments, while blocks of the array are marked by changes in the violin's modes of playing.[26] The first and last sections provide a dramatic contrast in that while each has the same distribution of numbers of lynes between instruments, their uses of the violin's playing modes are quite different. This is illustrated in Example 3.8.

As may be seen, pairs of blocks of the array in the first section are distinguished by playing mode and articulation while hexachordal lynes are distinguished by register. The final section employs pairs of playing modes to distinguish lynes, with changes of blocks indicated by new pairs of articulation modes. Register is freed up for other purposes in the final section.

Dual is even more dramatic in its instrumental assignment of lynes, as illustrated in Example 3.9. In this work, changes of block are marked by the change in the number of lynes in the two instruments. Twice in the course of the work the cello overwhelms the piano by

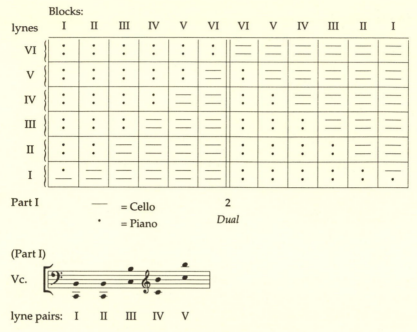

Example 3.9.   *Dual*: lyne assignment

assuming progressively more of the lynes of the array. As may be seen in the example, each instrument's portions of each array are complementary, so that in the course of the work each instrument plays through all the partitional pathways of the underlying array type. Both register and playing mode are used to distinguish lynes in the cello part. At the beginning, the cello has one lyne played pizzicato in its lowest register. As more lynes are added in subsequent blocks, they are initially packed into the lowest octave of the instrument, and only after a fair share of music has gone by does the cello get the chance to lift itself out of its grunting state. It more than makes up for its initial suppression in the soaring eloquence of later passages, where in one instance it forces the piano to tinkle away in its highest register, and at the end has reduced it to a few taciturn utterances in the bass. The whole tussling dialogue of the work, implied by a pun on its title, is not imposed on its structure but is the direct result of the ways sections are articulated by the changing projection of its underlying arrays.

The Fourth String Quartet combines both playing style and muting to articulate changes of array and block, moving from unmuted arco and pizzicato eventually to muted arco, pizzicato and sul ponticello.

Array I	Array II blocks:						Array III blocks:						Array IV
	1	2	3	4	5	6	1	2	3	4	5	6	
tutti	con sord.:						con sord.:						tutti
senza sord.	V1	V2	Vc	Va	V1	Va	V2	V1	V1	V1	V2	V1	con sord.
					V2	Vc	Va	Vc	Va	V2	Va	V2	
									Vc	Va	Vc	Vc	

4 lyne pairs				
arco	arco		arco*	arco/sul pont.
				by pair

2 lyne pairs				
pizz.	sul pont.		pizz.	pizz.

Example 3.10.   String Quartet no. 4: progression of muting and articulation

This, combined with the shift to weighted aggregates in the middle of the work, lends the end of the piece an otherworldly character enormously changed from the opening. This is summarized in Example 3.10.

Arie da Capo carries differentiation still further in its distribution of all the trios and quartets derivable from its five-member ensemble among its five sections. Each section is treated as an aria featuring one of the five instruments. During its aria, the solo instrument plays a lyne pair throughout, while the blocks of the array are articulated by changes in the size and makeup of the accompanying ensemble. The result is five parallel sections, each with the same distributions of instruments, but each with its own complement of ensembles. The second and fourth arias are further distinguished by the use of the bass clarinet in place of the regular instrument. Example 3.11 summarizes the instrumental progression of the work. The changes between and within the arias are clearly audible in the course of the work because of their stark differentiation by instrumentation and ensemble.

Lyne assignment and projection can reveal various compositional strategies for interpreting the abstract structure of the array. In the Fourth Quartet the six distinct hexachordal areas are each always associated with the pathways of a particular pair of lynes running through the four transformations of the array. However, the instrumental assignment of the lynes changes from transformation to transformation. The composition uses a twelve-part seventy-seven-partition array, whose row class is based on the B-type hexachord. At the outset, each instrument carries three lynes. Two belong to a given

Ensembles in *Arie da Capo*

Section	Soloist	Trio I	Quartet	Trio II
1	Cl.	+ Fl., Vn.	+ Fl., Vc., Pn.	+ Vn., Pn.
2	Vc.	+ Fl., B. Cl.	+ Fl., Vn., Pn.	+ B. Cl., Vn.
3	Fl.	+ Vc., Pn.	+ Cl., Vn., Vc.	+ Cl., Pn.
4	Vn.	+ Fl., Vc.	+ B. Cl., Vc., Pn.	+ Fl., Pn.
5	Pn.	+ Cl., Vc.	+ Fl., Cl., Vn.	+ Vn., Vc.

Example 3.11. *Arie da Capo*: instrumental ensembles

combinatorial pair, played arco and distinguished by register. The remaining four lynes are played pizzicato and are combinatorially paired between the first violin and the viola, and the second violin and the cello. In the course of the work, each instrument moves through all four of the resulting three-lyne strata of the array, in a pattern not totally dissimilar to the distribution of trichords in the trichordal arrays of Babbitt's earlier music.[27] As a result, each instrument in the course of the work plays through all of the hexachordal areas, effectively playing its own unfolded and transformed version of the work's array. The assignment of lynes among the instruments of the Fourth Quartet is illustrated in Example 3.12.

In *A Solo Requiem*, (1977) for soprano and two pianos, the vocal part or its instrumental representative also moves through the pathways of all six lyne pairs in the course of the work, but unlike the Fourth Quartet, the work's six different array transformations are transposed so that the vocal part always employs the same hexachordal area. This changes the orientation toward the array dramatically in that the focal part, the voice, is constantly recycling the same small repertoire of pitch class material through a variety of different partitional and combinational situations. While this affects the entire composition, it is particularly vivid in the two settings of the Shakespeare's Sonnet no. 71 that frame the work, using arrays that are related by retrogression and transposition. Babbitt has chosen the lyne pair pathways of the two arrays so that the voice uses the exact same sequence of combinatorial row pairs in the two settings, contrasted solely by the ways the two different strata fit into the partitions of their arrays. Joseph Dubiel has discussed the subtlety of the prosody of these passages as well as of the rest of the composition.[28] The array employed, a twelve-part seventy-seven-partition array, is a circle-of-fifths transformation of the array described in conjunction with Example 3.2. Thus, it pos-

Lyne Pairs		P	RT6	$I^{weighted}$	$RI^{weighted}$
arco	a	Vn. 1	Va.	Vn. 2	Vc.
	b	Vn. 2	Vn. 1	Vc.	Va.
	c	Va.	Vc.	Vn. 1	Vn. 2
	d	Vc.	Vn. 2	Va.	Vn. 1
pizz.	e1	Vn. 1	Va.	Vn. 2	Vc.
(sul pont.)	e2	Va.	Vc.	Vn. 1	Vn. 2
	f1	Vn. 2	Vn. 1	Vc.	Va.
	f2	Vc.	Vn. 2	Va.	Vn. 1
Bar		①	⑫⑧ (128)	②①⑤ (215)	③②⑦ (327)

Example 3.12.   String Quartet no. 4:
distribution of lynes in instruments

sesses the property that replicates certain segmental dyads in the
dyads found between combinatorial rows. As the work plays with
different degrees of lyne separation in the voice, intervallic relations
between lynes become extremely crucial in the music's progression,
and the fixed hexachordal area used in the vocal line emphasizes a
particular set of dyads and collections.

Still another orientation toward the array may be found in *Arie da
Capo*. As we discussed above, the work consists of five arias, each
featuring one of the instruments of the ensemble. The solo instrument always traces the same lyne pair, and hexachordal areas are preserved throughout the transformations of the array. As we noted
above, the fundamental hexachord of the work can be inverted onto
itself at more than one index number, so Babbitt is able to vary the
relations between rows of combinatorial pairs in the two arrays using
weighted aggregates, while maintaining the desired constancy of the
hexachordal content in lynes and lyne pairs. This is illustrated in Example 3.13.

Both the Fourth Quartet and *Arie da Capo* direct each instrument
through fixed partitions associated with fixed hexachordal areas, but
the former piece invites us to contemplate an essentially egalitarian
ensemble's changing orientation toward a set of pathways, whereas
the latter composition focuses our attention on a particular pathway,
reinterpreted by a series of different instrumental passes. *A Solo Re-
qiuem* offers still another interpretation by using the constant assignment of a hexachordal area to the principal part as a fixed horizon
against which to change the orientation of the work's arrays.

Example 3.13. *Arie da Capo*: two aggregate weighting strategies

The preceding remarks hardly exhaust the variety of strategies Babbitt has used to deploy arrays in his compositions, and by no means tells the whole story for any of the pieces mentioned. For example, the division of the array in the Fourth Quartet into lyne pairs played by a single instrument and pairs found between instruments obviously creates a particular orientation to its material that will affect the progress of the composition, and creates different emphases among the hexachordal areas. In *Arie da Capo* the number of lynes played by the instruments in each aria's accompaniment changes from section to section, altering our orientation to the array. The central quartet section of each aria will be of particular interest due to the unequal assignment of lynes within the subsidiary instruments. In both *Arie da Capo* and *A Solo Requiem*, the degree to which lynes are distinguished within parts changes, altering our orientation toward the material. In the earlier work, lynes are clearly separated at the outset but dramatically mixed in the solo of the final aria, whereas in the latter work the lynes are separated only after their initial mixture in the vocal part. Even such a brief look suggests the considerable differences that can be achieved solely by the ways an array is deployed in a composition.

COMPOSITION OF DETAILS

The richest and most varied aspect of Babbitt's music has always been in the ways surface details interact with the global structure of a composition. All-partition arrays only partly determine the surface config-urations of their constituent aggregates, and how the details are com-posed out has a profound influence over the course of a work.[29] There are virtually as many strategies to composing out the implications of an array as there are compositions in Babbitt's oeuvre, and it is his inventiveness and flexibility that allows him to reuse the same ab-stract structure in piece after piece. Before turning to a discussion of larger stretches of compositions, we shall illustrate some of the ways details unfold on Babbitt's musical surfaces. The following is hardly complete and can at best only suggest the richness and subtlety of his compositional manner.

Surface detail in Babbitt's music creates association and hierarchiza-tion through a variety of referential means, involving both collec-tional content and order. Significant details occur both within the span of a single aggregate and over larger time spans. More long-range details frequently involve the composition of aggregates formed by lyne or lyne pair, just as in his earlier music. Manifold reference is possible through the variety of ways one can interpret the musical surface. Notes in a violin part, for example, may be grouped significantly not only with other notes in the violin but with notes in other instruments that are rhythmically or registrally or even dynam-ically or articulatively similar in a network of simultaneous associa-tions forging both local and long-range connections.

Almost as varied as the strategic paths of Babbitt's details across the musical surface are their underlying abstract structural sources. De-tails may be traced back to the structural implications of the row, but this covers a wide variety of interpretations. Surface details may in-voke collectional aspects of the row, such as discrete hexachords, tet-rachords, or trichords. They may reproduce row segments, or they may project nonsegmental orderings of rows. This last is particularly interesting, as it emphasizes that a row is the ordering of the twelve pitch classes with regard to *all* of one another, not merely a series of adjacencies. A thorough investigation of a twelve-tone row entails more than a look at its segmental components but should also encom-pass the location and order of collections of all sizes. Babbitt was not the first to exploit this compositional resource; Schoenberg's composi-tions are filled with examples of relationships based on nonsegmental ordered collections.[30]

Special properties of rows may motivate certain kinds of surface elaborations not directly related to their ordering constraints, and ag-gregates may be composed to represent complete rows themselves. The partial orderings found between combinatorial row pairs also provide the source of surface details, as do the partial orderings of

Example 3.14. *Sextets*: composition of lynes in the violin in part 1.
Reprinted by permission of C. F. Peters Corporation

partitions in the array. Hierarchies based on many-to-one references of various types can be established to inform the progression through the underlying structure of Babbitt's compositions. We shall look at a few examples.

Sextets, as we have discussed above, is a work for violin and piano employing five array transformations.[31] The array is unusual in that it is constructued from an ordered hexachord rather than a complete row.[32] While there are twelve hexachordal lynes in the array, each lyne is paired with another so that the array may be construed as six composite lynes, each forming an aggregate over the span of a block. The array, when read in this manner, can be interpreted as a six-part all-partition array, with fifty-eight aggregates. The array is also unusual in that it employs only three hexachordal areas of a possible six.

In the opening and closing sections of the composition, the violin has two hexachordal lynes forming one composite lyne, while the piano plays the remaining material. Sections two and four assign two

Example 3.15. *Sextets*: derived B-type hexachords.
Reprinted by permission of C. F. Peters Corporation

composite lynes to the violin, while the central section divides the material equally between the two instruments.

In virtually every block of the opening section, the partial orderings of the violin's part have been composed to produce B-type hexachords, the basic hexachord type of the work. This is illustrated in Example 3.14. They are not ordered in the same way as the lyne hexachords (they cannot be), but they reproduce the hexachordal areas found in the other lynes.

Several points may be made. The array employs combinatorial pairs of ordered hexachords related in three ways: retrogression, inversion, and retrograde inversion. Of these three relationships, only the retrograde relation permits the construction of B-type hexachords between lynes. Fixing the hexachordal area for a pair of hexachords combined in such a fashion will in turn yield certain additional hexachordal areas as combinatorial by-products. This is illustrated in Example 3.15.

As mentioned, the array of *Sextets*, unlike Babbitt's other B hexachord arrays, employs only three hexachordal areas. Of all the ways Babbitt could have chosen three hexachordal areas from the six possible ones to construct his array, he has chosen the two that show up as by-products in Example 3.15. Thus the composition of the opening section of the work tells us a great deal about its underlying structure. Not only is a particular composite lyne given special treatment through its exclusive projection by the violin, it is also a lyne that itself can be and is composed to project the collections underlying the structure of the composition. The composition of the violin part is nontrivial, furthermore, as there are many places where other decisions could have been made to obscure the hexachordal collections.

The preceding hardly exhausts the opening passage of *Sextets*. The piano itself contains myriad details, as do the combinations of the two instruments. Nevertheless, our observation highlights a particularly important aspect of the initial role of the violin and allows us to hear the contrast with that instrument's function during later sections of

Example 3.16.   String Quartet no. 4:
all-combinatorial tetrachords

the work. The final section, for example, returns to the gross distribution of material found at the outset. We noted before that the final section uses the violin's articulations differently; we can note here that the final section also assigns the instrument a composite lyne whose ordered hexachords are related by retrograde inversion so that the sorts of hexachordal collections generated in the violin in the opening section cannot be produced by that instrument in the final section. The role of the two instruments with regard to each other and to the underlying material is drastically changed, a result of the overall progression of the piece.

The Fourth String Quartet provides even more elaborate examples of collectional reference in its details to abstract features of its row class. Example 3.16 reproduces a row from the work.

As may be seen, the row not only contains B hexachords segmentally but also is made of three discrete all-combinatorial tetrachords. These all-combinatorial tetrachords invert onto themselves at the same index number that maps the hexachords onto themselves, so that a given hexachordal area can also be referred to by a fixed tetrachord of one of the types so appearing. The work is filled with such references, both in its aggregate sections and in its weighted aggregate passages. Particularly lovely is the close of the work. A few selected passages are found in Example 3.17. The Fourth Quartet's row class shares the tetrachordal property with the row class of *More Phonemena*; compare with Example 3.3.

It will be remembered that the projection of the lynes of the array puts particular emphasis on two lyne pairs, the pizzicato pairs distributed among the instruments of the ensemble. The two hexachordal areas so highlighted in the array receive special emphasis in the way they are referred to in the composition of the details of the work and serve to focus references to other hexachordal areas.[33]

Still another form of reference emerges in the Fourth Quartet. Although the array of the work employs combinatorial pairs related

Example 3.17. String Quartet no. 4: tetrachordal details.
Reprinted by permission of C. F. Peters Corporation

solely by inversion, Babbitt has composed the details of the surface to reflect partial orderings that arise from other combinatorial relations and properties of the underlying row class. Two examples will suffice: the opening of the work and much that follows contain both types of all-interval tetrachords projected in a variety of ways. Examples 3.18a and b illustrate a few of these.

All-interval tetrachords do not appear segmentally in the work's row class, nor can they appear at like order numbers between inversionally related rows; however, they do fall out of combinatorial pairs related by retrogression, and because they are inversionally paired by the index number that maps a row's hexachords and onto themselves, they can firmly fix the hexachordal area of a reference. This is illustrated in Example 3.19.

Examples 3.18a and b.   String Quartet no. 4: all-interval tetrachordal details.
Reprinted by permission of C. F. Peters Corporation

Example 3.18b.

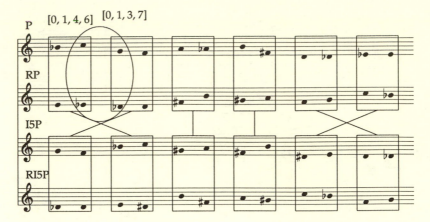

Example 3.19.   String Quartet no. 4: all-interval tetrachord derivation

The composition also contains a wealth of [0, 4, 8] trichords, or augmented triads. Babbitt has even gone so far as to violate the distinction of performance mode on the first page of the work to project one.[34] Collections of this type do not show up in the segments of the work's rows but are certainly implied by the segmental presence of the all-combinatorial tetrachords. This is illustrated in Example 3.20.

Although the array forms the basis for these compositions, one cannot ignore the other compositional properties of the row when considering the details. The musical surfaces are not just convenient or arbitrary solutions to the partial orderings of the background structures but offer their own pathways through and insights into the properties of a composition's row class. Much of the power of Babbitt's music is generated from the interaction, even opposition, between the surface and background.

My Complements to Roger demonstrates a number of ways details are derived both from the underlying row structure and from the ways row segments are deployed in the aggregates of the array. As mentioned above, the composition is based on a single four-part all-partition array of thirty-four aggregates. Each aggregate lasts one bar and is partitioned into time spans based on the conjugate of its pitch class partition. The opening bar, for example, is based on the partition $4^2\ 3\ 1$, and it is rhythmically divided into $4\ 3^2\ 2$, the conjugate of its pitch partition. This was illustrated in Example 1.30. The time spans of each aggregate are filled with equal note value strings. These strings carry sequences of pitch classes that represent segments of the work's underlying row class. What is more, the number of equal note values in a string is determined by the way its particular pitch class

Example 3.20.   String Quartet no. 4: [0, 4, 8] trichord derivation

sequence appears in an aggregate of the underlying array. Thus, for example, a five-note segment will represent some specific five-element segment from a particular partition of the work's array. This is illustrated in Example 3.21.

Every detail in the surface of the composition has a particular source in some aggregate from the underlying array. The details are composed by shifting among the various lynes present in a given aggregate. When a complete row segment cannot be formed, incomplete segments representing notes in order but not necessarily adjacent within a row segment are formed. The rhythms reflect this, as illustrated in Example 3.22.

The composition weaves a complex web not only between the details and their sources in the array but among the ways details are compounded in the surface of various aggregates themselves. The overall progression, made of the web of details working in concert with the changing registral patterns discussed above, reaches a climax of reference in the aggregates surrounding the single lyne partition, the registral climax of the piece.[35]

Another particularly nice example of segmental reference occurs in the final section of *Paraphrases* (1979), a composition for nine winds and piano. This work is in some ways a transitional composition, and we shall examine it in more detail in the following chapter, but the final section is fully representative of the compositional practices of Babbitt's second period. The passage in question is remarkable for its simplicity and for the immediate way in which it produces its results. The work is composed of a hyperaggregate array of twelve lynes consisting of the fifty-eight partitions of twelve into segments of length six or less. In the final section lynes are assigned individually to instruments, with the piano taking three.

Each aggregate of the passage is composed out as a simple polyrhythmic presentation of its underlying partition. The 5 4 3 partition, for example, is played as five against four against three. The duration of each aggregate, on the other hand, varies, representing simple

Example 3.21.   *My Complements to Roger*:
details and the array. Copyright © 1991 by Sonic
Art Editions. Used by permission of Smith
Publications, 2617 Gwynndale Ave.,
Baltimore, Md. 21207, U.S.A.

statements of the series of time intervals from the work's time point
row. The instrumental parts are woven together so that the resulting
verticalities, articulated and distinguished from one another by dynamics, represent row segments ordered in register. The resulting
chords thus represent the same sorts of interval patterns as those
found in the instrumental lines, and since the composition's array is a
hyperaggregate, every surface detail is reflected by some instrumental part in the passage. The fact that the array can be so composed is
an unusual property, based on certain particular qualities of its underlying row class. A portion of the passage is found in Example 3.23.

In addition to the sorts of details we have examined so far, Babbitt
frequently shapes aggregates to reflect some realization of the partial
ordering of another aggregate. Sometimes he is able to compose an
aggregate to reflect the partition of another aggregate. The following
example is drawn from *My Ends Are My Beginnings*. We shall deal with
this work at greater length later in the chapter. In the passage in ques-

Example 3.22.   *My Complements to Roger*:
incomplete equal note value strings

tion, the aggregate is composed as a string of five notes forming a row segment, and three groupings of septuplets over different time spans. Each grouping of seven represents a different discrete subset of the seven attack points in a septuplet. When the three groupings are compounded, the resulting ordered seven-note string is also a row segment. The two segments are themselves found elsewhere in the composition's arrays as a 7 5 partition aggregate. In the passage in question, they are derived from the counterpoint of lynes in a 6 4 1^2 partition. This is illustrated in Example 3.24. It should be noted in addition that the two slurred trichords themselves represent row segments, other than those reflected in the details discussed above. This serves merely to underline the multiplicity of reference afforded by Babbitt's compositional manner.

Details may stem from still other aspects of a composition's premises. Special structural features of the work's underlying row class motivate the composition of the aggregates at the outset of *Dual*. In a number of recent compositions, including *Paraphrases*, Babbitt has employed a special kind of row in which each of the ten successive

Example 3.23. *Paraphrases*: registrally
ordered details. Reprinted by permission
of C. F. Peters Corporation

segmental trichords represents a different collection class. Of the twelve different trichordal collection classes, the two left out are [0, 4, 8] and [0, 3, 6], the augmented and diminished triads. The former cannot be ordered to represent the four classical transformations un-ambiguously, and the latter is the single trichord type that cannot generate an aggregate. These so-called *all-trichord rows* have enticed Babbitt into reinvoking a number of features of his first-period com-positions in the context of his more developed technique. This is not to say that the trichord disappears in his second-period compositions, but its significance is more strongly felt beneath the surface than on it. All-trichord rows provided a means to bring the synthesis of his two practices to the surface of the music. As we shall see in the next chap-ter, the all-trichord row was but one stimulus to Babbitt's ultimate compositional synthesis of his various practices through his career.

The opening aggregates of *Dual* are composed to yield aggregates that are generated from single trichord types, working through the ten trichord types found segmentally in the underlying row's interval pattern. This is illustrated in Example 3.25.

The resulting aggregates bear a distinct similarity to those dis-

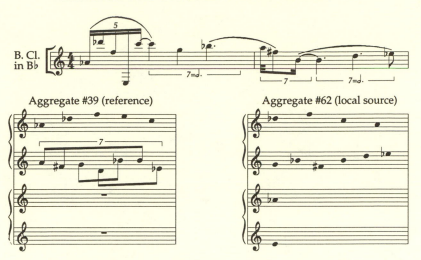

Example 3.24.   *My Ends Are My Beginnings*: details and the array.
Reprinted by permission of C. F. Peters Corporation

cussed in the previous chapter, such as the opening passage of *Du*, while participating in the unfolding of a more complex background array. The entire composition does not maintain this particular strategy all through, but like the opening violin part of *Sextets*, this passage lays out a wealth of information about the work's underlying structure.

All-trichord rows possess powerful means for creating references among the details of compositions using them. With the exception of the two excluded trichord types, any collection of three pitch classes, without regard to order, can index a very small number of rows—four in the case of those trichords that are inversionally symmetrical, and two for those that are not.

Many compositions contain one or more aggregates that have been simply composed so that they themselves represent a member of the work's row class. Obviously, whether or not this can be done varies with the nature of the partition in question. Extremely long and extremely tall aggregates yield the easiest sources for composing complete rows, but examples abound throughout the partition types. We can cite many examples, including ones from *Dual* and *Paraphrases*.[36] The following, Example 3.26, is drawn from the opening of *Images* (1979) for saxophonist and synthesized tape.

The foregoing hardly exhausts Babbitt's repertoire of techniques for composing out the aggregates of his arrays but suggests the richness and variety to be found in his music.[37]

Dual

for Violoncello and Piano

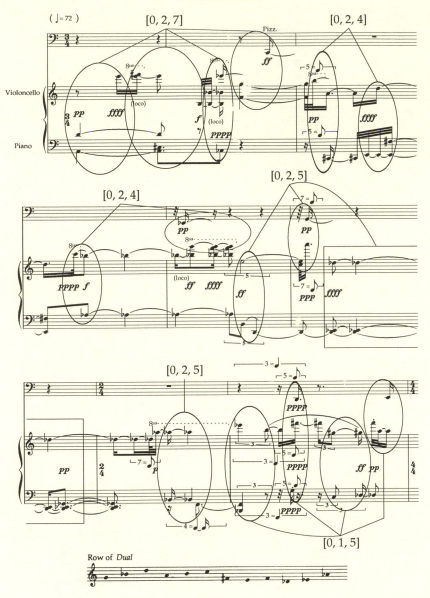

Example 3.25.   *Dual*: trichordal details. Reprinted by permission of C. F. Peters Corporation

Example 3.26. *Images*: opening aggregate. Reprinted
by permission of C. F. Peters Corporation

Pitch-class array, first three aggregates

e, i	e 9 8 t	6 1		
a, e	2 4 ——— 4		5	
a, ah	0 7			
aw, o	3 ——— 3 8			
u, u		2 9 e ——— e 4 0 1		
uh, u	5		t 8 3 7	
Acc.				
High				
Acc.			9	
Mid.	0		2	
Acc.		t 5 7		
Low	1 6 ——————— 6			

Time-point array, first three aggregates

p, b	3			
t, d	0			
ch, j	4 9 ——————— 9 7 2 6 5			
k, g				1 8 t 3 e
f, v		6 e 9 4 8 7		
th, th		3 t 0 5		
s, z	e	1 2	0 4	
sh, zh	8 6 5 7			
m, n	1			
l, ng	t			
r, y	2			
w, h				

Example 3.27a.   *Phonemena*: pitch class and time point
articulations by vowels and consonants. Reprinted
by permission of C. F. Peters Corporation

RHYTHMIC STRUCTURE

Coincident with his development of the all-partition array was Babbitt's compositional use of the time point system. We have already examined the basic premises of the time point system in the opening chapter and suggested some of the perceptual implications of Babbitt's translation of abstract structures in the pitch domain to the rhythmic domain. Much of what we have already discussed with regard to composition with all-partition arrays in the pitch domain also applies to the time point system. The structure of the array itself will have a profound effect upon the way a composition unfolds, as will the means of lyne projection and the composition of the details.

How the rhythmic structure is coordinated with the pitch structure forms still another layer in the composition of Babbitt's music. Generally, the time point arrays are not coordinated in a one-to-one manner with the pitch class arrays, and frequently the ratio of aggregates in one domain to the other changes. This itself forms a dramatic feature of a number of works, especially when conjoined with changes in the absolute duration of pitch class aggregates or the insertion of equal note value strings filling in time point intervals. *Arie da Capo* combines these changes into an overall acceleration that is breathtaking.[38]

As mentioned earlier, many compositions use dynamic levels to project time point lynes, and frequently the registral distribution of

Example 3.27b.

lynes in the pitch class array is echoed by the distribution of time point lynes from low to high dynamics. However, Babbitt has used other means to distinguish time point lynes in some compositions. In *Phonemena*, for example, just as he distinguished pitch class lynes by means of vowels in the voice, so he distinguishes time point lynes by means of consonants. This is illustrated in Examples 3.27a and b.

Whereas in many compositions Babbitt has restricted himself to straightforward interpretations of time point moduli, in some works he has played with using different-sized moduli simultaneously, each projecting a different lyne pair.[39] The opening sections of *Arie da Capo* employ this technique. One consequence of such an approach is that because the various time points of different-sized moduli will coincide from time to time, a given attack point in a composition may represent different time point values for different strata employing different-sized moduli. In compositions using dynamic levels to articulate time point lynes, this will permit a given attack to have more than one dynamic level and thus provide the composer with still another means for distinguishing pitch relationships.[40] This is illustrated in Example 3.28.

A number of compositional interpretations of the time point system are found in Babbitt's work, frequently in combination with certain other rhythmic approaches we have discussed, to yield a multitude of ways the musical surface may be composed to project relations both locally and over long spans of time.

A Brief Venture into Comparative Anatomy

Babbitt's compositional approach is not a simple realization of certain generative techniques but represents a constant lively reinterpretation of the primitives that he has elected to explore. The richness of his second period can be dramatically illustrated by comparing the opening aggregates of a number of compositions all of which employ the same underlying abstract array structure in the pitch domain. Each of the five pieces we shall look at represents a different combination of instrumental, rhythmic, and interpretive approaches to its basic material, and each composes out a different set of implications derived from the basic array. We shall not offer a complete analysis of any of these pieces but shall simply suggest the different trajectories initiated from their common origin.

The pieces are *Tableaux, Arie da Capo, Playing for Time, An Elizabethan Sextette*, and *Melismata*. The first and third are for solo piano, while the remainder are for mixed quintet, female sextet, and solo violin,

Example 3.28.   *Arie da Capo*: articulation by dynamic level.
Reprinted by permission of C. F. Peters Corporation

respectively.[41] Their opening aggregates and their analyses are found in Examples 3.29–33.

Each work is based on some transformation or set of transformations of a six-part all-partition array of fifty-eight aggregates, itself a hyperaggregate of its underlying row class.[42] The only transformational differences found among the arrays of the pieces are the classical twelve-tone operations plus the circle-of-fifth operation that preserves the basic partitional structure of the array while exchanging intervals in predictable ways.

The underlying abstract array has a peculiarity that, although it does not immediately affect our discussion, is worth mentioning in light of certain issues we shall raise later.[43] In the orientation found at the outset of each of these works, the final aggregate of the array requires the addition of a single pitch class for completion. This little

* Published score reads *mp* but is contradicted in bar 2

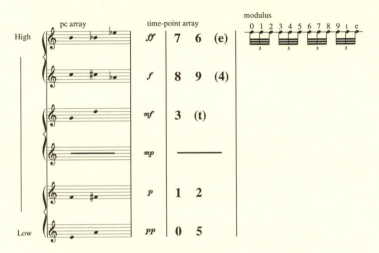

Example 3.29. *Tableaux*: initial aggregate and underlying arrays.
Reprinted by permission of C. F. Peters Corporation

hitch prompts a variety of solutions in the works using transformations of this array and also suggests why all five of these compositions open with the same partition.

As may be seen, each piece interprets the basic material in radically different ways, using a variety of different rhythmic techniques. The arrays themselves represent different kinds of transformations. Taking *Tableaux* as containing the basic array, *Arie da Capo* employs a circle-of-fifths transformation, while the remaining pieces use inversions of two kinds. *Playing for Time* and *Melismata* both employ an inversion of the entire array using a single index number, while *An Elizabethan Sextette* uses a weighted-aggregate array. This last represents a series of transpositions of *Tableaux*'s array lynes but is better understood as being derived from an inversion of the form of the array found in the solo violin piece. It is interesting to note that the

Example 3.30.   *Arie da Capo*: initial aggregate and underlying arrays.
Reprinted by permission of C. F. Peters Corporation

Example 3.31. *Playing for Time*: initial aggregate and underlying array. Used by permission of Alfred Publishing Co., Inc.

weighted aggregate array takes advantage of the D hexachord's ability to be inverted onto itself at more than one index number; one may see that while the lyne pair containing trichordal segments has been inverted by a single index number, the difference in collection types formed by the dyad pairs in the weighted array and the original array reveals that each lyne of this pair has been inverted by its own index number.

Array projection varies among the pieces considerably. Although the two ensemble pieces will obviously offer the greatest differences, even the solo pieces deploy the array in individual ways. An obvious instrumental weighting of the array is offered in *Arie da Capo*, and we have already commented on the way the shifting solos of this work will change instrumental emphases throughout. In stark contrast, the female voices of the choral work pair up at the outset to obscure lyne differentiation, already obscured by general similarity of the women's voices and the use of weighted aggregates. This is part of the mark-

* should by chart be *f* but for other reasons is *p* in score

Example 3.32. *An Elizabethan Sextette*: initial aggregate and underlying arrays.
Reprinted by permission of C. F. Peters Corporation

Example 3.33.   *Melismata*: initial aggregate and underlying array.
Reprinted by permission of C. F. Peters Corporation

edly different strategy of this composition, which only gradually reveals its underlying array structure in the progress of the work. It is
amusing to note that the ultimate unobscured appearance of the single row partition in the second, unweighted array of the composition
coincides with the line "All is Heav'n that you behold, and all your
thoughts are blesséd." The entire piece is a divestment of obscurity,
from the regret and denial of the opening poem to the final cry of
"Shall I a virgin die? Fie no!"

In the two piano pieces, the earlier work at the outset differentiates
lynes by register, while the later work combines lyne pairs in register.
Furthermore, the two works stack the lyne pairs of the array in a different order, so that the registral placement of the lower two pairs is
exchanged. It should be noted that the works are very different in size
and character, with the earlier composition containing four array
transformations to the latter's one. *Melismata* and *Playing for Time* both
use the same array, but the solo violin work reverses the registral
order of the lyne pairs and contains a second transformation of the
array.

Opening ordered aggregate of *Tableaux*:

Row P :

Opening ordered aggregate of *Playing for Time*:

RT$_t$ P:

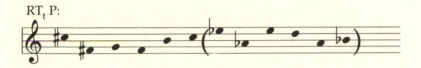

RI$_5$ P: etc.

Example 3.34.   *Tableaux, Playing for Time*: ordered details

Each composition uses a different strategy for composing out the aggregate. Both piano pieces order the elements of the aggregate to form approximations of the underlying row class but do so in different ways, with different results. *Tableaux* retains both hexachordal contents and discrete trichordal order, retrograding each of the inner two trichords, while in *Playing for Time* the first hexachord is retained in order and the second represents its inversion. This is illustrated in Example 3.34.

Melismata contains a series of segments from different members of the work's row class, articulated rhythmically to tag them to specific locations in the composition's arrays. *An Elizabethan Sextette* also contains row segments, but articulated within the context of the

weighted aggregate and its resulting doublings, and representing different interpretations of the elements of the aggregate.

Perhaps the most radically different interpretation of the aggregate
is found in *Arie da Capo*. Here, temporal grouping breaks the aggregate into a pair of chromatic (A-type) hexachords, while attention to
the solo instrument in contrast to its accompaniment parses the aggregate as a pair of B-type hexachords. Simultaneous attacks are limited exclusively to [0, 2] and [0, 4]-type dyads and [0, 2, 4] trichords.
This work approaches the array from a very different point of view,
with few explicit references to row segments in its composed details
at the outset. It is worth noting that the two all-combinatorial hexachord types found at the outset, along with the C-type hexachords
found in the following aggregate, can be derived from like order
numbers in combinatorial pairs of the work's row class, not unlike the
examples above, drawn from the Fourth String Quartet.

Finally, the works represent an overview of the wide variety of
rhythmic approaches Babbitt has used in his career. Even though *Tableaux*, *Arie da Capo*, and the vocal work all use the time point system,
each interprets it in a different way, and the remaining two pieces
employ two additional related techniques. *Tableaux* uses the most direct interpretation of the time point system at the outset, with the
same lynes as the pitch class array articulated in six dynamic levels
from *pp* to *ff* corresponding to register from lowest to highest.[44] The
modular length is one beat, so that even the fastest strings of notes
are structural time points in the array. *Arie da Capo* also uses dynamics
to distinguish the lynes of its time point array, but uses different modular lengths for each lyne pair as well as employing a weighted inversion of the array.[45] *An Elizabethan Sextette* uses a nonweighted inversion of its array for its time point lynes at the outset, but, in contrast to
Tableaux, lynes are paired by dynamics, just as the pitch class lynes
are paired by voice.[46] This is one further manifestation of the work's
initial obscurantism. The modulus is a full bar, much slower than that
of the piano work, and the resulting time spans are filled in with
subdivisions of equal note values.

Playing for Time and *Melismata* use different approaches. In the piano piece, each aggregate is exactly one bar long in $\frac{3}{4}$ time, and each
bar is partitioned into time spans representing the partition of the
aggregate. These time spans are differentiated by changes of subdivision, much like those of the duration rows of the *Composition for Viola
and Piano* and the Second String Quartet, discussed in the previous
chapter. In the violin work, the length of each aggregate is determined by the succession of intervals of a lyne of the array interpreted
as a series of time points, using the beat as the unit.[47] Thus, the first

aggregate is seven beats long, corresponding to the interval between D and A in the appropriate lyne of the opening aggregate. The resulting string of pulses is filled in with some subdivision reflecting certain aspects of the pitch string being articulated. The two works provide contrasting approaches to aggregate rhythm. The piano composition presents regularly spaced aggregates whose internal rhythms are broken up into irregular pulses, while in the violin piece the regular pulses are clearly audible despite their internal irregularities. The aggregates, on the other hand, unfold at a variety of rates, determined by the temporal interpretation of the intervals of the work's rows.

All told, the five compositions represent a variety of perspectives on the shared structural entity, the array. Rhythmically, instrumentally, and strategically, each piece sets out across the same terrain with a different set of both goals and means to achieve them. That it is not hard to recognize simply from listening that the pieces are all based on the same underlying structure makes their differences more vivid and dramatizes the depth of relationships from surface to background in Babbitt's music. Once again we can appreciate the balance between individuality and universality so elegantly maintained throughout his work.

Two (Short) Analyses

The preceding discussion has been largely anecdotal in order to illustrate the breadth of Babbitt's compositional approach; an understanding of its depth can only begin to emerge with the examination of whole pieces. We shall take a look at two complete compositions from his second period. The first, *Post-Partitions*, is from the mid-1960s and still reflects his experimentation with the various new tools at his disposal. The second, *My Ends Are My Beginnings*, is one of his most sophisticated works rhythmically, but its relatively small four-part all-partition array makes tracing relations through its transformations comparatively manageable.

POST-PARTITIONS

Post-Partitions is a short but by no means small solo piano piece from 1966.[48] It was written in celebration of Roger Sessions's seventieth birthday and is based on the same ordered hexachord type as *Partitions*. In fact, the performance instructions state that it may be played immediately following the earlier work, as well as independently.

While *Post-Partitions* is based on the same interval pattern as the earlier piano piece, it is not of the same compositional practice. As we noted in the previous chapter, the earlier work is based on trichordal arrays, derived from combinations of the successive segmental tri-chords of the fundamental hexachordal ordering, and the arrays are deployed to present the eight partitions of four distinct elements into two or fewer parts. *Post-Partitions*, on the other hand, contains a single presentation of an all-partition array, rhythmically articulated by a single presentation of the same array interpreted as lynes of time points.

Although the basic materials of *Post-Partitions* are those that Babbitt codified in his second period, the work is in many ways experimental and contains many compositional features peculiar to it. The structure of the array and the ways time point lynes are projected are not typical of later compositions; nevertheless, the work's concision and strongly articulated progression of details help illuminate Babbitt's musical thinking for a range of compositions. Many of the approaches found in the work were later taken up in different contexts, applied to materials more typical of his established practice.

The array of *Post-Partitions* is closely related to that of *Sextets*, the piece Babbitt composed immediately following the piano work. The array of *Sextets* was derived from that of *Post-Partitions* by means of the circle-of-fifths operation, combined with the rearrangement of the constituent blocks. There is one other difference between the arrays, reflecting the composition of the details at the outset of *Sextets*. The distribution of lyne segments in the piano work's array would not permit the construction of the desired B-type hexachord collections in the appropriate lyne pair. (The circle-of-fifths operations has no effect on this property, other than changing the interior order of the derived collections.) Babbitt rearranged some elements in the first few aggregates, preserving the order of the individual lynes, in order to achieve the sorts of details he desired for the larger composition's opening section. In doing so he was able to swap the locations of two partitions, thus preserving the array's all-partition property.

As mentioned above, the array is constructed of six composite lynes each made of two ordered hexachords related by inversion, retrograde, or retrograde inversion, and contains three hexachordal areas. The eight blocks of the array are distinct; in other words, there is no overlapping of ends of lynes of one array into another. The array contains the fifty-eight partitions of twelve into six or fewer parts. The six composite lynes of the array are projected in six registers of the piano, with a certain amount of overlap between adjacent registers. The hexachordal lynes in each register are distinguished by articulation. One set of lynes is sustained or legato, the other short or stac-

Stems up: staccato

Stems down: legato

Example 3.35. *Post-Partitions*: initial array block

cato. Because there are only three hexachordal areas, not only do the individual composite lynes form aggregates over the span of a block but so do the composite lynes formed by staccato and legato pairs of a given hexachordal area. The two composite lynes of a given hexachordal area are always registrally adjacent. The resulting quartets of hexachordal lynes always contain one each of the four classical transformations. This last explains the exclusion of combinatorial pairs related by transposition in the composite lynes of the array. The first block of the array is found in Example 3.35; the whole array is found in the list of all-partition arrays at the back of this volume.

The work uses a simple translation of the pitch class array as its time point array, and aggregates in the pitch class array are coordinated one-to-one with the time point aggregates. This is not typical of Babbitt's later practice, in which the number of pitch class aggregates usually exceeds the number of time point aggregates, nor is the strict coordination of aggregate boundaries between the two domains found in the present work always maintained. Furthermore, Babbitt has chosen an unusual manner of projecting the elements and lynes of his time point array. In most time point compositions, time point lynes unfold against a fixed grid of concatenated moduli and are distinguished by dynamic levels. In *Post-Partitions*, each composite time point lyne unfolds against its own modular grid, distinguished from the others by modular length, and each *element* is assigned a dynamic level![49]

This has several consequences for the nature of the piece. Every aggregate of the time point array, and consequently of the pitch class array, runs the dynamic gamut from *ppppp* to *fffff*, contributing to the work's flamboyant surface. This contrasts with other time point pieces in which the change of participating lynes in the stream of aggregates will cause some passages to be predominantly loud, others predominantly soft, and still others highly varied. The opening of the Fourth Quartet is an excellent example of Babbitt's more general practice, moving gradually from predominantly soft aggregates to predominantly loud ones over the course of the first block of the pitch class array.

Using dynamics to distinguish time points virtually necessitated the use of different-sized moduli. Had a single modular size associated with the meter been used for all time point lynes, each dynamic level would have had a fixed location within the bar. As it is, Babbitt has constructed a long-range polymeter of six different tempi based on modular length. The six layers consist of moduli whose lengths are four quarter-notes, three quarter-notes, two quarter-notes, three eighth-notes, as well as two and two-fifths quarter-notes and one and five-sevenths quarter notes. The resulting quarter-note subdivisions, representing the elements of each modular layer, are, respectively, triplets, sixteenths, sextuplets, thirty-seconds, quintuplets, and septuplets. As these six different layers cycle against one another, the possible placement of dynamics within the bar changes, but in ways that still create limits and create cycles within the piece. Certain locations are always available for each dynamic; the others shift at various rates. One result of the cycling is the occurrence of attack points in the score that represent different elements in different lynes, allowing certain simultaneities to have more than one dynamic level. Example 3.36 summarizes the mechanics of the rhythmic structure of *Post-Partitions*.

In this work, different regions of the time point array are distinguished by the sorts of subdivisions present in the surface, rather than by dynamic level. We can trace the progress of a time point from lyne to lyne by seeing what sorts of subdivisions are associated with it. Example 3.37 illustrates the time point aggregates of the first few bars of *Post-Partitions*.

Since each dynamic level in the composition is associated with a single element in the time point domain, it is possible to express an equivalence between dynamic levels in the temporal array with pitch

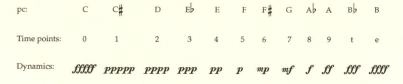

pc:	C	C♯	D	E♭	E	F	F♯	G	A♭	A	B♭	B
Time points:	0	1	2	3	4	5	6	7	8	9	t	e
Dynamics:	*fffff*	*ppppp*	*pppp*	*ppp*	*pp*	*p*	*mp*	*mf*	*f*	*ff*	*fff*	*ffff*

Example 3.36. *Post-Partitions*: rhythmic rates

classes in their array. A direct translation equates C with *fffff*, descending in value through B = *ffff*, G = *mf*, and so forth, to D♭ = *ppppp*. This is not to say that pitch classes and dynamic levels are perceptually equivalent, but that the values of elements in each domain are shifted around in analogous manners. The path of the pitch class C through the lynes of its array will be equivalent to the trace of *fffff* through the lynes of the time point array. The relations among pitch classes and those among dynamic levels will have certain simlarities, but these will not extinguish the profound differences between the two domains.

It is worth digressing briefly here to clarify some misunderstandings about dynamic levels in general in Babbitt's scores. On the face of it, notated dynamic ranges of *ppppp* to *fffff* in such works as *Sextets*,

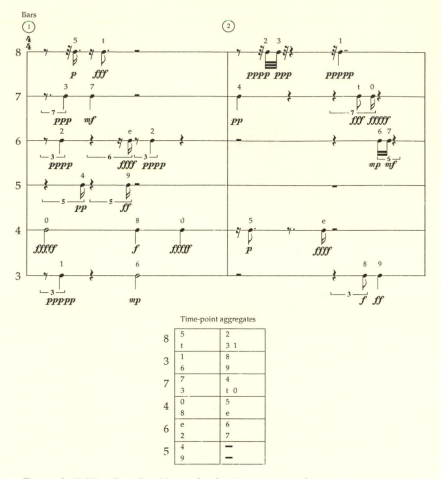

Example 3.37.   *Post-Partitions*: rhythmic structure, first two aggregates.
Reprinted by permission of C. F. Peters Corporation

Relata, or the one under consideration would seem to demand an extension of performance practice from impossible hush to excruciating roar. Supposedly absolute dynamic values among disparate instruments in the larger ensemble works might also suggest the need to match *fff* in a harp in one bar with the same dynamic level in a tuba some bars later. Clearly, this is futile, and it does not represent how we perceive dynamic levels. If, on the other hand, we read Babbitt's dynamic notation to indicate inflections within a normal range of dynamics, we can hear in his music a series of contours of intensity that maintain their identity under various sorts of transformations.

These notated contours reflect the flexibility available within the

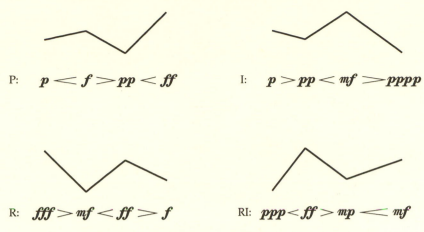

P: $p < f > pp < ff$

I: $p > pp < mf > pppp$

R: $fff > mf < ff > f$

RI: $ppp < ff > mp < mf$

Example 3.38.   Dynamic contour transformations

dynamic range, a quality found in performances of, if not precisely notated in, the more familiar repertoire. Because of the nature of the domain, we can associate dynamic contours derived from different absolute dynamic values and recognize transformations that preserve contour qualities without necessarily preserving absolute differences between values. Contour transformations can replicate the four classic twelve-tone operations without necessarily preserving absolute values. A number of different sorts of contour-preserving transformations are found in Example 3.38.

Thus we need not hear Babbitt's dynamic values as absolute from one instrument to another over long time spans. Rather, we are being asked to hear whether a given event is stronger or weaker than previous events. The number of places back to which we would want to be able to do this will vary contextually. The absolute value of a dynamic level comes into play when creating balances within an ensemble, a crucial factor in those passages where a given attack point has events of more than one dynamic level.

It is important to realize that Babbitt's musical thinking respects the profound perceptual differences between the various musical domains. His use of analogous abstract structures in perceptually different dimensions always takes advantage of the possibilities unique to each dimension. Thus, while his rhythmic and pitch structures may be based on the same abstract array, the ways details are composed out in each domain reflect the properties of that domain. The analogy between domains remains at the abstract level of similar distributions of material and patterns of recurrence.

The general description of the underlying array structure and

Example 3.39. *Post-Partitions*: first aggregate.
Reprinted by permission of C. F. Peters Corporation

modes of projection of *Post-Partitions* allows us to begin to look at the details and how they are derived. We shall follow one particular aspect of the composition of the surface, with allusions to certain other features. A clue to the progress of the piece is found in the first bar, reproduced in Example 3.39.

The work erupts with a gesture covering the full range of the instrument, made of a set of six discrete dyads alternating with one another. Each dyad consists of a sustained note and a short note. The six dyads represent the initial elements of each hexachordal lyne, paired by composite lyne. Thus, the first aggregate consists of a representation of its underlying partition, 2^6. When we look at the subsequent aggregates of the first block, we can see that, in one way or another, each projects the same dyadic mosaic found in the first bar.[50] Example 3.40 reproduces the continuation of the composition.

As may be seen, the second aggregate maintains the dyads as simultaneities, although, in contrast to the first aggregate, elements will not only be in different registers but may also both be of the same durational quality. In the third aggregate, each pitch class is attacked individually, so that while the six dyads of the opening are present, additional pitch class pairs are projected by the same means. The rhythmic composition of the aggregate also emphasizes some of the new dyads by placing their elements in adjacent dynamic levels. These new materials will become important later on.

Example 3.40. *Post-Partitions*: aggregates two, three and four.
Reprinted by permission of C. F. Peters Corporation

The fourth aggregate restores the dyadic attacks of the first two, with one exception. One pair of pitch classes appears as nonadjacent elements of the same lyne and so cannot be attacked simultaneously without the inclusion of the interposed pitch class. Nevertheless, the preceding aggregate's projection of dyads has taught us a way of grouping the two individually attacked notes of the aggregate in time.

The remaining aggregates of the block similarly preserve the set of dyads found at the outset, juxtaposing them in various ways. Thus, not only does the opening of the composition preserve a mosaic through all its aggregates but that mosaic represents the initial partition of the array.

The second block of the array introduces a new mosaic of dyads,

Example 3.41.   *Post-Partitions*: dyadic links
between blocks one and two. Reprinted
by permission of C. F. Peters Corporation

which are used to compose out its aggregates and the aggregates of
the third block as well. The first aggregate of the second block is
found in Example 3.41. As may be seen, the aggregate can be interpreted as the new set of dyads, but it can also be heard in terms of the
dyads of the first block. This is typical of Babbitt's music: virtually
every aggregate participates in a multitude of trajectories over different time spans. This is implicit in the duality of detail and array, but
also includes, as we have seen, unfoldings in lyne pairs as well as
different levels of detail.

The second and third blocks are composed to project the new mosaic as much as possible. As aggregates grow longer—that is, contain

more elements ordered in a single lyne—it becomes more difficult to project desired groupings. If two notes of a dyad are nonadjacent members of the same lyne, Babbitt must resort to filling in the dyad gradually with the intervening elements and their appropriate pairs, gradually building up larger collections. Frequently these larger collections can be alternatively parsed into dyads including some from the earlier section, keeping them alive in the surface of the composition.

Another feature that emerges in the musical surface is the generation of B-type hexachords, or their subsets. These collections may or may not represent hexachordal areas found in the underlying array. This is illustrated in Example 3.42.

The fourth block of the array introduces a new dyadic mosaic, as does each subsequent block of the array. Example 3.43 is a summary of the dyadic mosaics found in all the sections of the piece, along with their sources in certain aggregates of the array.

An overview of the mosaics of the work reveals the progressive, accretive nature of the composition. A number of wonderful details emerge when we start examining relations among the mosaics. Some of the richest connections emerge from the initial aggregate of the fifth block, the 12^1 partition of the array. The passage acts as a catalyst for the work's overall progression. It is reproduced in Example 3.44.

The passage presents the dyads arising from like order numbers of the two complete hexachords in a single register. These dyads will form the mosaic of the subsequent aggregates, but there is a lot more here. Because the two hexachordal lynes are distinguished by playing manner we are able to follow them through the aggregate, but the two voices cross, yielding an additional pair of hexachords distinguished by register. This pair of new hexachords, however, are themselves type B, the type underlying the whole array! These new hexachords are not a product of combinatorial generation, as are the derived B-type hexachords in the first section of *Sextets*; rather, they are details arising from the composition of the aggregate and the restrictions imposed by its partial ordering. The fact that they represent a hexachordal area outside the array is a matter of compositional choice, as one could construct a registral pair based on the same vertical dyads that would have been part of the array's set of areas. The choice reflects other aspects of the progress of the piece, as we shall see.

In addition to the dyads formed between lynes, the passage at the beginning of the fifth section of *Post-Partitions* has been composed to project both dyads within the hexachords distinguished by register and those of the lynes themselves. Babbitt has used the twelve time

Example 3.42. *Post Partitions*. B-type hexachordal details.
Reprinted by permission of C. F. Peters Corporation

Example 3.43: *Post-Partitions*: dyad mosaics and blocks

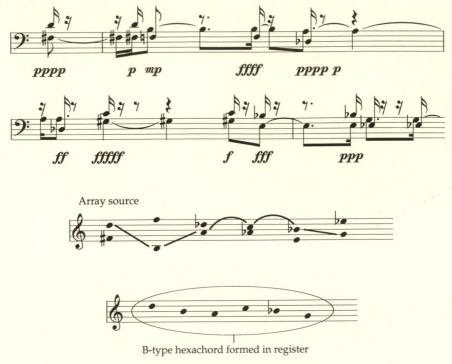

Example 3.44. *Post Partitions*: the 12^1 partition. Reprinted
by permission of C. F. Peters Corporation

points of the aggregate to repeat each of the simultaneous dyads, so
that it is easy to associate pitch classes with both preceding and following pitch classes. The resulting catalog of dyads has resonance
throughout the work.

This particular passage allows us to illustrate Babbitt's debt to
Schoenberg. The multivalent interpretations of this aggregate echo a
similar pattern at the outset of the second movement of Schoenberg's
Third String Quartet, in which an aggregate is played as a series of
dyads between two instruments and in which the voices cross to produce a rich network of interpretations that inform the progress of the
whole movement.[51] This same work is more subtly echoed in the previously discussed aggregate containing the mosaics of both the first
and second blocks. The row of Schoenberg's quartet may itself be
interpreted as two sets of discrete dyads, both of which have invariance properties exploited in the composition. Despite the surface dis-
similarities between Babbitt's music and that of Schoenberg, the older
composer is never too distant.[52]

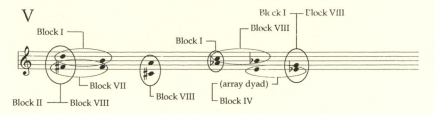

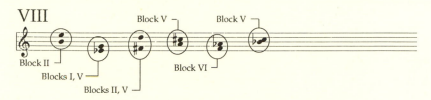

Example 3.45. *Post-Partitions*: dyadic detail sources

The dyad content of the 12^1 partition aggregate is a nexus of relations that make up the progress of the piece. While the three mosaics composed out in the first four sections of the composition have no dyads in common, the catalog found in the center of the work has several in common with each, forging links among them. The next two mosaics, found in blocks six and seven, also contain certain dyads in common both with earlier mosaics and with each other; they also contain some of the dyads formed as a by-product in the third aggregate of the first section, discussed above, not to mention a number that have similarly appeared in aggregates throughout the work. The real conjunction of material, however, is saved for the final section. Every single dyad of the last section's mosaic has at least one previous source in the mosaics of the piece or in the central catalog. This is illustrated in Example 3.45.

The whole effect of the last section is to summarize the piece by juxtaposing selected dyads from throughout its length. The last bar dramatizes this, and highlights another layer of compositional detail, the presence of B-type hexachords arising from combinations of lynes on the surface. The passage is found in Example 3.46.

Example 3.46. *Post Partitions*: final aggregate. Reprinted by permission of C. F. Peters Corporation

As can be seen, the closing gesture is strongly reminiscent of the opening gesture, with alternating dyads for the most part grouped by register. The opening three dyads are simultaneities from the central 12^1 partition; the first dyad is from the mosaic of the first section. The next dyad to enter, B and E, was the first dyad heralding the initiation of the second sections. The subsequent dyad, C and B♭, is the only dyad not directly from any of the mosaics of the earlier sections (it is found earlier as a segmental dyad in the 12^1 partition), and its role in the aggregate itself is different from the others in that its span extends across several registers. The final dyad of the mosaic, F and A♭, is also the last dyad of the mosaic to have been introduced in the other mosaics of the work.

Most interesting is the final attack of the work, a dyad that does not appear in the last section's mosaic but is from the opening section and, incidentally, is found at the end of *Partitions*. Its role here emerges in conjunction with the preceding dyad and the sustained E in the highest register. The resulting five-note collection is a subset of a B-type hexachord, all played in the higher dynamic levels. The hexachord is completed with the high E♭, separated from the rest of the aggregate by duration and dynamic level, and associated with the final notes because of its high dynamic level. The hexachordal area so invoked is the same as the one produced by voice crossing in the central 12^1 partition aggregate. Thus, the final aggregate echoes significant portions of the work in a number of ways, using a variety of criteria that invoke the rhythmic, and consequently the dynamic, structure of the composition. The final event's *fffff* on the downbeat simply brings the work full circle to the rhythmic point of its initiation.

The preceding remarks do not by any means cover all that can be said about the sequence of mosaics, let alone the wealth of additional details that flow over the surface of the work. For example, we have not really looked at the ways dyads are compounded into larger collections, nor have we done more than suggest the other layers of collectional details built up within aggregates. But we can make a couple of points about the way the work progresses based on what we have observed. First, the preservation of given mosaics from aggregate to aggregate creates groupings of aggregates in the surface that may themselves be grouped in various ways. As we have seen, the progression of the piece is accumulative. All three of the initial mosaics are invoked at the central passage, and the final passage sweeps up material from the entire work. The accretive process is crystallized in the final aggregate, with its multiple references to different processes and places in the piece.

Second, it is worth noting that in addition to the hierarchical relationship established by dyadic content among the mosaics, a distinction is made in the piece with regard to the sources in the array. All the mosaics belong to the same partition class; they all consist of six dyads. However, while each is a solution to the partial orderings of the sections of the array in which it appears, only the first, the fourth, and the last mosaic strongly represent the partitions of specific aggregates of the array. The first is the dyads formed between lynes of the composite lynes in the first aggregate, the fourth is also formed of the dyads of a composite lyne, and the last, with one exception, is once again a similar set of dyads, from the final aggregate of the piece. This difference in their structural source is echoed in the roles of the mosaics in the piece. Although all seven mosaics are composed out in their respective spans, the three just discussed have additional significance. The first mosaic establishes the processes of the work, while the central and final mosaics each sum up the music up to their respective appearances.

From the most abstract aspects of its underlying structure to its surface details, *Post-Partitions* is composed to project a rich web of relations through which the listener is propelled. Successive hearings allow one to explore the dense network of pathways that span the composition, the better to enjoy its exuberance and progressive accumulation of musical momentum.

MY ENDS ARE MY BEGINNINGS

My Ends Are My Beginnings of 1978 is an extended triptych for solo clarinetist, who doubles on bass clarinet for its central panel. Despite the work's instrumentation, it is richly contrapuntal, and its highly contorted single line is the heard surface of a multiplicity of compositional unfoldings in many layers over a variety of spans.

The three sections of the piece, separated by measured pauses, are each based on a different transformation of a four-part all-partition array of thirty-four aggregates. The two lyne pairs of the array represent the two distinct transpositional regions derived from complementary pairs of the E-type hexachord, the composition's fundamental collectional structure. Taking the array of the inital section as A, the central section is the retrograde inversion of A at index number two, and the final section is the inversion of A at index number nine. In both cases, the entire array is inverted so that aggregates are maintained, although the locations of hexachordal areas in the array are switched around. The two lyne pairs are each given a single register within which to operate, articulated at the instrument's registral

Example 3.47. *My Ends Are My Beginnings*:
lyne location of hexachordal areas

break. Within register, however, lynes are usually intermingled. Babbitt consistently maintains one hexachordal region in each register, and this occasions the exchange of the registral locations for the partitional pathways of the lyne pairs between the first and second sections. The third section returns to the registral locations of the first section, restoring the hexachordal sequence of the upper lynes, while reversing that of the lower lynes. This is illustrated in Example 3.47.

Because of its relative brevity, the array is not a hyperaggregate, and a complete presentation of all the members of the row class only gradually emerges in the course of the work. This has a considerable consequence in the composition of the details, because it becomes possible to invoke rows that do not appear in the local array. Example 3.48 is a chart of the rows as they appear in the lynes and blocks of the array, without regard to partitioning. It should be noted that because the array contains relatively many long partitions, there is a great deal of swapping over the block boundaries.

One aspect that will appear familiar is the disposition of row transformations in the blocks, lyne pairs, and lynes of the array: because the array contains thirty-two rows, Babbitt can duplicate the sorts of relationships he employed among transformations of trichords in his trichordal arrays. However, this also means that combinatorial pairs of rows will always be related by inversion in the body of the array.

One of the principal strategies in the composition of the work's details is the invocation of specific rows by means of segmental reference, and the row class has been ordered to facilitate this. It will be remembered that the E-type hexachord, unlike the first-order all-combinatorial hexachords, is extremely limited in its interval and tri-

Lyne

(1)

High
| I | T_e | RI_8 | I_6 | R_5 | T_3 | RI_0 | I_2 | R_1 |
| II | I_8 | R_7 | T_5 | RI_6 | I_4 | R_e | T_1 | RI_t |

Low
| III | RI_3 | T_6 | R_0 | I_9 | RI_7 | T_2 | R_8 | I_5 |
| IV | R_6 | I_e | RI_1 | T_4 | R_2 | I_7 | RI_5 | T_4 |

(2)

High
| III | R_9 | I_6 | RI_0 | T_7 | R_5 | I_2 | RI_8 | T_e |
| IV | RI_t | T_9 | R_7 | I_0 | RT_t | T_1 | R_3 | I_8 |

Low
| I | I_1 | R_0 | T_2 | RI_e | I_9 | R_8 | T_6 | RI_3 |
| II | T_4 | RI_1 | I_3 | R_t | T_8 | RI_9 | I_7 | R_6 |

(3)

High
| I | I_t | R_1 | T_3 | RI_4 | I_6 | R_9 | T_7 | RI_8 |
| II | T_1 | RI_2 | I_4 | R_3 | T_5 | RI_t | I_8 | R_e |

Low
| III | R_6 | I_3 | RI_9 | T_0 | R_2 | I_7 | RI_1 | T_4 |
| IV | RI_3 | T_t | R_8 | I_5 | RI_7 | T_2 | R_4 | I_5 |

T_0 0   e   4   8   7   3   5   6   9   2   t   1

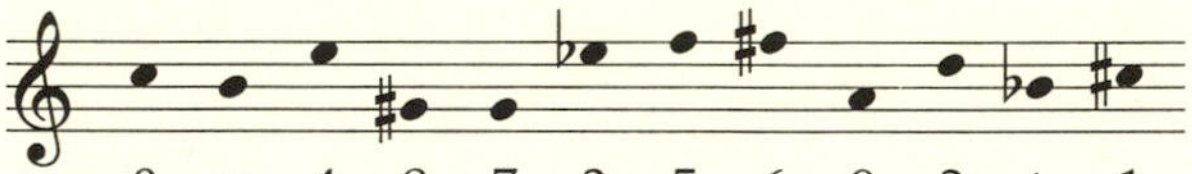

Example 3.48. *My Ends Are My Beginnings*:
array locations of row class members

chordal contents, so such things as all-interval rows or all-trichord rows cannot be constructed with them. Babbitt uses a different approach in this row, however, harking back to the row of the *Composition for Viola and Piano*. As with that row, also built of E-type hexachords, each segmental trichord of a given type is ordered uniquely. This means that although a given trichordal collection may appear in three different rows, its ordering will associate it with a single member of the row class. A single three-note segment can therefore indicate a row synecdochically, providing possibilities for reference over the span of the work. The initial trichord of the piece, for example, invokes a row that appears only in the arrays of the central and final

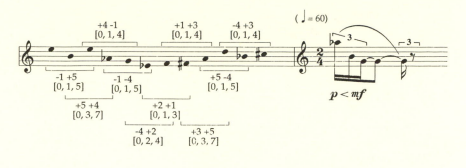

Example 3.49. *My Ends Are My Beginnings*: unique trichordal orderings.
Reprinted by permission of C. F. Peters Corporation

sections. This is illustrated in Example 3.49, along with a diagram of
the structure of the row. Once again, we can see that the sorts of
compositional preoccupations of Babbitt's first period were not abandoned in the second period but inform some of the deeper aspects of
his musical structures.

While the ordering of the row allows recurring segmental collections to be associated with specific members of the row class, their
redundancy allows us to divide up the row class into families based
on various types of collectional invariance. Hexachordal area, of
course, divides the row class into two families, each of which can be
further divided by the relative order of the two hexachords. This is
directly reflected by the array's division into lyne pairs and lynes.
Further criteria produce additional subfamilies within hexachordal
areas or between areas. For example, there will be pairs of rows related by hexachordal area that also exchange the contents of their discrete trichords within the hexachords. Similarly, the row contains segmentally two members of a tetrachord type that can be inverted onto
itself. Thus, there will be pairs of rows related by various invariance
relations involving these tetrachords.[53] This is illustrated in Example
3.50. Thus, various strategies may be brought to bear to place a
greater significance on part of the row class through the ways other
parts may invoke it. That part may be a row, or a complex of rows,
depending on the context.

The rhythmic structure of *My Ends Are My Beginnings* is probably
the most complex that Babbitt has ever devised. There is a time point

Example 3.50. *My Ends Are My Beginnings*:
segmental collectional invariants

array, representing a simple translation of the first pitch class array into the temporal domain. Throughout the composition three pitch class aggregates are composed with each of the aggregates of the time point array. As is the case in most of Babbitt's second-period compositions, lynes of the time point array are projected by dynamic level and unfold against a single modular grid. However, in this piece the size of the modular grid changes frequently, as often as every pitch class aggregate. The modular grids are changed within a fixed tempo, and although the meter changes frequently to accommodate some of the moduli, others are built of five- and seven-unit subdivisions of the beat. In these cases, the metrical placement of the time point elements shifts so that their qualitative differentiation is constantly changing.[54]

The fixed tempo allows Babbitt to embed his unfolding time point array in a larger rhythmic scheme. The duration of each pitch class aggregate is controlled by the intervals of a sequence of time point rows whose unit length is the quarter-note, the basic pulse of the piece. The sequence used is equivalent to the interval sequence of the top lyne of the time point array, including the eighty-eight (eleven times eight) intervals of the rows, the seven intervals between the ends of rows, and the intervals produced by repetitions of elements in the lyne. In terms of time point class, these last would be of zero duration, but Babbitt uses twelve units as its equivalent. Because the array contains thirty-two rows, but thirty-four aggregates, a total of twenty-four elements must be repeated. The top lyne of the array repeats seven elements, while two of the others repeat six and one repeats five. Thus the top lyne alone has 102 intervals, the number of aggregates in the composition. Not only is this lyne of particular importance in the rhythmic structure, it is also important in the pitch structure of the piece, containing as it does the 12^1 partition.

In addition to the larger scheme opperating over the span of the time point and pitch class aggregates, Babbitt has composed details within spans created by the time point array. The four lynes of the array are carried by the four dynamic levels *ppp, p, mf,* and *ff.* Additional dynamic levels between, above, and below these also appear in the piece, however, and inflect a wealth of equal-note-value subdivisions filling out intervals from the time point array. While it is always contextually clear whether a rhythmic event is part of the time point scheme or part of a subdivision, the frequent changes of moduli permit given subdivisions of the basic pulse to represent both kinds of events at different places in the piece. Recontextualizing subdivisions is one of the strategies of the rhythmic composition of *My Ends Are My Beginnings.*

As one might imagine, the interaction of the three different levels of rhythmic structure with the pitch class array is quite complex, and produces a score that looks quite fiendish on the page. Once we understand just how the different levels interact, however, we can begin to hear the rhythmic changes and inflections in ways akin to the complex rhythmic structures of Brahms, or the elaborate rubato against a more regular underlying beat in certain forms of jazz.

Example 3.51 contains a portion of the array of the first section of *My Ends Are My Beginnings*, with its share of the time point array, the modular size, and the overarching durational lyne superimposed.[55]The complete array may be found in the list of all-partition arrays at the end of this volume.

It should come as no surprise that, having provided himself with a richly layered background structure, Babbitt endows the details of the work with a multitude of ways of invoking the lynes and aggregates of the arrays. As the piece progresses, the ways details may refer to the array, as well as the portions of the array to which they refer, change frequently. Usually, change of strategy is coordinated with changes in the blocks of the array. In the process, the significance of certain aspects of the surface is altered. All this takes place within the restraints of the background rhythmic and pitch structures, which frequently motivate the sorts of details that are projected on the surface.

We shall present two related details of the interaction between background and foreground before taking a closer look at three different detail strategies. First, an examination of the aggregate durations reveals that the twenty-ninth duration, associated with the 12^1 partition of the first array, is one quarter-note, the shortest possible duration for an aggregate in the work. This is not the only aggregate projected by the interval between two time elements a step apart, but in other such situations Babbitt compounds the interval by adding twelve, the equivalent of an octave, to it. In the passage in question, the aggregate is played as a burst of twelve notes in a single beat. This is the only rhythmic event of its kind in the first part of the work and so is a vivid moment in the progress of the piece. As we shall see, this particular ordering is strongly invoked by the details of an earlier section, so its emergence here has more than local significance. Second, in the middle section of the piece, Babbitt composes the details of several aggregates to invoke a portion of the array that includes, among other things, the 11 +1 partition of that section. This aggregate uses for its eleven-note segment the same row as is found in the 12^1 partition of the third and final section of the piece. Turning to this last aggregate, we can see that although its duration is ten beats long, Babbitt subdivides the first beat in the identical manner to that used in the analogous spot of the first section of the piece. We can further

Example 3.51. *My Ends Are My Beginnings*:
first two blocks of the array

Example 3.52.   *My Ends Are My Beginnings*: 12[1] partition relations

Example 3.53. *My Ends Are My Beginnings*: details and row references. Reprinted by permission of C. F. Peters Corporation

see that the two rows used at the analogous spots of the outer sections not only are members of the same hexachordal family but share discrete trichord content as well. Thus, the final section picks up a reference to the details and array of the middle section in a rhythmic figure that invokes a striking moment in the first section, with a collectional echo of the same spot. This is illustrated in Example 3.52.

All the various cross-references of the passage under discussion depend on a variety of different aspects of the work's underlying structures, in both the pitch and rhythmic domains. These details are in turn embedded in larger webs of reference and association that span the entire composition. To shake the web a little further, we can point out that the time point aggregate containing the 12^1 partition, the dynamic high point of the piece, is coordinated with the three pitch class aggregates in the third section analogous to the source aggregates for the detail references in the second section that we have just discussed. Thus, the climactic moments of analogous structures in various domains are all composed to interconnect. The more we explore the work, the more richly entwined become the pathways through it.

A complete analysis of *My Ends Are My Beginnings* would be far beyond the scope of this volume, but we shall try to suggest the richness and variety of its details by looking at three sections. The first is the opening of the piece. As may be seen in Example 3.53, the se-

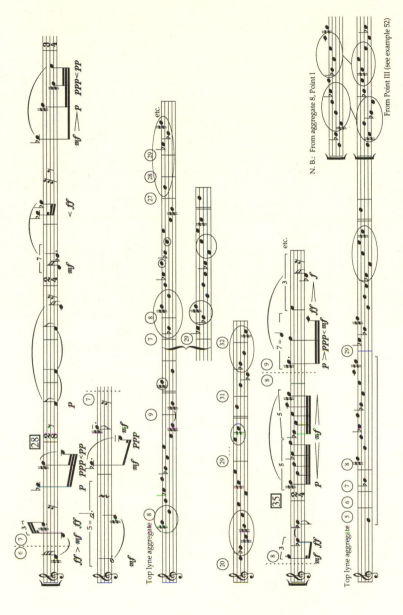

Example 3.54. *My Ends Are My Beginnings*: details and lyne references. Reprinted by permission of C. F. Peters Corporation

quences of pitches may all be associated with specific members of the row class.[56] Some of these rows appear in more than one array transformation, but some are found only in later sections of the work. For the most part, articulation and slurs are used to denote aggregate boundaries where these segments appear in the underlying arrays.

The following passage, beginning with the fifth aggregate of the piece, and coordinated with the start of the second block of the array, changes strategies in terms both of its mode of reference and of the references' sources in the array. In this passage, ordered nonsegmental collections are projected on the surface, all making reference to portions of the top lyne of the initial section's array. Here, slurs and articulation group pitches that are found within aggregates but are not necessarily adjacent. Particular emphasis is given to the 12^1 partition's segment, which, as we briefly noted above, eventually itself emerges as a brilliant flourish. That flourish is rhythmically prepared in the local passage as well, at the point in which for the first time an entire row unfolds on the surface of the music. The local flourish, however, itself projects a row powerfully linked by collectional invariance to the row found in the 12^1 partition of the third section! The passage is analyzed in Example 3.54.

Still another technique for and source of reference can be found in the opening passage of the second section, for bass clarinet, to which we referred briefly above. In this passage, the rhythmic subdivisions of the time point intervals are used to make ordered nonsegmental references to strands from particular pitch aggregates later in the array. The recurring subdivisions of nine, ten, and eleven are particularly vivid in this passage, and we have already alluded to the long-range significance of the $11 + 1$ partition and its references in this section. The incomplete rhythms of the subdivisions act in the same way as those we examined in *My Complements to Roger*, which, incidently, was composed immediately after the work under consideration and uses a circle-of-fifths transformation of the array.

In addition to the rhythmic references of the passage, slurs that cross rhythmic boundaries set up a second set of references to other segments of the array, to create a counterpoint of details. The two sorts of reference and their sources are illustrated in Example 3.55.

The preceding examples only begin to hint at ways the structure of the array shapes the details and progress of the piece. Other passages in the various sections refer variously to lynes, lyne pairs, and aggregates, using a wide gamut of means to create reference. In contrast to *Post-Partitions*, we can see that the larger composition changes not only the contents of the details of its various passages but their very nature, as well. Nevertheless, as in the other piece, one can sense the

Example 3.55. *My Ends Are My Beginnings*: details and equal note value strings.
Reprinted by permission of C. F. Peters Corporation

Example 3.56. *My Ends Are My Beginnings*: 12¹ partitions and the final aggregate. Reprinted by permission of C. F. Peters Corporation

sort of accumulation of reference that occurs locally when the details of a passage all invoke some small set of sources, and globally, as a particular hexachordal area or a set of smaller invariant collections emerges repeatedly. The preceding discussion certainly suggests the significance, for example, of the the top lyne of the initial array, its hexachordal area, and the pair of rows in the two outer sections' 12¹ partitions sharing trichordal collections. In both the rhythmic and pitch domains, in decisions involving duration, dynamics, and details, the work has been composed to project cumulatively a view of its part of the chromatic universe from the perspective of these materials. We should not be surprised to find that the final aggregate is rife with references to collections both ordered and unordered from the rows of the 12¹ partition aggregates of the work's outer sections. This is illustrated in Example 3.56.

And what about the work's title? Like his music, Babbitt's titles have many levels at which they may be understood. The 12¹ partition of the array type is made of the last eleven elements of a row followed by the first element of the following row, the same, of course, as the first element of the row completed in the partition. The relations among the transformations of the arrays guarantees that each subsequent section opens with the reversed sequence of aggregates of the end of the preceding section. A glance at the abstract structure of the opening and closing aggregates of the entire work reveals another interpretation. Nor is it merely a coincidence that the initial and final gestures are related by retrograde inversion. The fact that the first and last notes of the piece are the same is just the most immediate, most obvious instance of the title's wide-ranging significance. Some of the above are illustrated in Example 3.57.

But just as we do not pretend to have done more than scratch the surface of the music, so we have not begun to exhaust the meanings of its title. One of the rewards of listening to and thinking about Mil-

Example 3.57.   *My Ends Are My Beginnings*: beginnings and ends.
Reprinted by permission of C. F. Peters Corporation

ton Babbitt's music is that it constantly offers up new interpretations. It invites active participation, and the engaged listener comes away exhilarated and refreshed from repeated hearings. Each traversal of a composition's geography brings new pathways and vistas through a rich musical world.

4

THE GRAND SYNTHESIS (1981–)

IN 1981 Milton Babbitt completed *Ars Combinatoria*, his first purely orchestral work since *Relata II* of 1968, and with it ushered in a new compositional period during which he has synthesized the practices and predilections of all his earlier work. Babbitt's production for the past decade has been marked by an increase in both the size and number of new pieces, not to mention the richness of their contents. In addition to *Ars Combinatoria*, he has written a large-scale piano concerto, *Transfigured Notes* for string orchestra, and several extended chamber works and solo piano pieces, as well as a wealth of shorter compositions. Several works exceed twenty minutes in length, which for the density of his music is a very large time span indeed.

Two technical developments underlie the compositional flowering of Babbitt's most recent period: the superarray and the all-trichord row. Each in its own way has allowed him to bring out some of the compositional practices of his earliest trichordal period in the context of the practices of his all-partitional music. This is not to say that all his most recent works employ superarrays or all-trichord rows; he has continued to write pieces that embody the techniques of his second period and even his first period, but his enriched repertoire of compositional practices has extended his range of approaches in all the music of the past ten years.

Some of the musical implications of all-trichordal rows and superarrays can be gathered from an examination of *Paraphrases* (1979), a work that prepared the way for Babbitt's latest developments.[1] It is scored for five winds, four brass, and piano, and uses the largest ensemble he had employed since the ill-fated *Concerti* of 1976. The work is in three sections, distinguished timbrally by the use of muted brass in the outer sections, and the unique presence of the English horn in the last section. We have briefly discussed the final, shortest section of this piece in the preceding chapter; it is a complex chorale-like presentation of the work's all-partition array in the manner of Babbitt's second-period compositional practice. The first two sections, however, contain features that adumbrate much of his more recent music.

Paraphrases is based on a twelve-part hyperaggregate all-partition array type containing all fifty partitions of twelve made of segments containing six or fewer elements. The work uses an all-trichord row class, which because of the nature of the array type appears complete in each of the three major sections. The first two sections each contain a single presentation of the all-partition array, the second section employing an inversion yielding weighted aggregates. Unfolding more slowly against the primary arrays are secondary trichordal arrays generated from the ordered trichords of the work's row class. These are arranged in the familiar partitions of four elements into two or fewer parts, in the practice of Babbitt's first period. We see emerging in this work the synthesis of his two principal compositional practices: trichordal arrays unfolding the partitions of four; and all-partition arrays, played out in the context of the superarray and motivated by the all-trichord row.

Both the first two sections of the piece use the same techniques for projecting lynes of the various arrays. For the first half of each section, the lyne pairs of the primary array are carried by the five winds and the piano. The four brass instruments play the lynes of the secondary array. In the second half, lyne pairs of the all-partition array are taken up by the brass and piano, while the secondary array unfolds in the double reeds and clarinets. The flute in these passages carries an additional secondary array, also built of segmental trichords. In the course of the first two sections of the work, the brass and reeds gradually play through arrays based on all the trichords found within the segmental hexachords of the row, while the flute projects arrays based on the two trichords that cross the hexachordal boundary, the two trichords in the row containing a tritone. This is summarized in Example 4.1.

A suggestion of some of the ways Babbitt makes this multiplicity of arrays work for him can be found at the openings of the work's first two major sections. For the duration of the first section, the notes from the secondary arrays are generally attacked simultaneously with the same pitch classes in the primary array, as octave or unison doublings. The effect is not unlike the sorts of compositional realizations found in sections of pieces using weighted aggregates, such as the second half of the Fourth String Quartet, discussed in the previous chapter.[2] The independence of the secondary arrays is withheld for much of the opening of the piece. Their completion, however, is delayed until after the last aggregate of the primary array, so in effect they are stripped away from their initial dependency by the end of the first section. In the second section, the secondary arrays are treated more independently, with significant effect upon the composition of the surface details.

Row of *Paraphrases:*

Example 4.1.   *Paraphrases*: trichords

The strategy for composing out the details of the initial aggregates of the work is to form complete row statements from the counterpoint of the lynes. In later segments of the opening section, aggregate details reflect the trichordal generation of the secondary arrays; this is the reverse of the progression we found in *Dual*, written immediately following *Paraphrases*. Still other strategies are used in further passages of the section. At the opening of the second section, Babbitt once again composes the initial passage to form a complete row statement, but as the aggregates of the section's primary array are weighted, he must use elements of the secondary array independently. Thus the two secondary arrays are used in complementary fashions in the two sections. In the first section, the secondary array tends to weight certain pitch classes in the context of complete aggregates, while the secondary array in the second section frequently counterbalances the effects of the primary array's weighted aggregates. This is illustrated in Example 4.2.

As *Paraphases* demonstrates, *Ars Combinatoria* was not the first composition in which Babbitt projected more than one array simultaneously, and in fact he had experimented with such procedures in the final section of *Reflections* (1975) for piano and tape.[3] The orchestral piece, however, is the first work in which he created what has become a hallmark of superarrays: the maximizing of combinations of constituent arrays. Once again Babbitt has found a way of employing his principle of maximal diversity, played out over a very broad span.

Ars Combinatoria is, like *Paraphrases*, based on a fifty-eight-partition twelve-part hyperaggregate array type, using an all-trichordal row class. It is not a transformation of the earlier work's array type, however, as it is based on an entirely different row, containing a different distribution of the ten trichord types found in both rows. The main

Example 4.2. *Paraphrases*: initial aggregates of sections one and two.
Reprinted by permission of C. F. Peters Corporation

Ensembles

1	I	II		III		IV		IV				III	II	I	
2		IV	III		II	I		I		II	III	IV			
3			I		II		III	IV		IV		III	II	I	
4				IV			III	II		I	I	II		III	IV

RN: Array Blocks

Example 4.3. *Ars Combinatoria*: superarray structure

body of the composition is a superarray containing eight complete transformations of the composition's underlying array type. Framing the superarray are tutti passages in which each instrument or section is limited to two pitch classes apiece.[4] For most of the work, the orchestra is divided into four discrete ensembles, each containing six instruments or instrumental sections. Each ensemble plays two concatenated array transformations, and each instrument or section plays a lyne pair. The superarray is constructed to yield every possible combination of from one to four ensembles.

Just as the orchestra is divided into four ensembles, so the underlying array type itself can be broken into four blocks, marked by the completion of the rows in each lyne. Babbitt has taken advantage of this by also constructing his superarray to represent all the possible combinations of different blocks of the array type, to within the familiar twelve-tone transformations. Thus each of the fifteen sections of the superarray represents both a unique combination of ensembles and one of blocks of partitions. This is illustrated in Example 4.3.

It is crucial to realize that the sort of structure found in Example 4.3 does not arise automatically when constructing superarrays and that the two patterns of combinations are not isomorphic.[5] Although the resulting dual pattern does not represent the partions of four elements into two or fewer parts, it shares with that familiar list the presentation of all the possible nonzero subsets of four things. Thus in one more way, Babbitt in his latest period has found the means to integrate the practices of his earlier compositional approaches.

The invention of the superarray, combined with a renewed attention to trichords expedited by all-trichordal rows, has opened the floodgates of creativity for Babbitt over the past several years. Each new work embodies familiar principles in fresh and interesting combinations, and the variety of compositional strategies, even at the level of large-scale design, is staggering. In the remainder of the chapter we shall survey some of the different paths Babbitt has followed in this, his most fruitful compositional period.

Superarray Structure and Projection

In the preceding chapter we looked at some of the ways the use of all-partition arrays affected how a piece unfolds. Among the various aspects discussed were the abstract nature of the array itself, how its constituent lynes are projected on the musical surface, and how the details of its aggregates are composed. All these issues remain important in superarray compositions, but to them we must add an analogous set determined by the superarray.

The abstract structure of a superarray will determine a great deal about a composition. In certain ways, the superarray is an extension of the concept of the array itself. Babbitt's all-partitional arrays are combinations of strata of hexachordally combinatorial two-part arrays, arranged to form columnar aggregates.[6] A superarray uses complete arrays as strata, but their disposition does not necessarily guarantee aggregates between strata. How blocks of constituent arrays can be arranged in superarrays varies from piece to piece. In some compositions, Babbitt simply writes both strata simultaneously throughout, but more often he arranges them to produce a maximum variety of subsets of the number of strata present. Sometimes, as in the superarray of *Ars Combinatoria*, he combines two patterns simultaneously, producing all the combinations of strata as well as all combinations of array block types. Different superarrays of this kind can be constructed to yield different pathways through the different combinations of strata. Thus, in some works, the passage combining all strata appears at the center, while in other works it appears near the end. We shall see examples of a variety of different superarray structures.

Modes of projection similarly have a big impact on the nature of a work. In some pieces, constituent arrays are projected by a particular instrument or ensemble throughout, their lynes or lyne pairs distinguished in the manners of Babbitt's earlier music. In others, arrays are projected by a particular register, either within an instrument or among a number of instruments. Still others combine various registers of various instruments to obtain distinctive ensembles for projecting constituent arrays.[7] Each of these approaches yields a markedly different compositional surface.

Composition of details now involves not only the points we examined in the previous chapter but also the problem of combining complete aggregates from more than one array. Babbitt's usual practice in superarray pieces is to align array boundaries where possible. We shall call the resulting combinations *composite aggregates*, referring to those vertical slices formed by aggregate boundaries across constituent arrays. In some compositions he has experimented with the occasional stretching of an aggregate in one array over more than one aggregate of another. We have seen this to a marked degree in *Paraphrases*, but it also appears in works involving superarrays made from transformations of a single type of array. Usually such situations arise when the blocks of the various constituent arrays forming a section of a superarray contain different numbers of aggregates. In other works, he simply lets the extra aggregate hang over the end to be composed out alone, although in certain works he keeps alive the presence of the empty strata with unpitched percussion.

A direct consequence of composite aggregates is the availability of pitch class doublings between arrays. This gives Babbitt an additional source for a means of projecting details that he had employed in some of his weighted aggregate pieces: the use of octave and unison doublings to associate strings of pitch classes on the musical surface.[8] Such practice not only enriches the referential potential of the surface but allows a wealth of spectacular sonic effects that still may be understood to be participating in the aggregate progression of a piece. While his recent compositions are full of unison and octave doublings, the aggregate is still the underlying structural unit, despite its distance from the surface. It is still possible to hear such pitch class duplications as structural boundaries, separating the different strata of the underlying superarray, while at the same time noting the ways they group details in the surface.

Superarray Compositions

A number of recent compositions offer contrasting approaches to the use of superarrays, in terms of both their projection and the ways the superarray is itself constructed. Two of the most recent, *The Joy of More Sextets* (1986) and *Whirled Series* (1987) show to what an extraordinary extent superarrays may be manipulated to produce interesting and suggestive compositional strategies.

The String Quartet no. 5, as William Lake has shown, is based on eight transformations of a four-part all-partition array type, the circle-of-fifths transformation of the array used in *My Ends Are My Beginnings*.[9] Like *Ars Combinatoria*, which it followed by a matter of months, the quartet employs a four-part superarray combining blocks of the constituent arrays. Because the quartet's array may be broken into eight blocks as opposed to the orchestral work's four, Babbitt has contrived to make two complete statements of all possible combinations of the constituent arrays. This is illustrated in Example 4.4.[10]

Part I
Strata

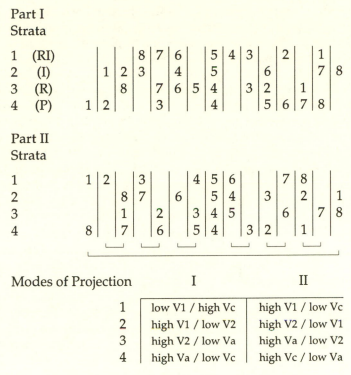

Part II
Strata

Modes of Projection

	I	II
1	low V1 / high Vc	high V1 / low Vc
2	high V1 / low V2	high V2 / low V1
3	high V2 / low Va	high Va / low V2
4	high Va / low Vc	high Vc / low Va

Example 4.4.   String Quartet no. 5: superarrays
and modes of projections (after William Lake)

As may be seen, the two patterns are strikingly different, the first always guaranteeing the continuation of an ensemble across sectional boundaries, while the latter moves through the partitions of four, placing one complementary pair of subsets at the opening and the close. The second half accordingly contains six points at which the ensembles carrying the constituent arrays are changed completely, by the complement of the ensemble as a whole.

One consequence of the structure of the quartet's superarray is that it cannot represent all possible combinations of blocks of its constituent arrays. Nevertheless, Babbitt has constructed it so that the eight solo statements represent the eight different blocks of partitions of the underlying array type.[11] Just as the structure of the array itself allows us gradually to infer the interval pattern of its row class through varied segments, so the structure of the superarray provides windows through to the individual partitions of its constituent arrays. It is worth noting that although the two halves of the composition are self-contained in terms of both completed arrays and presentations of all possible combinations of constituent arrays, the eight solo statements that add up to a complete picture of the underlying array's partitions span the entire work.

The ways the constituent arrays of the Fifth Quartet are projected also contrast with *Ars Combinatoria*. While the earlier piece divides its ensemble into four discrete groups of instruments, the constituent arrays of the quartet are each played by a different set of duos, allowing each instrument to participate in more than one array at a time. Within instruments, register distinguishes lyne pairs from different arrays rather than separating lynes within pairs as in the orchestra piece. As a consequence, the pathways of individual instruments through the quartet are considerably different from instrumental pathways in the orchestra piece, and their relative degree of participation will shift according to both the disposition of the partitions of the arrays and the number of arrays present.

Two large-scale piano works composed shortly after the quartet offer contrasting approaches to superarrays. *About Time* (1982) forms the centerpiece of a larger composition, *Time Series*, which opens with *Playing for Time* (1977) and closes with *Overtime* (1987). Both *Playing for Time* and *About Time* are based on transformations of the same six-part array we discussed in the previous chapter, while the last work employs different ways of using related material. *Canonical Form* (1983) returns once again to the array type of *My Ends Are My Beginnings*, which also underlies the Fifth String Quartet. *About Time* uses only two arrays at a time in its superarray but gradually exposes all the different partitions of its underlying array type in its eight solo statements. By contrast, *Canonical Form* contains three strata, and although each half of the work contains each combination of strata in multiples equal to the number of arrays present, the superarray has been constructed to reproduce the same combinations of array sections in each half.[12] Thus, unlike the other works we have discussed, the overall partitional structure of the underlying array type is obscured, and certain partitions are given a privileged status in the solo sections. The patterns of the superarrays for the two compositions are illustrated in Example 4.5.

In both compositions register is used to separate constituent arrays as well as lyne pairs. As may be guessed from the layout of arrays in Example 4.5, the two pieces enter and move in the world of the piano in radically different ways. *About Time* opens with an extended passage covering the instrument's complete registral span before dealing individually with the two halves of the keyboard. Babbitt has also composed the opening composite aggregate so that the two registers

About Time

Part I:	high	P	1		2	3	4	5	6	7	8		(Array Blocks)
	low	I	1	2	3		4		5	6	7	8	

Part II:	high	RI	8	7	6		5		4	3	2	1
	low	R	8		7	6	5	4	3	2	1	

Canonical Form

High		C C C	C	C C C C	C C C C	C	C C C
Mid.		B B B B B	B	B B	B B	B	B B B B B
Low	A A A	A A A		A A	A A		A A A	A A A

Example 4.5.   *About Time, Canonical Form*: superarray structure

unfold the same ordering, slightly out of sync with each other. This produces the effect of spaciousness at the outset, and it also informs the listener of the dual nature of the work's composite aggregates. It also provides a sonic link with the preceding piece in *Time Series*. As noted in the last chapter, the array type underlying both works is completed with an extra note that must be added from outside the array; at the close of *Playing for Time*, the extra note is the initial element of a final row played in multiple octaves. There are many more intimations of the progression of *About Time* contained in its opening, such as the nature of the hexachords and trichords grouped by time and register, as well as their rhythmic dispositions, but we cannot pursue this in any detail at present.[13] The opening bars are illustrated in Example 4.6.

In stark contrast, *Canonical Form* opens with a prolonged rumbling in the lowest register and only gradually climbs into the higher reaches of the instrument. As Joseph Dubiel has discussed at far greater length, the emergence of the remaining strata of activity as separate entities happens only gradually.[14] For example, the initial array, in the lowest register, continues through the first entrance of the middle register, and they both continue through the entrance of the high register. It is not until later in the first half that one can sense the music as an interplay amongst three different registral continuities rather than a single continuity gradually taking over the whole keyboard. The result is music that reveals itself retrospectively and concedes its underlying properties much more grudgingly than the earlier work.

Example 4.6.   *About Time*: initial composite aggregate.
Reprinted by permission of C. F. Peters Corporation

So far we have concentrated on the large-scale design of these works, and because of the constraints of space, we must continue to do so for the most part. However, Babbitt's new large-scale techniques have by no means supplanted his composition of detail, which when combined with the overall design of a piece yields the propulsive force of his music. *About Time* uses equal subdivisions of quarter-note pulses to index the source of strings of pitch classes, both segmental and nonadjacent, in the underlying partitions of the work's constituent arrays. The dynamics used reflect the temporal distance between a detail and its source, with greater distances eliciting higher dynamic levels. The changing degree to which the two arrays yield octave doublings, or reflect each other's surface orderings, forms another continuity through the piece, with a great contrast made between the work's opening and the conjunction of the two 12^1 partitions, happily combined in the first half of the composition. Babbitt has composed the work so that the two rows at this latter spot are hexachordally combinatorial, and the surface reflects this echo of Schoenberg's fundamental twelve-tone technique. The passage is found in Example 4.7 and may be compared with the opening found in Example 4.6.

Example 4.7. *About Time*: 12^1 partitions. Reprinted by permission of C. F. Peters Corporation

Two chamber works from this period—*Four Play* (1984), for clarinet, violin, cello, and piano; and *The Joy of More Sextets* (1986), for violin and piano—dramatize the subtlety and variety of structure and projection with which Babbitt has used superarrays.[15] The earlier composition uses circle-of-fifths transformations of the array type found in *Paraphrases*. The work's superarray consists of four transformations of the underlying array type, arranged into two strata. The four blocks of each of the constituent arrays are combined to yield the six pairs of different partitional block types as well as solo presentations of each block type. This, however, necessitates a very unusual transformation for one of the constituent arrays.

As usual, Babbitt desires that each constituent array represent one of the four classical transformations of the twelve-tone system, and in this piece he has used the weighted forms of the inverted arrays. However, the resulting distributions of partitional block types would prevent the construction of the desired superarray pattern of combinations, so Babbitt has had to come up with a special solution. The first, third, and fourth arrays to enter represent the prime, retrograde, and inverted forms of the array type. The second, however, is different. Its partitions are ordered in the same way as the prime and the inverted forms of the array, but within each block, not only has each row been inverted onto itself to preserve hexachordal content, it

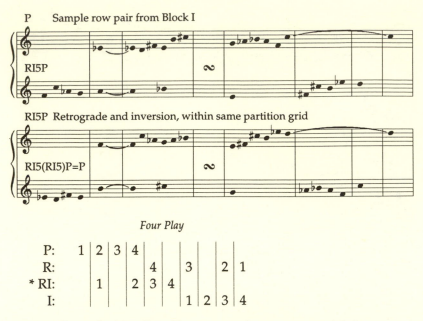

Example 4.8.   *Four Play*: retrograde aggregate weighting
and superarray structure

has also been retrograded against the fixed pattern of partitions. Aggregates are potentially weighted by the familiar inversional operation, but such a retrogression also creates certain weightings while preserving both hexachordal areas to within lyne pairs and preserving the hyperaggregate quality of the array itself. The resulting rather peculiar transformation can be seen two ways: as a whole, it permits the construction of the superarray, but seen by the row content of each block, it contributes to the whole pattern of the piece the distribution of the row class within blocks of the array contributed by a more straightforward weighted retrograde inversion. Example 4.8 illustrates the operation described and diagrams the overall distribution of blocks and constituent arrays in the composition's superarray.[16]

It is easy to notice that in both inversional forms of the array type not only has Babbitt used weighted aggregates but he has done so in a way that maps the hexachords of given lynes onto each other. This is a crucial part of the overall design of the piece, which becomes clear when we examine the projection of its superarray. In *Four Play*, all four instruments participate in both strata of the superarray identically. The clarinet, violin, and cello each contain one lyne pair from each array, while the piano, divided into high, middle, and low regis-

Example 4.9. *Four Play*: registral articulation.
Reprinted by permission of C. F. Peters Corporation

ters, has three. Each instrument, or piano register, plays the same lyne pair, in terms of both hexachordal area and partitional pathway, in each of the four arrays. Within each instrument, lynes of a given array are separated by register, and the assignment of lyne pathway to register is also maintained throughout. This is true also of the piano, where the three registral divisions are big enough to separate lynes. We can now understand the reasons for the use of both weighted aggregates and the exchange of hexachords: the four arrays have been constructed so that in all sections of the work involving two array blocks, the lynes combined in register in each instrument (one from each participating array) are hexachordally combinatorial. This is illustrated in Example 4.9.

Four Play's mode of projecting its arrays has profound consequences for the surface of the music and manifests some of the interpretations of its title. All four instruments play throughout, with differentiations in instrumental participation based on the partitional structure of the constituent arrays rather than on the progression of the superarray. When two arrays are present, each instrument or registral division in the piano plays a quartet of rows all based on the same hexachordal area, with combinatorial pairs within a single array separated registrally and pairs formed between arrays combined in register. Sectional changes are not signaled by changes of ensemble, register, or some combination thereof; rather, they are marked by alterations in the intervallic configurations within or between instruments. In passages of single unweighted array blocks, each instrument gradually unfolds aggregates within a string of aggregates formed by the whole ensemble. Passages based on single blocks of weighted aggregates also contain aggregates unfolded within instruments (or registral division in the case of the piano), but octaves and unisons arise between instruments. The six duos, each of which contains one weighted and one unweighted block of aggregates, contain octaves both between instruments and within instruments, between registers. The sanctity of the hexachordal boundary in the work's array guarantees that aggregates will still gradually unfold within registers of instruments in the passages of composite aggregates. Example 4.10 contains a passage from the work, along with an analysis of its underlying composite aggregates.

In distinct contrast to such works as the String Quartet no. 5 or *Ars Combinatoria*, *Four Play* depends entirely on the changes in its intervallic qualities to articulate its sections. *The Joy of More Sextets* attempts an even subtler approach to the reinterpretation and projection of its underlying material. This enormous duo, lasting well over twenty minutes, is one of Babbitt's most compelling works in its endless flow of lyricism, and it deserves far greater attention than we can afford here. However, our brief examination of its strategies for assembling and projecting its superarray can at least suggest pathways for listeners to follow into the work beyond its ravishing surface.

The composition is based on a six-part all-partition hyperaggregate array type, exhausting a row class constructed from the D-type hexachord. Although similar to the sort of array used in the several compositions whose openings we compared in the previous chapter, it is not a simple transformation but represents a new structure with its own sequence of partitions. The rows of the two array types, however, are closely related. One can derive the row class of one from the other by simply inverting one of the segmental hexachords at the proper index numbers. Unlike the older structure, which required the addition of an extra note for completion, the new array, found in *Sheer Pluck* and *Groupwise* as well as the violin and piano composition, is entirely self-contained.[17]

Block 2, aggregate 15 from P

(stems seperate lynes in parts)

Block 1, aggregate 1 from * RI

Example 4.10. *Four Play*: composition of a composite aggregate.
Reprinted by permission of C. F. Peters Corporation

P	1 2 3 4 5 6 7 8	RI7P	8 7 6 5 4 3 2 1
RT7P	8 7 6 5 4 3 2 1	TtP	1 2 3 4 5 6 7 8
I4P	1 2 3 4 5 6 7 8	RT3P	8 7 6 5 4 3 2 1

Part I   Part II

Example 4.11. *The Joy of More Sextets*: superarray structure

This type of array, along with three others Babbitt has used in recent years, was constructed by David Smalley, a composer and math-
ematician studying with Babbitt in the early 1980s. Smalley, who has
an intense interest in the fundamental constraints underlying all-
partition array structures, has challenged himself to construct arrays
with certain desired properties that Babbitt has used in building other
arrays.

The Joy of More Sextets is in two parts, labeled I and II in the score,
but played without a break. The reentrance of the violin after the only
lengthy piano solo marks the beginning of part II. The two halves of
the composition are each based on superarrays containing three strata
of one constituent array each, and the three constituent arrays of part
II are transposed retrogrades of those of the first part. However, both
the structure and the projection of the two superarrays are highly
contrasted, as are the resulting musical surfaces. Nevertheless, Babbitt in his disposition of the materials of the second half has preserved
certain sorts of relationships from the first half that create continuities
spanning the entire composition. Example 4.11 illustrates schemat-
ically the layout of blocks of the constituent arrays within the superarrays of the two halves.

A few points can be noted. The first half consists almost entirely of
trios of array blocks, with the exception of three sections. The second
half, however, combines its blocks into two presentations of the
solos, duos, and trios of the constituent arrays. The eight blocks of
the underlying array must in combination contain fifty-eight aggregates, so that while six contain seven aggregates, two must contain
eight. In this array, those labeled four and eight in Example 4.11 are
the long ones. Babbitt has elected to compose out the extra aggregate
separately rather than stretch aggregates from other arrays across two
aggregates. In the first half of the piece, in which the top array is
carried by the violin while the other two occupy the two halves of the
keyboard, this means that the violin part not only contains a brief solo
in its middle but that the instrument also departs the scene with a solo
aggregate. It further means that the piano's extended solo closing part
I is foreshadowed by a similar moment in its center, where two of the
longer blocks are conjoined in the superarray.

Part I

lyne pair
partition stratum

hexachordal
area

Part II

array stratum area

```
                  h.  ⎧ I    A ⎫              ┌─ c─  II   A
Violin            m.  ⎨ II   B ⎬ array        ├─ b─  I    B
                  l.  ⎩ III  C ⎭              │  ┌─ a─  III  C
                                             │  │
                  h.  ⎧ III  A ⎫             │  │        ⎧ I   A
       (upper)    m.  ⎨ I    B ⎬ array       └─ a─ ⎨ II  B
                  l.  ⎩ II   C ⎭                          ⎩
Piano  ⎨                                                  ⎧ II  C
                        ⎧ II   A ⎫              └─ b─ ⎨ III A
       (lower)    m.  ⎨ III  C ⎬ array                    ⎩
                  l.  ⎩ I    B ⎭                          ⎧ III C
                                               └─ c─ ⎨ I   B
```

Example 4.12. *The Joy of More Sextets*:
distribution of lyne pairs and arrays

While the mode of presentation of the superarray is straightforward in the first half of the composition, the second half uses a different strategy. In part II, each constituent array is divided between the violin and piano, so that neither instrument contains a complete simple transformation of the underlying array type. This results in a proliferation of octaves within the violin part as well as over narrower registral spans of the piano part. It also means that the violin is never absent for long in the second half. However, a look at the specific ways that the constituent arrays and their lyne pair strata are projected in the two halves of the piece reveals a wonderfully subtle connection. Example 4.12 contains a diagram of the disposition of the arrays and their strata within the work.

The three strata represent the three lyne pairs of the array, defined by hexachordal region and partitional participation. As may be seen in the first half, the violin separates the three strata of its array into three distinct registers. Meanwhile, the piano's two constituent arrays, occupying the two halves of the keyboard, are themselves sliced into three registrally distinct strata, representing two additional distributions of lyne pairs. Note that the three distinct partitional pathways each occupy all of the three registral slots among the three instances of the underlying array type. Because of the use of inversionally related arrays in the superarray, the three hexachordal regions cannot be similarly distributed, given the initial distribution of partitional pathways. In the second half, Babbitt has also used register to distinguish lyne pairs in both the violin and the piano, and another look at Example 4.12 reveals something remarkable. For the

violin part, Babbitt has extracted three lyne pairs from the three constituent arrays so that the resulting combination represents the three
distinct strata of the underlying array type, in terms of both hexachordal region and partitional participation! He has further distributed the
strata of both instrumental parts to replicate the same registral configuration of hexachordal regions found in the first half of the piece.
Because each lyne pair of the underlying array exhausts the rows of its
hexachordal region, the violin part of the second half is a hyperaggregate, as are the two registral halves of the piano part. Furthermore,
the violin part of the second half can be construed as a very strange
transformation of the underlying array, with the separate strata reversed and displaced with regard to each other.

The structure and projection of the second half of the work have
considerable effect upon the musical surface. In the first half, the violin's registral shifts are controlled by the disposition of partitions in
the array, so that changes tend to happen over relatively short periods
while in general the instrument maintains a steady occupation of its
whole range. In the second half, the structure of the superarray and
the violin's unusual distribution of materials cause it to shift among
different combinations of registers more slowly and maintain a given
combination for a more extended period. This is true of the piano part
as well and is the source of the closing section's prolonged high violin
line and the piano's low rumbling. On the other hand, the constant
assignment of hexachordal area to register guarantees the frequent
recurrence of particular groupings of pitch classes in certain registers
throughout the composition.

An even more radical manipulation of superarrays occurs in one of
Babbitt's most recent compositions, *Whirled Series*, for alto saxophone
and piano. Babbitt has again used the four-part all-partition array
type of the String Quartet no. 5 and several other works, in two superarrays each containing three constituent arrays. As at the outset of
the violin and piano duo, the saxophone projects one array, while the
piano contains two. Here, however, the similarity stops. Instead of
being separated registrally, the piano's arrays have been thrust together so that one has split the other, like an incursion of foreign rock
between adjacent sedimentary layers. One array occupies the middle
register, while the two lyne pairs of the other are spread to the extremes of the keyboard.

But this is the least of it. As its title confirms, *Whirled Series* is based
on even greater deformations of its constituent arrays. While the resultant strange array in the violin part of *The Joy of More Sextets* arose
from an unusual method of presenting otherwise intact arrays, some
remarkable qualities of the saxophone piece are produced by actually

lyne

Saxophone	high	1	—	—	—	— —	—	—	—
		2	—	—	— —	—	—	—	—
	low	3	— —	—	—	— —	—	—
		4	—	—	— —	—	—	—	—

lyne pair

Piano	higher	array 2	III	— —	— —	—	—	—	—
	high		array 1 I	—	—	—	— —	—	— —
	low		II	—	—	—	—	—	—	—
	lower		IV	—	— —	—	— —	—	—

Example 4.13. *Whirled Series*: the partitions of four
applied to lynes and lyne pairs in part 1

decomposing its constituent arrays. The piece is in two halves, the second containing transposed retrogrades of the first's constituent arrays. In both halves, the array of the saxophone part has been broken into eight blocks marked (approximately) by row boundaries. The eight blocks have then been treated in the same way as Babbitt has treated the eight aggregates in his trichordal arrays: like the trichords of his earliest pieces, the four lynes of each block have been variously displaced to represent all the partitions of four elements into two or fewer parts!

Needless to say, this plays havoc with the alignment of lyne segments within aggregates. To make matters even more interesting, Babbitt has applied the same process to the piano's arrays, only instead of the lynes of the individual arrays, he has treated the four lyne pairs of the two arrays as his constituent elements. Example 4.13 is a diagram of the first half of the piece.

Although the processes of *Whirled Series* do much to obscure the underlying arrays' structure, they also reveal a great deal about the roots of that structure. The partition of the initial block of the saxophone's array into two and two preserves the combinatorial lyne pairs, yielding aggregates in the instrument's slowly unfolding part. Similarly, the partition of the piano's opening section preserves complete array blocks in its pair of lyne pair duos. In a further example, the final block of the first half uses the partition of lynes into one and three that contains the instrument's final aggregate, a 4^3 partition. These are illustrated in Example 4.14.

The opening of the composition reveals its heritage both in the segment of the all-partition array in the piano and in the inversionally

1st Block, superarray
2 lynes in saxophone,
2 lyne pairs in piano.

Example 4.14. *Whirled Series*: sample portions
of the arrays and superarray

Example 4.15. *Whirled Series*: excerpt.
Reprinted by permission of C. F. Peters Corporation

combinatorial pair of rows in the saxophone. In preparation for the more unusual twists and turns of its structure, *Whirled Series* takes its departure both from Babbitt's compositional hallmark and from its progenitor, Schoenberg's fundamental twelve-tone technique.

The structure of the piece produces a wonderful surface, with all sorts of bizarre textures and juxtapositions. While the pattern of partitions into duos, solos, trios, and quartets of lynes and lyne pairs is maintained between the two instruments, the juxtaposition of parts within the partitions alters in the course of the work. Thus, in the first set of blocks divided into three and one, the trio of lynes in the saxophone is accompanied by the trio of lyne pairs in the piano, and the following solos juxtapose a lyne in the saxophone's lowest register with a lyne pair in the piano's lowest register. In the next set of blocks so partitioned, however, the two instruments accompany each other with complementary ensembles, the piano plinking away in the highest octaves against an active series of licks in the saxophone at one point. A couple of bars of each passage are illustrated in Example 4.15.

Clearly the treatment of the constituent arrays of *Whirled Series* pushes the aggregate very far from the surface in most places in the work, but nevertheless it informs the music at many levels. In the second half of the piece, Babbitt has rearranged the sequence of lyne and lyne pair partitions so that the final section is based on the combination of all four elements in both instruments. The end, therefore, presents composite aggregates from complete array blocks in both parts. Pinning the work in place, and bringing it to a ferocious conclusion, is the final composite aggregate, composed out over an extraordinary twenty-four bars! The reluctance of each instrument at the end to relinquish each note of its lynes belies the insouciance with which they have slipped and slid around in their materials for most of the piece. A section of the final composite aggregate is found in Example 4.16.

Whirled Series marks the present limit to which Babbitt has allowed the interaction of his various compositional predilections to carry him in the underlying design of his compositions. Here the differing partitional preoccupations of his first two periods have created a composition whose underlying structures can frequently only be discerned by inference, but that too has its source in his earliest music. Just as the complete ordering of the row of the *Composition for Four Instruments* never literally appears in that work, so the complete array type underlying the saxophone and piano duo never emerges unobscured in the musical surface. While Babbitt has traveled a great distance in the span of his creative life, he has always been able to take his bearings using the small set of navigational constants with which he surveys his compositional world.

Concerted Superarray Compositions

Our brief examination of some of Babbitt's recent works has shown us the variety of ways superarrays may be treated and so affect the nature of a composition and the way it progresses. Babbitt has not stopped with the superarray, however, and his imagination has extended its implications in a number of directions. Some of the most dramatic manifestations of Babbitt's latest compositional period are three concerted works, *The Head of the Bed* (1982), *Groupwise* (1983), and the Piano Concerto (1985). All three of these pieces involve a soloist accompanied by an ensemble of some sort: in the case of the first work, a solo voice with the ensemble of the *Composition for Four Instruments*; in the second, a flautist with three strings and piano; and in the last, a soloist with orchestra. In each case, the accompaniment

Example 4.16. *Whirled Seires*: final bars. Reprinted by
permission of C. F. Peters Corporation

is itself formed of a complete four-part superarray based on some sort of all-partition array type, while the soloist's music is derived in some other manner.

The Piano Concerto is perhaps the most elaborate work Babbitt has ever undertaken, rivaled only by *Relata*, the title given the concatenation of his first two orchestra pieces. The concerto is vast in scope and uses a large orchestra, although not as large as in the earlier composition. Structurally, however, it is unparalleled in its complexity. The orchestral part of the work, like *Ars Combinatoria*, is based on a four-part superarray, containing in its fifteen sections both the complete combinations of the different ensembles carrying the constituent arrays and the repertoire of combinations of the array type's four partitional blocks. Like the earlier work, the concerto is based on a twelve-part all-partition hyperaggregate array type containing the fifty-eight partitions made of segments up through six elements in length. The row, as in so many of his later works, is all-trichordal.

Despite these similarities, the works are very different. Most remarkably, even though the two compositions share the same row class, the arrays of the two works are not simple transformations of each other, despite the fact that they contain exactly the same rows and partitional shapes! As was the case with *The Joy of More Sextets*, Babbitt in the Piano Concerto has used an array type constructed by David Smalley, in which Smalley has dealt with similar partitional issues to those used by Babbitt in *Ars Combinatoria* and *Paraphrases*, with the same row class as that in the orchestral piece. The two array types, however, represent two distinct structures. The distributions of partitions throughout their four blocks are different and can yield different pathways for composing out the details of individual aggregates. Nor do the two array types arise simply from a few exchanges of pitch classes back and forth across aggregate boundaries, like the differences between the arrays of *Post-Partitions* and *Sextets*. The very distribution of rows within blocks is different. In both arrays, each block is made of three quartets of rows, each quartet containing one each of the four classical transformations in two combinatorial pairs. Like the array of *More Phonemena* mentioned in the previous chapter, the three quartets of both arrays represent inversional, retrograde, and retrograde inversional combinatoriality in their combinatorial pairs. However, the relationships between hexachordal areas of the quartets is different in the two arrays, as are the ways the quartets are transformed in subsequent blocks. This is illustrated in Example 4.17.

To make matters even more interesting, the very same row class is used in still another all-partition array constructed by Babbitt, the twelve-part seventy-seven-partition array that underlies *Dual* and the

Ars Combinatoria Array   *Piano Concerto* Array
(Babbitt)   (Smalley)

Quartets   Quartet Transformations   Quartets

hex. area

I $\left\{\begin{array}{l}P \\ I \\ R \\ RI\end{array}\right.$ $\begin{array}{l}X \\ \\ T1X\end{array}$ P   R   I   RI   I $\left\{\begin{array}{l}P \\ I \\ R \\ RI\end{array}\right.$ $\begin{array}{l}X \\ \\ T1X\end{array}$ P   RI   I   R

R $\left\{\begin{array}{l}I \\ RI \\ P \\ R\end{array}\right.$ $\begin{array}{l}T4X \\ \\ T2X\end{array}$ P   R   I   RI   R $\left\{\begin{array}{l}I \\ RI \\ P \\ R\end{array}\right.$ $\begin{array}{l}T4X \\ \\ T5X\end{array}$ P   RI   I   R

RI $\left\{\begin{array}{l}P \\ RI \\ I \\ R\end{array}\right.$ $\begin{array}{l}T3X \\ \\ T5X\end{array}$ P   R   I   RI   RI $\left\{\begin{array}{l}RI \\ P \\ R \\ I\end{array}\right.$ $\begin{array}{l}T6X \\ \\ T3X\end{array}$ P   R   I   RI

Blocks: I   II   III   IV   Blocks: I   II   III   IV

Example 4.17.   Contrasting array structures

recent *Consortini*. This type of intense scrutiny of the possibilities
available from a particular structure has informed Babbitt's music
from the outset. We need only remember the constantly recurring trichordal arrays in his first period, or his multiple use of his four- and
six-part arrays in a variety of compositions to remind us of this aspect
of his work. A more abstract sign of this tendency is the frequency
with which his underlying materials share certain properties, such as
the unique trichordal orderings underlying the row class of the *Composition for Viola and Piano* and that found in his four-part array, of *My
Ends Are My Beginnings* and *My Complements to Roger*, and of many
other pieces. As another example, the row of *Reflections*, as we noted,
is a rearrangement of the row of the String Quartet no. 2, the unique
all-interval ordering, to within reversal of hexachords, using A-type
hexachords in which the interior order of the two hexachords is not
equivalent under the classical twelve-tone transformations. That
same row, in its original configuration, underlies still another all-
partition array constructed by David Smalley and used by Babbitt in
the recent work *Fanfare* (1987), for double brass sextet.[18] This all goes

to emphasize the variety of possibilities inherent in the fundamental structures of the chromatic universe and the importance of the activity of *composition* in twelve-tone composition: this is not music that arises automatically from a few fundamental decisions, but at its best, twelve-tone music *takes advantage* of the structuring possibilities within the chromatic universe to project rich, satisfying complex pathways.

Not only are the array types of *Ars Combinatoria* and the Piano Concerto different but the patterns of their superarrays are also markedly dissimilar. In the purely orchestral work, the combination of all four strata occurs in the center, while the analogous passage in the concerto falls in the penultimate section. Although both superarrays contain less dense combinations during their earlier sections, the concerto's sequence groups its solos into two pairs separated by a pair of duos at the very outset, shoving the weight of the denser sections even more dramatically toward the end of the piece. It is worth noting here, incidentally, that the third orchestral work of Babbitt's most recent period, *Transfigured Notes*, is based on the circle-of-fifths transformation of the concerto's array type, disposed in a superarray of the same design as *Ars Combinatoria*. A detailed study of these three massive works would reveal a great deal about Babbitt's compositional thinking at a significant moment in his career.

Still another feature differentiates the orchestral portions of the concerto from *Ars Combinatoria*. In the earlier work, the four constituent arrays were each carried by a different discrete ensemble extracted from the orchestra as a whole. In the later piece, each array occupies its own register, and individual instruments may participate in a variety of arrays. Instruments in *Ars Combinatoria* play lyne pairs, with lynes distinguished by register. Depending on the passage, lyne pairs in the concerto may be carried by a single instrument, a pair of similar or dissimilar instruments, or even, in the solo block statements, by dynamic levels. This last is particularly unusual, as Babbitt, when using dynamics to index lynes of an array, almost exclusively associates them with the time point domain.[19] Although the two works have many parallels and are based on the same row class, the ways their structures have been built up through arrays into superarrays, and projected through their ensembles, have yielded wildly different musical surfaces in strikingly different dramatic progressions.

Parenthetically, we might mention that *Transfigured Notes* uses still another approach to project its constituent arrays. In that work, each section of the string orchestra, with the exception of the basses, is divided into two parts, and each of the resulting eight subsections is further divided into three registers. The resulting twenty-four instru-

Concerto for Piano and Orchestra

Orchestral Registers (high to low)

1:		IV	III	II			I				I	II			III	IV
2:				I		II	III	IV		IV	III		II	I		
3:			IV		III		II	I	I	II			III		IV	
4:	I							II	III		IV	IV	III	II	I	

Piano arrays

weighted:	I	II			IV	III								
solo:					IV	III			II	I				
super-imposed		I	III				*II*	*III*			IV		II	
		II	IV				*IV*	*I*			I		III	

(Each line of the superimposed arrays represents a different array transformation, with the italicized group in the center a single folded transformation. Note that in the weighted-aggregate piano array and in the superimposed arrays the block order is not preserved.)

Example 4.18.   Piano Concerto: orchestral superarray and solo superarray

mental regions are divided into a quartet of six-part ensembles, each a distinct distribution of instrument and register. The lyne pairs of the constituent arrays are each assigned a location in the string ensemble, providing a multitude of reinterpretations based on instrumental, registral, and temporal groupings. The basses do not participate in the basic superarray but project still another stratum based at the outset on combinatorial pairs from the underlying row class.

So far we have not even mentioned the most obvious difference between the concerto and the orchestral work: the almost endlessly busy soloist (a discarded title for the concerto was *Moving Right Along*). The solo part is also built of blocks of arrays, frequently taken out of order. Nevertheless, each array is complete, and of the same type as the orchestral music. Example 4.18 is a diagram of the superarray of the work, including the soloist's arrays.[20]

During the four solo statements of the orchestra's superarray, the piano's array blocks are made of weighted aggregates. The initial passage of the concerto pairs a series of aggregate partitions in the orchestra with their weighted inversional images in the piano. The six lyne pairs in the piano, arranged from low to high in register, are obliquely reflected by their counterparts arranged analogously from *pp* to *ff* in the lower depths of the orchestra. This is illustrated in Example 4.19.

In the remaining sections of the work, the piano plays transforma-

Example 4.19.   Piano Concerto: piano and orchestra arrays, first block

tions of the blocks that do not appear in the orchestra, so that in one way or another all the partitions of the array are present for all but four of the sections of the piece. The result is a dense but dramatic progression, articulated by drastic changes in the orchestra and subtler changes in the piano. The first two opening sections provide the greatest contrast between registers in the orchestra, whereas the subsequent section marks the first emergence of distinct individual voices in the accompanying ensemble. The fact that the orchestra's lowest register is initially featured but then abandoned for nearly half the piece makes its return striking, and its previous absence guarantees its presence for all but one section of the rest of the work. The presence of the lowest register, combined with the greater concentration of duos and trios of registers during the later parts of the concerto, culminates in the eventual expulsion of the soloist in the penultimate section, where the orchestra emerges in full panoply across its entire registral span. The soloist's return parts the orchestra, forcing it into the extremes of its register, whence it originally came. In the final section, however, the lynes of the orchestra's arrays are projected by instrument, rather than in the manner of their initial presentations, by dynamic level.

A lovely detail of the close arises from the unequal lengths of the underlying array type's blocks. In the concerto, Babbitt has not stretched aggregates when combining blocks of different lengths but has marked the inequalities with unpitched percussion in the middle and at the end of sections. In the last section, the long block is in the piano, which allows the soloist the last word, accompanied by a few clicks from the percussion.

The preceding discussion is only the most general overview of this vast work, but it demonstrates once again the ways Babbitt's large-scale designs can shape the dramatic processes of his compositions. The specific details of the various sections of the piece and the interaction of the soloist and the various massings of the orchestral ensemble create additional networks of pathways through the music, which repeated listening gradually assembles into an impression of the whole.

While the Piano Concerto represents an extreme, the work did not emerge from nothing. Obviously, Babbitt's experiences with the compositional procedures of his middle period and such works as *Ars Combinatoria* prepared the way for the concerto, but he had already experimented with superarrays as accompaniments in two earlier concerted works. Two years before the Piano Concerto Babbitt had written a chamber concerto for flautist and instruments, titled *Groupwise*. In this work, a solo instrumentalist, playing flute, alto flute, and piccolo, is accompanied by a four-part superarray divided among an

Bar	1	28	61	103	136	171	203	243	267	298	339	368	398	456	494
Soloist	F 1	F 2	F 3	F 4		A	A	F 5	F 6	P		A	A	F 7	F 8
Vn. 1 ⎧ Vn. 3 ⎨ Va. 2 ⎩	8	7	6				5		4			3	2	1	
Va. 3 ⎧ Vc. 1 ⎨ Vc. 2 ⎩		1			2		3			4	5		6	7	8
Vn. 2 ⎧ Va. 1 ⎨ Vc. 3 ⎩			8	7	6	5	4		3		2		1		
high ⎧ Pno. mid. ⎨ low ⎩	1	2				3		4		5	6			7	8

F: Flute   P: Piccolo   A: Alto Flute

Example 4.20.   *Groupwise*: superarray structure

ensemble of violin, viola, cello, and piano. The accompaniment's superarray is based on the four classic forms of a slightly varied circle-of-fifths transformation of the array type found in *The Joy of More Sextets*.[21] As may be seen in Example 4.20, the four constituent arrays are laid out to yield the ubiquitous fifteen subsets of the four projecting ensembles.

It is of particular interest to note the way the piano and strings are divided into ensembles and how they articulate their constituent arrays. While the piano has its own array, laid out across six octaves, the string instruments are each divided into three registers and combined into two duos and a trio. Each instrumental register has its own lyne pair, and each of the three string ensembles has its own constituent array. However, the assignment of lyne pair to instrument leads each instrument in the course of the composition through each of the three hexachordal regions as well as the three lyne pair partitional strata of the underlying array type, echoing the procedures of the String Quartet no. 4 and foreshadowing the composite array of the violin part of the second half of *The Joy of More Sextets*.

An immediate consequence of Babbitt's instrumental assignments in the accompanying ensemble is the frequent presence of all three string instruments on the musical surface. Nevertheless, the various sections can be differentiated by the changing ways instrumental registers enter and depart. Thus, for example, it is not until the third section that we finally hear the lowest register of the cello, and the fourth and fifth sections (in addition to a change in the solo part) are contrasted by the dramatic expansion of the cello part throughout its full registral compass in the latter section. The different constitutions of the three string ensembles guarantees a wide range of relative instrumental participation from section to section.

Entrances and departures are also affected by the disposition of the array blocks in register and by the composition of the surface. The piano's reentrance in the sixth section floats at the top of the ensemble because the partition of its array at that point falls exclusively in its higest register, while the multiple octaves that mark its final departure in the penultimate section of the work are composed into the surface to highlight its closing move.

As one may guess, the details of the accompaniment provide Babbitt with a rich tapestry against which to display his soloist. As in the Piano Concerto, the solo part is built of its own material. While *Groupwise* does not ever achieve the density of the orchestral work, it nevertheless does provide some surprises. The soloist plays during thirteen of the fifteen sections of the composition, with two breaks. This is shown in Example 4.20. Eight of those sections are played on the flute, while four of the remaining five employ the alto flute, and the fifth, the piccolo. The flute part, taken as a whole, is a complete statement of a transformation of the underlying array type, interrupted by the other two instruments. What is remarkable in the flute part is the fact that the array is not a simple twelve-tone transformation of the arrays of the accompaniment but is itself a circle-of-fifths transformation. Babbitt had for all intents and purposes avoided employing such transformations in the same piece since the early 1950s, so it is worth taking a moment to inspect the changes wrought upon the row by this operation. The two versions are shown in Example 4.21, along with brief segments of the two arrays.

Note that many features of the row are preserved, including the collection types of the segmental hexachords and discrete trichords, while certain other segmental trichords change places. The operation also preserves some mosaics in the array. Such forms of invariance are not limited to the collections or ordering pattern of this row or the array type: the array of *More Phonemena*, discussed in the previous chapter, would also make an excellent candidate. Although the underlying hexachords would change type, the dyadic properties and the segmental tetrachords of its rows would be retained, as would a number of collections derived between combinatorial pairs.

In contrast to soloist's passages for flute, the alto flute sections and the piccolo section employ a different strategy, one that is the second

Flute row

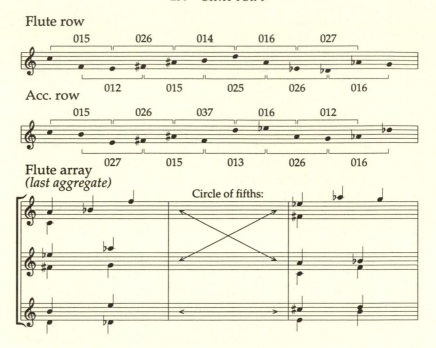

Example 4.21. *Groupwise*: circle-of-fifths transformation

great thrust of Babbitt's most recent compositional style. This, of course, is the reemergence of trichordal arrays deployed as the eight partitions of four into two or fewer parts, the abstract structure that informed virtually all the music of his earliest period. As we shall see, combinations of trichordal arrays within superarrays underlie a number of his recent works, just as we have seen their more subtle influence manifested in the patterns of the superarrays we have already discussed.

The trichords used in the alto flute's section, interestingly, are not those of the solo flute's rows but rather are from the rows of the accompaniment, except for those that are of invariant order in both. The piccolo's material is based on the two [0, 2, 6] trichords whose two orderings are invariant in the two arrays. The opening of the piece makes explicit the relationship between the two transformations and intimates the use of trichordal derivation later in the music. As is illustrated in Example 4.22, the soloist's opening phrase spells out one of the accompaniment's hexachords in order, followed by a trichordally derived hexachord, while the strings and piano spell out ordered hexachords of their arrays.

Example 4.22.   *Groupwise*: opening bars. Reprinted
by permission of C. F. Peters Corporation

In *Groupwise*, trichordal arrays are limited to the passages using the
secondary solo instruments, where they are constructed from the segmental trichords of the work's underlying row class. The earliest of
the concerted compositions, *The Head of the Bed*, makes even greater
use of them. This composition is a setting of a poem by John Hollander, Babbitt's collaborator for *Philomel*. The poem of the later work
was not written expressly for setting, unlike that of the earlier composition. One aspect that may have attracted Babbitt to it is its structure
of fifteen sections of fifteen lines each. The nature of Babbitt's setting
clearly takes advantage of the significance of this number in a variety
of ways.

Like the two works we have examined, *The Head of the Bed* pits a
solo line against an accompaniment built from a superarray. In this
work, the superarray is built of eight transformations of the four-part
all-partition array type familiar from so many earlier compositions,
including *My Ends Are My Beginnings, Canonical Form*, and the String
Quartet no. 5. The arrays in question are simple transformations of
those used in the solo clarinet work discussed in the last chapter. In
contrast with the procedures Babbitt used immediately afterward in

Instrumental Superarray   (RN = Blocks)

Fl.				IV		III	II		I	I	II		III	IV
Cl.		I			II	III	IV			IV	III	II	I	
Vn.	IV	III		II	I		I		II	III			IV	
Vc.	I	II		III	IV				IV	III	II	I		

Example 4.23.   *The Head of the Bed*: instrumental superarray

the composition of the String Quartet no. 5, the constituent arrays of
the vocal work are broken into four double blocks, each containing
two rows per lyne and combined as in Example 4.23.[22]

We can immediately recognize that once again, as in the Piano Concerto and *Ars Combinatoria*, not only has Babbitt produced all the
solos, duos, and trios as well as the tutti of the ensemble projecting
the array but he has also done so with the partitional blocks of the
array. A comparison with the patterns of the other works' superarrays
shows that *The Head of the Bed* is a combination of the two. The first
half duplicates the pattern of the opening of *Ars Combinatoria*, while
the last few sections represent a distribution closely related to that of
the concerto. The three works together suggest the range of dramatic
succession that such patterning can lead to.

The conscious evocation of his earliest procedures is only empha-
sized by Babbitt's choice of ensemble for the vocal work and its assignment to the constituent arrays. Babbitt accompanies the soloist
with the same four instruments that first articulated subsets of four
elements back in the late 1940s and has assigned them simply, with
one instrument for each constituent array, so that once again flute,
clarinet, violin, and cello can play out their various combinations
within his musical universe.

The fifteen sections of the poem are distributed among the fifteen
instrumental sections, set in a manner that evokes still further the
music of his earliest practice. The vocal setting throughout is based on
trichordal arrays, whose fifteen subsections are used to set the fifteen
lines of each stanza. This is illustrated in Example 4.24.

Through the various sections of the piece, the vocal line employs
various combinations of the ten segmental trichords derived from the
rows of the constituent arrays. The trichords are distinguished by
type and order. Further variety in the vocal part is accomplished by
altering both the sequence of the partitions of four within its trichordal arrays and the order of the subsets within partitions. With the

The Head of the Bed

Example 4.24.   *The Head of the Bed*: vocal array, first stanza, and initial aggregate.
Reprinted by permission of C. F. Peters Corporation

combination of all-partition arrays, superarrays, and the extensive use of trichordally derived rows within trichordal arrays, *The Head of the Bed* evokes structural and strategic aspects of music from throughout Babbitt's career.

We have treated this work very briefly, but clearly much more could be said. Joseph Dubiel has observed the critical differences of ensemble sequence between this work and the *Composition for Four Instruments*,[23] and as in all of Babbitt's vocal music, the setting of the text is subtle and deeply intertwined with the musical structure. Fortunately, an excellent recording allows the repeated hearings needed to offer up the composition's musical riches.

Trichordal Arrays and Superarrays

Trichordal arrays, whose influence is so strongly felt in so many ways in his superarrays, and which actually emerge in the early superarray of *Paraphrases*, never completely disappeared from Babbitt's compositional repertoire. As we have mentioned, the *Minute Waltz* of 1978 and a few smaller recent pieces are straightforward trichordal array compositions. In a couple of recent works, foreshadowed by the pieces we have just discussed, Babbitt has experimented with more elaborate interactions among trichordal arrays, all-partition arrays and superarrays.

Lagniappe (1985), for solo piano, was written to round out a recording of some of the composer's piano music played by Robert Taub. As its title suggests, the piece is a little extra something tossed in as a savory treat at the end of a substantial meal of compositions that span Babbitt's entire career. While *Lagniappe* can stand successfully as a self-contained work, it also acts as a whirlwind tour of Babbitt's compositional development and evokes the earlier works on the recording.[24]

The piece is in eleven sections of varying length but all relatively brief. The final, and longest, section is based on the first two blocks of a circle-of-fifths transformation of the array type found in the Piano Concerto. The fleeting penultimate section is based on two-part counterpoint of members of the row class, skewed to create a sequence of overlapping row statements. The first nine sections, however, are based on trichordal arrays derived from the segmental trichords of the final section's rows, which themselves are, of course, all-trichordal. The use of an all-trichordal row facilitates the construction of trichordal arrays that can run over the gamut of trichordal combinations found in his early music, while the all-partition section evokes the techniques of his middle period. The two-part counterpoint of the penultimate section echoes his earliest published work, the first of the *Three Compositions for Piano*.

Some of the trichordal sections contain simple presentations of single trichordal arrays, but others present two simultaneously, one in each half of the keyboard. The selection of trichords, their resulting hexachordal mosaics, and the composition of the details all suggest his earlier music and gradually prepare for the climactic appearance of complete rows in the composition. Example 4.25 is a chart of the trichordal arrays and superarrays of the piece.

As we can see, the first two sections work through a trio of trichordal arrays based on the first three successive trichords of the underlying row type, but that are themselves related by hexachordal mosaic in the way the underlying structures of the *Composition for Four Instruments*, the *Composition for Viola and Piano*, and *Two Sonnets* are related. In fact, the collectional structures are simply the circle-of-fifths transformations of those in the works we discussed in an earlier chapter. Here, they invoke the ways trichordal arrays were used in the *Three Compositions for Piano*, a work predating the *Composition for Four Instruments*.

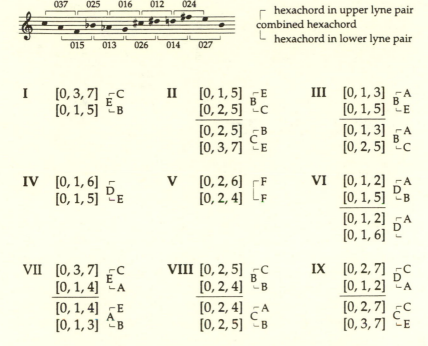

Example 4.25. *Lagniappe*: underlying trichordal distributions

The third section of *Lagniappe* is formed of two trichordal arrays containing the second, third, and fourth successive trichords of the underlying row type. The mosaics of the arrays themselves replicate those found in two sections of *Partitions*. Their realization not only is similar to the analogous passages in the early piano work, with various combinations of individual attack, single notes and dyads, and trichords derived from the counterpoint of lynes, but also at the outset emphasizes both the B-type hexachords later to appear in the work's complete rows and the discrete trichordal partitioning of one segmental hexachord. This is illustrated in Example 4.26.

These are just anecdotal examples of *Lagniappe*'s means of suggesting the other compositions on the recording, but the piece evokes Babbitt's earlier music in more general ways. Not only do the techniques of the piano work echo the underlying structures of his earlier compositions but the overall strategy will also seem familiar from such works as the Woodwind Quartet and the String Quartet no. 2. As in those pieces, the materials of the row are gradually exposed, both in terms of interval patterns and by collection and collection type, ultimately bursting forth in a finale made of combinatorial webs

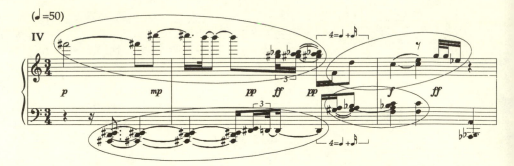

Example 4.26. *Lagniappe*: excerpt. Reprinted by permission of
C. F. Peters Corporation

of complete rows. *Lagniappe* traces the history of Babbitt's compositional development, showing the integration of his various techniques—whose differences are not so much stylistic as they are different regions in or paths across a single rich, complex musical world—within a systematic whole.

Consortini (1989), a very recent composition, also carries with it echoes of Babbitt's earlier practices as well as evoking even earlier music. This sizable work (about eighteen minutes) is scored for flute, piano, vibraphone, marimba, and cello, with the two percussionists additionally playing an array of twelve nonpitched instruments. There is the suggestion of a Baroque ensemble whose continuo instrument has undergone an expansive and colorful transformation implied in the layout of the score, but more significantly, the large-scale structure of the piece invokes Baroque practice, much in the way that *All Set* is imbued with the spirit of jazz.

The work is based on the circle-of-fifths transformation of the seventy-seven-partition twelve-part array type used in *Dual*, the third of the three distinct array types sharing a common row class. *Consortini* is in eleven sections, with five extended soloistic sections interposed between briefer tutti presentations of the six blocks of the array. The effect is very much like a Baroque concerto, with extended solo passages punctuated by the varied return of a ripieno.

In a manner reminiscent of *Arie da Capo*, the five soloistic sections exhaust the repertoire of subsets of the ensemble, in this case including the duos and solos in addition to the trios and quartets. In passages where both percussionists are unoccupied with their tuned instruments, Babbitt adds a counterpoint of strokes on drums and cymbals. Example 4.27 illustrates the overall pattern of instrumental ensembles in the course of the work.

tutti	duo 1	duo 2	trio 1	trio 2	solo	quartet
I	F,'C	V,M	F,P,'C	P,M,V	F	M,V,P,'C
II	F,P	M,'C	F,V,P	M,V,'C	M	F,V,P,'C
III	P,V	F,M	P,V,'C	F,M,'C	V	F,M,P,'C
IV	V,'C	P,M	F,V,'C	F,M,P	P	F,M,V,'C
V	F,V	P,'C	F,V,M	P,M,'C	'C	F,M,V,P
VI						

Blocks of the array	F: Flute
	M: Marimba
	V: Violin
	P: Piano
	'C: 'Cello

Example 4.27.   *Consortini*: instrumental ensembles.
Reprinted by permission of C. F. Peters Corporation

The five extended solo sections are not built from transformations of the array of the tutti sections but consist of trichordal arrays piled into superarrays. The trichords are derived segmentally from the work's all-trichord row class. Thus, like the Baroque works it echoes, *Consortini*'s solo passages are elaborations of the materials of its ripieni.

Miniatures, Piéces D'Occasion

In the preceding sections of this chapter we have for the most part concentrated on the large-scale works of Babbitt's most recent compositional period, without taking time to look at some of the briefer pieces. However, this is not to suggest that good things do not come in small packages; some of his most charming conceptions are among these more intimately scaled works, and a certain few show the ways that the composer has expressed his regards to other musicians past and present whose worlds intersect with his own.

Overtime (1987) is the third piece in *Time Series* and returns to the materials of *Playing for Time* and *About Time*. Unlike the earlier parts of the series, *Overtime* is not constructed from the same underlying array type found in *Arie da Capo*, *Melismata*, and those other works we briefly examined in the previous chapter. Rather, it consists of a remarkable superarray in two completely different strata, framed by

Example 4.28.   *Overtime*: initial aggregates

presentations of inversionally combinatorial row pairs. The row class underlying the piece is closely related to that in the earlier compositions, except that one of the segmental hexachords has been transposed onto itself by a tritone. The layout of the opening row statements prepares the way for the two strata of the superarray. Example 4.28 contains the opening passage of the piece.

The first pair of hexachords is presented so that the upper one initially exposes more of its elements than the lower, while the second pair unfolds more nearly note-against-note. The two presentations are consistent with what immediately follows in the superarray and determine the initial pitch class collections. In the main body of the composition, the lower stratum of the superarray consists of a four-part array using a single partition, $4^2 2^2$, made of four classical transformations of the row. This echoes the array at the outset of *All Set*, found in Example 2.64, which was also based on the D hexachord type. The upper array, on the other hand, contains three derived rows based on the all-combinatorial tetrachord types, [0, 1, 2, 3], [0, 2, 3, 5], and [0, 2, 5, 7]. The partition scheme of the lower array is compatible with the first aggregate of the introduction, while the counterpoint of the second aggregate yields the three all-combinatorial tetrachords of the upper array, in their initial tranpositions. Example 4.29 illustrates the opening of the main body of the piece, along with its underlying array structures.

Throughout the piece, the lynes based on derived tetrachords cycle through their various transpositions and their various order transformations at different rates and in different sequences. New orderings are employed later in the array as well. One interesting consequence of these changes in the upper array is the interplay of segmental intervals so formed with both segmental and combinatorially derived intervals in the lower array. At the outset, for example, the segmental dyads of the tetrachords in the upper array's first aggregate correspond to the dyads formed between inversionally combinatorial row pairs in the lower array's lynes. In the next two aggregates of the

Example 4.29.   *Overtime*: superarray structure

upper array, this is no longer true, but with the return in the fourth
aggregate to the transposition levels of the first, once again the significant dyads reappear. There are similar reciprocal relations between
the segmental dyads of the lower array and the combinatorially derived dyads of the upper. The later reorderings of the all-
combinatorial tetrachords create relations between the segmental
dyads of both strata. The piece closes with the tritone transposition of
the introduction, spread in register and realigned to reverse the patterns of the opening.

Although *Overtime* is not based on the same array type as the two
earlier works in *Time Series*, it nevertheless echoes their structures in
its details. This can be most readily suggested by a comparison of
their openings, in which B-type hexachords figure prominently. In
Playing for Time, these may be heard in the registral distribution of the
opening aggregate; in *About Time*, in the temporal order of the opening composite aggregate, unfolded in both registers. In *Overtime*, the
compounding of three all-combinatorial tetrachords in the second aggregate may be alternatively sliced into two B-type hexachords, mimicking the row of the String Quartet no. 4.

Babbitt's recent shorter pieces frequently visit old ground in new ways. The piano piece just discussed brings tetrachordally derived aggregates to the fore in a way not seen at the surface of a piece since certain compositions of the 1950s, although the repertoire of tetrachords used will be recognized as those found in the row of the Fourth Quartet as well as in that of *More Phonemena*. *Fanfare*, as we mentioned earlier, returns to the row of the Second String Quartet, but in a context of all-partition arrays in a superarray. *Homily* (1987), for solo snare drum, is based on exactly the same time point array as that spanning *My Ends Are My Beginnings*, but without all the rhythmic interpolations of that work. The short percussion solo closes with a coda of two combinatorially paired rows, related by retrogression and transposition. Its aggregates are marked throughout by changes in the modular length, creating changes of tempi and metrical grouping. Larger sections are marked by changes in snares, sticks, and playing manner, as well as dynamic span. The result is a constant evolution of textures and timbres, with frequently recurring rhythmic patterns at different tempi unfolding through a variety of dynamic contours.

Beaten Paths (1988) for solo marimba also uses the familiar four-part all-partition array type, in the form found in *My Complements to Roger*, played out against its transposed retrograde in a superarray whose strata are distinguished by register, its title perhaps reflecting the well-tried character of its underlying structure. *Play It Again, Sam* (1989), a solo viola composition dedicated to Samuel Rhodes, returns once again to the array type of *Melismata* for one more pass through the webs of possible relations in that segment of Babbitt's compositional world. Its title is engendered at least in part by the familiarity of the underlying array type but also reflects an aspect of the surface. In pursuing the particular paths of relations through its aggregates, Babbitt has composed the details with a great deal of repetition of notes and dyads within short spans of time. Both works illuminate fresh ways of creating accumulations of association over background spans familiar from a wealth of other compositions.

Scattered across Babbitt's list of works are a number of occasional pieces written to celebrate other composers' birthdays or commemorate their music. *Post-Partitions* and *My Complements to Roger* are dedicated to Roger Sessions, and *Don* celebrates Donald Martino's fiftieth birthday. Not infrequently, Babbitt has been able to introduce a quotation, either of a piece or of a technique associated with the celebrant. In *My Complements to Roger*, he manages to import a melody from one of Sessions's own compositions, the section of *From My Diary* dedicated to Babbitt himself. Of greater structural consequence is the relationship between Sessions's final chord and the row class of Babbitt's piece. These are both illustrated in Example 4.30.

Roger Sessions   *From My Diary*

My Complements to Roger

Example 4.30. *My Complements to Roger*. Copyright © 1991 by Sonic Art Editions. Used by permission of Smith Publications, 2617 Gwynndale Ave., Baltimore, Md. 21207, U.S.A. Quotation from Roger Sessions, *From My Diary*, used by permission of Edward B. Marks Music Company

More recent quotations include brief snippets of Schoenberg's *Pierrot Lunaire* in *Souper* (1987), one of a series of settings, commissioned by the Arnold Schoenberg Institute from a number of composers, of poems not used by Schoenberg out of the Albert Giraud cycle.[25] *In His Own Words* (1988), written in celebration of Mel Powell's sixty-fifth birthday, contains a number of sly rhythmic and intervallic references to several composers with whom Powell has been associated, including Paul Hindemith, but the work also includes a technical reference to Stravinsky. In what is otherwise a straightforward albeit sometimes strangely articulated trichord piece, there appears a passage composed with the sort of rotational array favored by Stravinsky in his last years. The passage, illustrated in Example 4.31, accompanies a quotation of a remark by the dedicatee, "Originality is merely one thing; mastery is something else. There is typical formal propriety in Stravinsky's departing just when the demons he abhorred, amateurism and slovenliness, are enjoying their season in the sun."

Lest the distance between Babbitt's practices and one of Stravinsky's major contributions to twelve-tone technique seem too

In His Own Words

Example 4.31.   *In His Own Words*: Stravinsky rotations

great, we need only remember the opening of *Philomel*, discussed briefly in the preceding chapter, to see the intersection of their thinking. The opening portion of Babbitt's work for voice and tape traces relations among an analogous sequence of transpositions of rows, which in their nonrotated state skew Stravinskian verticals over the span of the passage, the elements of each collection fixed with regard to their order number interval from the recurring note in the voice. While the means of interpreting the abstract structure derived by Stravinsky's rotations differ to a great degree between *Philomel* and *In His Own Words*, the implications of the operation in terms of the distribution of pitch classes and intervals, be it within a simultaneity or spread over a series of aggregates, are similar and show the influence of the Russian composer upon Babbitt's thinking.[26]

One of his most elaborate birthday greetings is *The Crowded Air* (1988), written in celebration of Elliott Carter's eightieth birthday. The

[0, 3, 7] [0, 1, 3] [0, 2, 5] [0, 1, 5] [0, 1, 5] [0, 2, 7] [0, 2, 4]   [0, 2, 6]   [0, 1, 6]   [0, 1, 2]
                    ([0, 1, 4])

Example 4.32.   *The Crowded Air*: initial piano aggregate.
Reprinted by permission of C. F. Peters Corporation

composition represents a synthesis of certain aspects of Carter's compositional techniques seen from the perspective of Babbitt's preoccupations. The work draws its title from the second line of Emily Dickinson's poem set in Carter's *Musicians Wrestle Everywhere*, which continues, "All day—among the crowded air."[27] The title is apt, given the music's density and the sheer amount of activity in its three-minute span.

While the work is based on an all-trichord row class, similarities to other compositions of this period are at best tangential. The ensemble consists of four winds, four strings, marimba, guitar, and piano. For the entirety of the composition the piano acts as a separate agent, playing with the rest of the ensemble but not part of it. The piano's material consists of complete row statements, sometimes paired combinatorially and sometimes alone. These frequently are ordered in register as well as in time, in imitation of Carter's own compositional practice.[28] As may be seen, the row is not constructed of all-combinatorial hexachords but is inversionally combinatorial. The opening bars of the piano part are found in Example 4.32.

The remaining ten members of the ensemble participate in a structural web that spans the work. In keeping with the nature of the occasion, the piece contains eighty bars in triple meter, at a tempo of eighty beats per minute. Bars are paired throughout the composition. The resulting forty equal sections underlie the pitch and rhythmic structure of the whole work. Each section contains three statements of a particular trichord played as a simultaneity. The trichord in question is the A-minor triad heard at the outset and is the first trichord of the piano's initial row. In its course, the music runs through all 120

Durations: 642   651   741   345   372   *(six times)*

552   822   633   *(three times)*

444   *(once)*

Opening bar's duration scheme:

642 | 651 | 741 | 345 | 372 | 282 | 624 | 615 | 714 | *and so forth*

Example 4.33. *The Crowded Air*: duration patterns

combinations of three instruments from the ensemble of ten in the projection of this trichord, as well as the variety of orderings and spacings available.

The rhythmic placement of the ubiquitous A-minor triads in each two-bar span determines the remaining rhythms for those spans. In the forty segments, the triads employ the six different orderings of five combinations of unequal durations, the three different orderings of three combinations of two equal and one odd duration, and the single ordering of three equal durations. Example 4.33 is a chart of the durations; it is not surprising that the equal duration span is at the center of the work.

The proportions of each rhythmic event within a span are equal to those of the triads covering the span. The resulting durations are frequently filled in with equal note values. Example 4.34 illustrates the first two spans.

The remaining instrumental parts are a curious admixture of Carter's and Babbitt's techniques. Viewed in detail, they cannot be interpreted as simple transformations of some row type, whether taken as single lynes or broken into combinatorial pairs, but they are formed so that for considerable stretches, each successive note forms with the two preceding notes a trichord ordered in the manner found in the underlying row class. This sort of approach echoes much of Carter's music, including his Piano Concerto and Third String Quartet.[29] The approach also has obvious ties with Babbitt's techniques right back to his earliest music, whose underlying rows could well be construed as the result of overlapping a certain set of ordered trichords used under various transformations in a series of trichordal arrays. A few instrumental segments of *The Crowded Air* are illustrated in Example 4.35.

Over longer spans, the instrumental parts yield a characteristic more readily associated with Babbitt's music, however. In the course of overlapping ordered trichords, Babbitt is frequently forced to repeat pitch classes, but he has composed each instrumental part so that

Example 4.34.   *The Crowded Air*: rhythmic details, first two spans

pitch class repetitions occur in a fixed register until all twelve pitch classes have sounded. Included within each instrument's part are the notes necessary for its participation in the constantly varied A-minor triad, a sound sustained through the entire piece. The process of composing the instrumental parts mimics the general properties of aggregates unfolding in all-partitional arrays, so it is possible to hear each instrument unfolding sets of complete aggregates over the span of the work. The resulting instrumental counterpoint itself does not yield complete aggregates, but the surface is not unlike those found in compositions using weighted aggregates or superarrays.

Although *The Crowded Air* is technically about as distant from his normal practice as any work in his oeuvre, Babbitt has been able to reconcile its features, both in detail and over long spans, with the ideas that have informed and sustained his composing since the earliest days of the *Composition for Four Instruments*. In doing so, he has once again revealed the communality that lies behind the particulars of each of his works, but he has also tapped that even deeper well of shared compositional constraints and possibilities that has nourished a variety of the century's musicians.

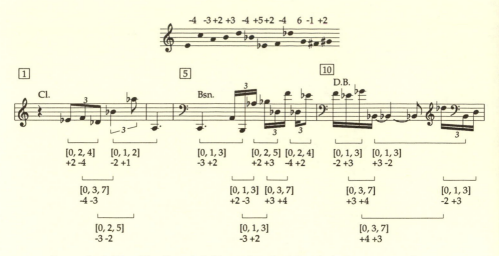

Example 4.35. *The Crowded Air*: ordered trichords in instrumental parts. Reprinted by permission of C. F. Peters Corporation

New Departures

In the past few years, Babbitt has continued to write works that both touch on his earlier music and open up new vistas in his compositional world. *Envoi* (1990), for piano four hands, returns to the materials of *A Solo Requiem*. Two large-scale piano works, *Emblems (Ars Emblematica)* and *Preludes, Interludes, and Postlude*, offer distinctly different approaches to the piano, and he has described the former as his equivalent of the *Art of the Fugue*. *Mehr "Du"*, for mezzo-soprano, viola, and piano, returns to the collection of poems by August Stramm that Babbitt had used for his 1951 song cycle. Recent years have also seen the composition of three works entitled *Soli e Duettini*, each a connected set of solos and duets. They are for two guitars, flute and guitar, and violin and viola respectively. While all these works embody familiar techniques, it is possible to discern the seeds of radical new developments germinating in many of them.

Mehr "Du" is a set of four songs that invokes the trichordal world of Babbitt's first period in ways that echo the beginnings of his second period while extending his most recent developments. Underlying these songs is a brand-new array in twelve parts, of segments no longer than six elements. This array was constructed by David Smalley and has several unusual features. Because no more than six lynes participate in any aggregate and because of certain other constraints, the array contains only twenty-nine different partitions. Like the array of *Sextets* and *Post-Partitions*, this new array is constructed from an ordered hexachord, but in contrast to the earlier array, each hexachordal lyne is considered a separate entity. Its twelve lynes exhaust the twelve transpositional regions of the A-type hexachord. The hexachord is ordered in the same manner as the second segmental hexachord of the row of the Woodwind Quartet, that unique ordering of the chromatic hexachord in which each of the four segmental trichords can also itself generate the chromatic hexachord.

Although the underlying materials recall earlier concerns, it is their deployment that suggests new directions. The four songs are constructed of a two-part superarray containing two instances of the twenty-nine-partition array. The resulting web of twenty-four lynes is divided up among the members of the ensemble in an unusual way. Each of the two instruments plays ten lynes of a block of the array, while the vocal part is composed of two lynes each from the two blocks. The voice's hexachords consist of two complementary pairs of the same transpositional area, representing the four classical transformations of the underlying order pattern. The results of these decisions have a profound effect upon the surface of the music. Because of the presence of the superarray, the piece tends not to have aggregates unfolding unobscured in time, and the choice of projection tends to obscure aggregates in the instruments in many passages. Most dramatic, however, is the resulting vocal line, which is full of octave leaps in a slow overturn of pitch classes. One soon becomes aware, however, of the intimate complementary relationships between the voice in its various registers and the surrounding instruments. A portion of the superarray and its disposition, along with a few bars of the first song, are found in Example 4.36.

The composite nature of the vocal line in *Mehr "Du"* has its precedents in the second half of *The Joy of More Sextets* or the accompaniment of *Groupwise*, but it takes a radical step in its persistent obscuring of the underlying array. Those earlier works have at least some passage where the underlying material is relatively near the surface, but here the underlying array emerges only by inference. This helps to reinforce a critical point about hearing Babbitt's music. While an awareness of the underlying structures can clarify the richness of his music, we are not listening merely to strip away the surface details to reveal the underlying array. The effect of the underlying array, like the effect of the row itself, is one that comes to permeate the work at many levels, creating a palpable resonance between specific moments and the piece as a whole.[30] What can lead us into the deeper layers of *Mehr "Du,"* as it does in all the rest of Babbitt's music, is an attention to the surface details, which in this case are constantly revealing frag-

S.P.			23e10t 976				6845	
pizz.		34021 5786t		1 (e) t9			9	
Vla. h.				754623	980te1		3	
m.			8 5	8	562		7e	e9t0 2431
l.	e98t67 023154							
Voice (high)		9e	4	0	437		0t21	7568
Voice (low)	20e1						7 9t	784653
high ↑			et2 467	201 598	3		8	
Pno.	5	786		34 6t	402		1e	t9
		9	980			7 te1	54 (6) 23	1
↓ low	79t8 643		351				0	0e 2
		te 104 (2) 35		e7	986 5			

Example 4.36.   *Mehr "Du"*: superarray structure and opening bars.
Reprinted by permission of C. F. Peters Corporation

ments of the fundamental hexachordal order. A glance at the opening bar, in Example 4.36, shows three instances of ordered fragments, two in the viola and one in the piano, the first in the viola immediately heard in retrograde in the voice, arising from an array lyne segment. Constant rehearing and remembering can ultimately reveal to us the underlying order as that simplest representation embodying the range of relationships in the piece; the presence of the array helps maximize that range over a variety of time spans.

For our final analytical vignette, we shall turn to two recent works written in close succession, *Soli e Duettini* for two guitars, and the work of the same name for flute and guitar. These two works in their similarities and differences encapsulate much of what is valuable in Babbitt's art, and the insights we may gain through their comparison are applicable to his work as a whole. While the two works are based on nearly identical background structures, decisions at virtually every level create differences between them both obvious and subtle.

Both works are based on superarrays constructed from the array type found in *The Joy of More Sextets* and its circle-of-fifths transformation. This approach, previously observed in *Groupwise*, is taken a step further here by giving both versions of the array more nearly equal status. As we discussed above, the two rows share certain ordered trichord types but are each distinguished both by sporting unique orderings of certain shared trichord types and by containing certain unique trichord types. This allows the construction of a language for each instrument that is unique but that can share a great deal with the language of its companion.

In both pieces, the upper instrument on the score presents the array in the order that it is found in the list of all-partition arrays at the back of this book, while the lower instrument presents the retrograde, under the circle-of-fifths transformation. The arrays of the two upper instruments are virtually identical: they are simply related by T_1. However, the relationships between the two arrays in each piece differ, in that to derive the double array structure of one piece from that of the other, one must transpose the lower array by T_6. This will have a very particular effect, however, in that the underlying hexachord type, D, maps onto itself under T_6. Thus hexachordal areas remain constant between the two double array dispositions, while specific smaller collections are shuffled.

A grosser differentiation occurs between the two works at the level of the superarray. Example 4.37 illustrates the two different dispositions of array blocks in the two superarrays, along with the still-different superarray of the third *Soli e Duettini*, for violin and viola. As one may note, not only will the two different pieces disclose their

				*				*	
Guitar 1	1	2	3	4	5	6		7	8
Guitar 2	8		7	6 5			4	3 2	1
	*					*			

				*				*	
Flute	1	2	3	4	5	6		7	8
Guitar		8	7	6 5			4	3 2	1
		*				*			

				*				*	
Violin	1		2	3 4	5	6		7	8
Viola	8	7	6	5	4			3 2	1
	*				*				

* Blocks with extra aggregate

Example 4.37. *Soli e Duettini*:
contrasting superarray structures

underlying materials in different ways but their solo sections will articulate different parts of the underlying array structure.

An obvious difference between the two pieces is their instrumentation: the earlier duo is for a pair of identical instruments, while the later work's instruments differ in ways as fundamental as register, articulation, and sheer sound production. What is more intriguing than the immediate timbral difference between the works is the way this difference interacts both with the fundamental dispositions of their two superarrays and with their contrasting strategies for assembling details on the musical surface.

Before taking a closer look at the surface details of the two works, we should briefly note still another difference in passing—which, incidentally, will serve to illustrate a recent development in Babbitt's rhythmic technique. Both works use a modified version of the time point system for their underlying rhythms, the later work opening with a straightforward presentation of the first aggregates of the upper array with each of the six lynes articulated by a different dynamic; the earlier work at its beginning employing a time point translation of the opening of its superarray's composite aggregates, with each of the six lyne *pairs* projected by a different dynamic. This difference has many consequences that we shall not pursue, but we shall take a moment to consider two significant results of certain subtle changes Babbitt has wrought upon the time point system. In both works, and quite prominently from the outset of the earlier one, Babbitt fills his time point intervals with additional attacks, derived by subdividing the spans with various complete and incomplete equal note value strings, a technique we observed in *My Ends Are My Beginnings*. In contrast to the earlier work, these added attacks frequently duplicate actual time point values, so, in general, Babbitt has tended to derive his sequences of time points by moving between lynes, thus generally signaling time point intervals by dynamic change. Babbitt has also greatly slowed the rate at which time point aggregates or composite aggregates flow by, especially at the outset of the guitar duo (the entire first duet and the opening of the first solo move through only two composite aggregates of the time point superarray), in order to allow a certain small repertoire of time intervals to be filled in a variety of ways using equal note value strings. The result is a vastly slowed dynamic rhythm in these compositions, with frequent long strings of events at a single dynamic level, or rocking regularly between two dynamic levels. By varying both the degree to which time intervals get filled in and the length of time to complete time point aggregates, Babbitt can produce a wide range of rates of dynamic change. This is particularly vivid in the opening flute solo of the later duo.

More radical still is Babbitt's changed approach to meter in these works. As we discussed in chapter 1, the time point system as originally conceived depended on a stable meter for its apprehension.[31] However, in a number of recent time point pieces from the past ten or so years, meter changes frequently, not only from $\frac{2}{4}$ to $\frac{3}{4}$ and $\frac{4}{4}$ but to bars that add or subtract sixteenth and eighth notes ($\frac{5}{8}$, $\frac{5}{16}$, $\frac{2}{4} + \frac{1}{16}$, and so forth). Now it might be argued that such changes simply allow Babbitt to dispense with some of the over-the-barline notational snarliness that can be seen in earlier works such as *An Elizabethan Sextette* or *Paraphrases*, but I believe that the new notation encourages us to hear constant metrical reinterpretations of the sequence of time points, so that the transposition of certain repeated intervals, for example, can itself shift our sense of the placement of downbeats. This becomes particularly vivid in those passages, such as the opening of the two-guitar work, in which the progression through time point aggregates is very slow. However it is interpreted, Babbitt's new approach invites a serious reconsideration of the perceptual possibilities of the time point system.[32]

How does the choice of instrumentation interact with the details and the disposition of the superarray to let each of these duos tell its own story? The two works approach their initial musical unfoldings in very different ways. The guitar duo is faced with the establishment of the identity of its two members. They are timbrally identical, and their initial appearance is in a duet. The music will have to go a distance to disentangle these two entities, and the very opening gestures, based on ordered trichords shared between the work's two row classes and formed both within and between instruments, further entwines their voices. As the music progresses, however, the upper instrument begins slowly to unwind a longish segment of one of its own rows, trichord by trichord, while the lower guitar forms a skewed paraphrase by gradually presenting a set of its own trichords. Those orderings and trichord types unique to each instrument are gradually exposed. The opening bars of the *Soli e Duettini* for two guitars are illustrated in Example 4.38.

Thus the instruments seek their own identity, gradually, through the material they play. The inherent possibility of confusion between the two instruments is never totally relinquished, and this is played with even in the simple alignment of aggregates between arrays. At the end of each instrument's first block, the lower guitar has an extra aggregate, which is played as a miniature solo before the first real solo, in the upper instrument. This little solo, played for the most part at the lower dynamic levels, is cut off by a fortissimo gesture from the "real" soloist, who then continues at the lower dynamic levels. The effect is to raise some confusion at the first significant juncture of the piece and smudge still another boundary.

In contrast, the flute and guitar duo raises what seem to be very different issues, merely from the fact that the two instruments are so immediately different. Their difference is directly underscored at the outset by the fact that the flute opens with its first solo. We are kept waiting to see what the guitar will bring, and further, once the guitar is playing, we are kept waiting even longer, through two blocks, before it achieves parity with the flute by means of its own first solo. Once again, the design of the superarray contributes to this drama, and the extra aggregate at the end of the guitar's first block helps to draw it out by promising, but not delivering, that instrument's awaited solo. The composition of the details enhances the effect of the opening. The flute seems obligingly forthcoming with its details; in contrast to the first composite aggregate of the guitar duo, which lasts about twenty-seven beats (both works are in roughly the same notated tempo) and contains a lot of repeated and reordered notes, the flute unfolds its opening aggregates in spans of five to eight beats, with unambiguous orderings and repetitions reduced to rearticulations of single tones. (This is not to say there is no ambiguity here; on the contrary, different groupings created by rhythm, register, and slurring allow multiple interpretations.) The ordering of the first two aggregates, we shall realize in retrospect, reproduces segmental hexachordal orderings from the flute's row class. This is illustrated in Example 4.39.

Example 4.38.   *Soli e Duettini* for Two Guitars: opening bars.
Reprinted by permission of C. F. Peters Corporation

Example 4.39.   *Soli e Duettini* for Flute and Guitar: opening bars.
Reprinted by permission of C. F. Peters Corporation

The guitar's entrance immediately asserts the instrument's own identity in several ways. Its first gesture is in its privileged register, the top note of its first trichord being the lowest note in the flute, and the trichord itself is one of its unique trichord types. This is almost immediately followed by a presentation of its other unique trichord type, played in what is perhaps the instrument's most privileged and inimitable manner (at least in contrast to the flute)—a chord. This is illustrated in Example 4.40. Just as the guitar duo had its work cut out to distinguish its members, so in contrast, the task here will be to assert the equality of the two very different players.

From the preceding we see that what makes these two pieces different is much more than just the obvious individual differences of their instrumentation, their superarrays, or the composition of their details. It has much more to do with the interaction of these various elements. Exchanging any one feature between the pieces would produce still new musical situations, new opportunities for entanglement. Where certain aspects are similar, other aspects of the two pieces create differences in interpretation. The dispositions of the superarray of both pieces' second halves are identical, but are composed to yield different results. One immediate similarity to note is the fact that both works contain a guitar solo based on the same block of the lower array. Although the composition of details and rhythmic articulation make these two passages very different, an even more funda-

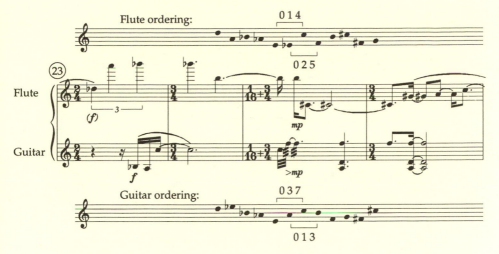

Example 4.40.   *Soli e Duettini* for Flute and Guitar: guitar entrance.
Reprinted by permission of C. F. Peters Corporation

mental difference ensures their individuality. While the sections of
the two arrays are identical to within transposition, their realizations
represent two different registral dispositions of the array's three strata
of lyne pairs. Thus the general registral unfolding of the two passages
is very different. Even the final lengthy duets of each piece work to
different ends, and this can be seen in miniature in the treatment of
the "extra" aggregate at the very end of the upper instruments' final
array blocks. In the guitar duo, the final aggregate of the lower instrument is stretched through the last two aggregates of the upper instrument, and the surface details, both within and between instruments,
concentrates on shared ordered trichords. In the later work, in contrast, the flute gets the last word, and its details are resolutely based
on unique order patterns from its own row class. The two passages
are shown and analyzed in Example 4.41.

Although their differences are multivalent, the two compositions'
similarities are also more complex than simply their shared materials.
Both works can be heard as dealing with the same issues—disclosure
and reconciliation—filtered through their more obvious constitutional differences. In the earlier work, the two instruments seek to
assert their individuality through their unique musical materials
while acknowledging and accepting their shared sound. In the later
duo, the flute's initial ascendency is shown to be less than the total
picture by the fact that the guitar has unique sounds, regions, and
materials of its own to bring forth. Both works trace a dynamic rela-

Shared ordered trichords:

Example 4.41.   *Soli e Duettini*: contrasting final bars.
Reprinted by permission of C. F. Peters Corporation

tionship between two entities with various shared and unique characteristics. It is the contrast between these two relationships, more than anything else, that captures the similarities and differences of these two compositions.

Clearly we have only hinted at the differences and similarities between the two duos, and there is a great deal about this music that we have had to ignore. An extended study of the issues raised by these pieces would have to include the third work in the series, the duo for violin and viola. This third *Soli e Duettini* falls somewhere between the first two in terms of instrumental differentiation, with neither the instrumental identity of the first nor the extreme differentiation of the second. Its superarray, while opening with a duet, nevertheless exposes different blocks of its constituent arrays in its solos and places its sole extended duet in the center of the work. A still more critical difference between the violin and viola duo and the other two pieces is the fact that its constituent arrays are not related by the circle-of-fifths transformation but are simple retrograde inversions of each other. Thus, unlike the other two works, both instruments speak the same language. This difference alone will raise a whole new series of questions of identity and contrast between the two protagonists.

The central lesson of our brief engagement with the set of pieces each entitled *Soli e Duettini* is that their individual qualities are not immediately captured by listing their constitutional similarities and differences. Rather, the choices involved in every compositional domain work in concert to produce the individualities of these works. Nothing is unconnected: twitch the web at any point, and the whole will vibrate. And this is true for Babbitt's music as a whole. Compositional decisions at any level ramify into every level, so that our sense of progression invokes not just our immediate sense of the moment but how that moment is echoed and reflected through the depths. There is no one correct level on which to hear Babbitt's music. The surface details are not simply a way of dressing up the "real music" of the array, nor is the array simply the hidden mechanics behind the surface dazzle: we are not asked to "pay no attention to that array behind the curtain." Babbitt's music depends on the tension between levels, the interplay between the specifics of a moment, or a passage, or a piece, and their contexts within a passage, a piece, or his work as a whole, and ultimately within the chromatic world of the twelve-tone system. It is this inclusiveness that makes his works most deeply and affectingly human.

EPILOGUE

THE PRECEDING CHAPTERS have given us a glimpse of Milton Babbitt's development as a composer over a period of more than four decades. It is hardly a complete picture, not merely because of its brevity but because Babbitt is still pursuing the implications of his chosen compositional constraints. As I write this, he has just completed a new composition for three clarinets, three strings, and piano, essentially the same ensemble used by Schoenberg in his *Suite* op. 29. The work promises to be enormous by Babbitt's standards, running to about twenty minutes, and in it he has extended his practice even farther than before. Each of the seven instruments carries a complete six-part array (the same type as we have just discussed with regard to the series of *Soli e Duettini*), with two in the piano. The eight arrays represent the four classical transformations applied to the array and its circle-of-fifths counterpart, thus extending the techniques of two of the duos. Like *All Set*, *Arie da Capo*, and *Consortini* before it, the work is a constantly changing patchwork of its various subensembles, with different solo instruments featured in its various sections. The work begins with a dizzying explosion of all seven instruments. This quickly dissolves to a solo in the cello, which then dominates the first big stretch of music, accompanied by an ever-changing retinue. Just as *Ars Combinatoria* opened up a whole new part of Babbitt's compositional world, so the new piece seems to contain within it many suggestive directions for future exploration.

Despite the incompleteness of the picture, there does emerge at least an intimation of the wholeness of Babbitt's work, from the *Three Compositions for Piano* and *Du*, through *Arie da Capo* and the Fourth String Quartet, right up to and beyond *The Joy of More Sextets* and *Consortini*. It is not merely the reappearance of the same instrumental ensemble that creates a resonance between the *Composition for Four Instruments* and *The Head of the Bed*; layer upon layer of musical invention has grown upon the patterning found in the early work, yet even the thickest encrustations of ramified ideas reveal by their lucidity the principles that have remained in effect in the thirty-five years that separate the two pieces.

But steadfast as these principles have been, they have not acted as a straitjacket. Although the seeds of Babbitt's development can be found in even his earliest music, the richness and profusion of his later periods have depended on the fertility of his imagination. His constant recombination of materials, structures, and strategies has led to the incredible luxuriance of his musical growth. And that growth has always been *musical*: no matter how he has extended the principles of the twelve-tone system, he has always done so from a perspective of their heard consequences.

Listeners attempting to trace the flowering of Babbitt's compositional garden are faced with a number of frustrating lacunae. A major work of his trichordal period, the *Composition for Tenor and Six Instruments*, has received few performances and remains unrecorded. The seminal song cycle *Du*, while recorded, is very difficult to obtain. Recent recordings of the Piano Concerto and *Relata I* provide a sample of the excitement of his orchestral music, but there seem to be no prospects for performances of *Ars Combinatoria* or *Relata II*. (At the time of writing, however, there are rumors that both *Correspondences* and *Transfigured Notes* may presently become available on compact disc.) The mysterious *Concerti*, a large-scale work for solo violin, synthesized tape, and small orchestra, is a tantalizing enigma at the center of his second compositional period. What will become of this concerto is not clear. Written for a synthesizer that no longer exists in its original state, it awaits a realization that will allow us to hear one of the major compositions of Babbitt's career.

Despite these frustrations, we can still come to know a wide range of the composer's music, thanks to the dedication and skill of a number of musicians who have found playing his works a rewarding challenge. They have been able to bring forth Babbitt's ideas with an immediacy we can but hope to suggest here, as they work directly in his music's natural environment: the world of sound. Their efforts allow us to roam through a body of work that is unsurpassed in its depth of conception, breadth of invention, and richness of detail, using the best possible means: our ears.

CATALOG OF COMPOSITIONS
BY MILTON BABBITT

UNPUBLISHED WORKS

1935	*Generatrix* for orchestra (unfinished)	Withdrawn
1940	*Composition for String Orchestra* (unfinished)	Withdrawn
1940	*Music for the Mass I* for mixed chorus	
1940	*Music for the Mass II*	
1941	Symphony (unfinished)	Withdrawn
1941	String Trio	
1948	String Quartet no. 1	Withdrawn
1949	Film music for *Into the Good Ground*	Withdrawn
1954	*Vision and Prayer* for soprano and piano	

PUBLISHED WORKS

1946	*Three Theatrical Songs* for voice and piano	C. F. Peters

First Period

1947	*Three Compositions for Piano*	Boelke-Bomart
1948	*Composition for Four Instruments* (flute, clarinet, violin, cello)	Presser
1948; 1954	*Composition for Twelve Instruments*	AMP
1950	*Composition for Viola and Piano*	C. F. Peters
1950	*The Widow's Lament in Springtime* for soprano and piano	Boelke-Bomart
1951	*Du* for soprano and piano	Boelke-Bomart
1953	Woodwind Quartet (flute, oboe, clarinet, bassoon)	AMP
1954	String Quartet no. 2	AMP
1955	*Two Sonnets* for baritone, clarinet, viola, and cello	C. F. Peters
1956	*Duet* for piano	E. B. Marks
1956	*Semi-Simple Variations* for piano	Presser
1957	*All Set* for alto saxophone, tenor saxophone, trumpet, trombone, contrabass, piano, vibraphone, and percussion	AMP
1957	*Partitions* for piano	Lawson-Gould
1960	*Sounds and Words* for soprano and piano	AMP
1960	*Composition for Tenor and Six Instruments* (flute, oboe, violin, viola, cello, harpsichord)	AMP
1961	*Composition for Synthesizer*	AMP
1961	*Vision and Prayer* for soprano and synthesized tape	AMP

Second Period

1964	*Philomel* for soprano and synthesized tape	AMP
1964	*Ensembles for Synthesizer*	AMP
1965	*Relata I* for orchestra	AMP
1966	*Post-Partitions* for piano	C. F. Peters
1966	*Sextets* for violin and piano	C. F. Peters
1967	*Correspondences* for string orchestra and synthesized tape	AMP
1968	*Relata II* for orchestra	AMP
1969	*Four Canons* for soprano and contralto	Broude
1969	*Phonemena* for soprano and piano	C. F. Peters
1970	String Quartet no. 3	C. F. Peters
1970	String Quartet no. 4	C. F. Peters
1971	*Occasional Variations* for synthesized tape	C. F. Peters
1972	*Tableaux* for piano	C. F. Peters
1974	*Arie da Capo* for five instrumentalists (flute, clarinet/bass clarinet, violin, cello, piano)	C. F. Peters
1975	*Reflections* for piano and synthesized tape	C. F. Peters
1975	*Phonemena* for soprano and synthesized tape	C. F. Peters
1976	*Concerti* for violin, small orchestra, and synthesized tape	C. F. Peters
1977	*A Solo Requiem* for soprano and two pianos	C. F. Peters
1977	*Minute Waltz (or $\frac{3}{4} + \frac{1}{8}$)* for piano	C. F. Peters
1977	*Playing for Time* for piano (part 1 of *Time Series*)	Hinshaw
1978	*My Ends Are My Beginnings* for solo clarinetist	C. F. Peters
1978	*My Complements to Roger* for piano	Perspectives of New Music
1978	*More Phonemena* for twelve-part chorus	C. F. Peters
1979	*An Elizabethan Sextette* for six-part women's chorus	C. F. Peters
1979	*Images* for saxophonist and synthesized tape	C. F. Peters
1979	*Paraphrases* for ten instrumentalists (flute, oboe/English horn, clarinet, bass clarinet, bassoon, horn, trumpet, trombone, tuba, piano)	C. F. Peters
1980	*Dual* for cello and piano	C. F. Peters

Third Period

1981	*Ars Combinatoria* for small orchestra	C. F. Peters
1981	*Don* for piano four hands	C. F. Peters
1982	*The Head of the Bed* for soprano and four instruments (flute, clarinet, violin, cello)	C. F. Peters
1982	String Quartet no. 5	C. F. Peters
1982	*Melismata* for solo violin	C. F. Peters
1982	*About Time* for piano (part 2 of *Time Series*)	C. F. Peters
1983	*Canonical Form* for piano	C. F. Peters
1983	*Groupwise* for flautist and four instruments (violin, viola, cello, piano)	C. F. Peters

1984	*Four Play* for four players (clarinet, violin, cello, piano)	C. F. Peters
1984	*It Takes Twelve to Tango* for piano	C. F. Peters
1984	*Sheer Pluck (Composition for Guitar)*	C. F. Peters
1985	Concerto for Piano and Orchestra	C. F. Peters
1985	*Lagniappe* for piano	C. F. Peters
1986	*Transfigured Notes* for string orchestra	C. F. Peters
1986	*The Joy of More Sextets* for violin and piano	C. F. Peters
1987	*Three Cultivated Choruses* for four-part chorus	
1987	*Fanfare* for double brass sextet	C. F. Peters
1987	*Overtime* for piano (part 3 of *Time Series*)	C. F. Peters
1987	*Souper* for speaker and ensemble (flute, clarinet, violin, cello, piano)	
1987	*Homily* for snare drum	Smith
1987	*Whirled Series* for alto saxophone and piano	C. F. Peters
1988	*In His Own Words* for speaker and piano	
1988	*The Virginal Book* for contralto and piano	C. F. Peters
1988	*Beaten Paths* for solo marimba	Smith
1988	*Glosses* for boys' choir	C. F. Peters
1988	*The Crowded Air* for eleven instruments (flute, oboe, clarinet, bassoon, marimba, guitar, piano, violin, viola, cello, bass)	C. F. Peters
1989	*Consortini* for five players (flute, piano, vibraphone, marimba, cello)	C. F. Peters
1989	*Play It Again, Sam* for solo viola	
1989	*Emblems (Ars Emblematica)* for piano	C. F. Peters
1989	*Soli e Duettini* for two guitars	C. F. Peters
1989	*Soli e Duettini* for flute and guitar	C. F. Peters
1990	*Soli e Duettini* for violin and viola	C. F. Peters
1990	*Envoi* for piano four hands	C. F. Peters
1991	*Four Cavalier Settings* for tenor and guitar	C. F. Peters
1991	*Preludes, Interludes, and Postlude* for piano	C. F. Peters
1991	*None but the Lonely Flute* for solo flute	C. F. Peters
1991	*Mehr "Du"* for mezzo-soprano, viola, and piano	C. F. Peters
1992	*Septet, but Equal* (clarinet 1, clarinet 2, bass clarinet/clarinet 3, violin, viola, cello, piano)	C. F. Peters
1992	*Counterparts* for brass quintet	C. F. Peters
1993	*Around the Horn* for solo horn	Smith
1993	*Quatrains* for soprano and two clarinets	Smith
1993	*Fanfare for All* for brass quintet	C. F. Peters
1993	String Quartet no. 6	C. F. Peters
1994	*Triad* for viola, clarinet, and piano	C. F. Peters

ALL-PARTITION ARRAYS

B ABBITT HAS USED a number of all-partition arrays in his music, based on the various different all-combinatorial hexachords. There is one four-part thirty-four-partition array, based on the E-type hexachord. The version of the array used in the opening section of *My Ends Are My Beginnings* appears here; circle-of-fifths transformations of this array are found in Mead 1983 and Lake 1986. There are three six-part arrays, containing fifty-eight partitions. One of these, used in *Post-Partitions* and *Sextets*, is based on composite lynes made of pairs of B-type hexachords. The form used in the piano work appears here. The other two are based on complete rows built of D-type hexachords. One of these, used under various transformations in *Arie da Capo, Tableaux, Playing for Time*, and other works, appears in Mead 1987a. The other, used in *Groupwise, The Joy of More Sextets*, and *Sheer Pluck* as well as in the more recent series of *Soli e Duetini*, appears here in the form found in the violin part of the first half of *The Joy of More Sextets*. This array is altered not only by the circle-of-fifths transformations but through a few relocations of partitions in *Groupwise*. There is one eight-part array, containing seventy partitions, used in the String Quartet no. 3 and published in Arnold and Hair 1976b.

There are two basic catagories of twelve-part arrays: those using all seventy-seven partitions of twelve and those using the fifty-eight partitions of twelve into twelve or fewer parts of six or fewer elements. Of the latter, there appear to be five distinct array types in Babbitt's work, including three based on all-trichordal rows, one based on the ordered A-type hexachord that contains segmentally all its generating trichords, and one based on the all-interval row used in the String Quartet no. 2. This last appears in *Fanfare*. Of the first three, one appears in *Paraphrases* and under circle-of-fifths transformation in *Four Play*. The other two are based on the same row class but are not isomorphic. These last two appear here.

In the other catagory of twelve-part arrays, there appear to be two basic formats for the distribution of rows. One sort contains combinatorial row pairs related solely by inversion. The arrays used in the String Quartet no. 4, using B-type hexachords, and those used in *Reflections* and *A Solo Requiem*, using A- and C-type hexachords and related by the circle-of-fifths transformations, are of this format. The array of *Reflections* appears in Peel and Cramer 1987, and portions of that of *A Solo Requiem* appear in Dubiel 1991.

The other format found in twelve-part arrays groups the rows into three quartets of four rows each, each quartet containing one each of the classical transformations and each exploiting a different kind of hexachordal combinatoriality. The arrays of *More Phonemena*, using A-type hexachords, and of *Dual* and *Consortini* employ such formats. The array of *Consortini*, using the same row class as that in the two twelve-part fifty-eight partition arrays discussed above, is found here. Arrays in this section are notated using integers for pitch classes, with 0=C, 1=C♯ and D♭, 2=D, and so forth, up to t (representing 10)=B♭, and e (representing 11)= B.

My Ends Are My Beginnings

Block I

et3	762	458	190	7		t	6e23510498
8940	15	32e6t7		859410t23	e	6	7
2561	9t	0	87e436		5t219	e03847	
7	4830e	91	2t5	6e	073486	5291	t
$4^2 31$	532^2	6321	63^2	921	651	641^2	$10\ 1^2$

Block II

867	2te3	1	1094	85637			72	et8019453
549	10	0	8te27365			58	49013et	276
1t2	965	3784e		e09t	t51264	4307e	86	
03e	478	t6592		214	380e79	9t162	5	
3^4	$43^2 2$	$5^2 1^2$	84	543	6^2	$5^2 2$	$72^2 1$	93

Block III

32	7	et6890514		4e2	t367	95	5	48102
6450891et7		2	63	30	091854	2	67	73te
	695t1240e38	7	21	16t9578	e	e403	9	6
		3	04e8759t			t61278	83e0421t	59
$10\ 2$	$11\ 1$	91^3	82^2	732	741	642	821^2	5421

Block IV

2		3t67e9850412		e3t7	6	48	9501
105	98467t3e			2908	145	73	26et
t	521		e340785	61	9t2	0e	8374
964738e	0		2t916	54	380e7	9t1625	
731^2	831	12	75	$4^2 2^2$	$53^2 1$	62^3	4^3

Post-Partitions

2^6	$3^2 2^3$	642	543	42^4	$3^3 1^3$	$3^2 2^2 1^2$
5 t	2 31			67	79 0	4 8e
1 6	8 9		te 954	3 2	2	0 7
7 3	4 t0	01		89e 5	e6 5	6 2
0	5 e		32 76	t 4	t1 4	9
e 2	6 7	89 54		1 0	3	1t 3
4 9		732 6te	0 18		8	5

5421	63^2	$4^2 31$	732	631^3	4321^3	$62^2 1^2$
	03 7245		3 59	e	t8 6	81
4976 e	6 e8	2	01	5	3	t
0532			2t 8e764	1	9	
		74 3t		489	0152	e6
t	t19	986			e	304572
81		1e 50		t6 0237	74	9

Post-Partitions

Block III

497 e8		76	2 801	2	1	5 3t
	03et 7245			5	8	1 96
1	9	t	9		467e t2350	e8 0
25 6	6		e	10t3 984		47
	8	1e 5023	t6 374		9	
30 t	1	4 98	5	7 6e		2
53^21	81^4	6321	541^3	731^2	91^3	3^321

Block IV

	1	8te3 6954	3 4	3	0 2	27	
5 t310	5 0		5 08	26	6794 8e	e	4
2 6e98	84			510 7	t3		
		71	9 1t	4 t		6 t	67e8 2350
47	732 96te	20		e	5 1	18	
			e6 27	89		9 5403	91t
52^2	72^21	82^2	432^2	42^31^2	62^3	52^31	831

Post-Partitions

		6 18te		954 e	42 30	27
	t	5		t3108 26	8e 67	94
		9	9467e8 1t23			350
2510t3 6e9847				7		
	e6891 275403				1t	
		47320	05		5 9	6te18
12	*11 1*	5^21^2	*10 2*	*741*	4^22^2	532^2

e8 4976	801 6	1	2		3	t 5
0	72459 3et	t	6		8	1
		2 6e9847	7		2510t	3
1t235		0	9		4	67e8 0
		3	304 t	457 1986	e	2
		5	81e 5	et 023	69 7	9 4
651	*84*	71^5	421^4	*75*	531^4	52^21^3

Post-Partitions

Block VII

724596 03e				et	t81	
	4976	e8 62	01 2	5	3	3t
		7	4 3t	8	9e6 0	0152
	0532	t	8e7	1 764	4	9
8	81et		69 5	9 023		74
t1		3045 19			572	86e
921	4^3	641^2	3^4	4^221^2	4321^2	43221

Block VIII

	52	t3108 2679	8			94	e 4
69 18te		54 e	2	2		e	7 30
	7			3t0 489e6	0	15 6	2 6
	0		05	5	8e7649 532t	t	9 1
	4		4 96te1	7 1	1	7320 8	5 8
275403	e6891t 3		3				t
6^2	721^3	93	621^4	821^2	$10\,1^2$	5321^2	32^41

Joy of More Sextets

Block I

29		9t8430	05		e	e1
1		1657	7	7e0		3t4298//
3te	954		4		4160278	
6	702		81	t	t953	
78	813		392et6	645		50
054	6te	e2		29318		7//6
$3^2\,2^2\,1^2$	3^4	642	$6\;2^2\,1^2$	$5\;3^2\,1$	741	$6\;2^3$

Block II

67//	43t	t8290	15			76e//
56e170					98	423t//50
8//5t9		e347		28610//		
34e//2	2	1	860	7te3549//	61	
0//1	89		9732e4t			
		65			50t4e237	981//
$4^2\,2^2$	6321	5421	732	75	$8\;2^2$	$6\;3^2$

Block III

		t	3	2489071e	e6	65
		1e76382	4			49t//7
	349e5t		7	6	20	01
	12087	49	9	35t		e//8
056//921378			8e60t		t54//	32
te4	6	05	521		19783	
93	651	$7\;2^2\,1$	$53\;1^4$	831	$53\;2^2$	$4\;2^4$

Block IV

5//		2	3	8t4965	51e	0	07//
76		61e5034	4		8t9	2	2//e
1//	et539478	8	0	0	2	1	16//
8	1026	7			7	7t5e94	43//
29		9	9718e	e	046	6	5t//
3//4e0t		t	t652	2713	3	38	89//
$5\;2^2\,1^3$	8.4	$7\;1^5$	$54\;1^3$	$64\;1^2$	$3^3\,1^3$	$62\;1^4$	2^6

Joy of More Sextets

Block V

	4	98t		23 ——			361750e//t
	e ——	e6 ——	67510928t34				4
	9t	35		5e410 ——	08 ——		8
		07		86 ——	621t39e45//		
387912 ——	2506	4	e	t//7 ——	7		2
45t06e	731 ——	12		9			9//
6²	4² 2 1²	3 2⁴ 1	11.1	5 2³ 1	921		8 1⁴

Block VI

t ——		t9428367e105					5//
4//e05	716			3 ——		3 ——	32t894//70e1
672 ——	2//e4359t			1	8 ——	82	
	8			72	0	61459et	
3198					5t46e	0//	
	0 ——			0e64t589 ——	91327 ——	7//	6
4² 31	73 1²	12		82 1²	5² 1²	72 1³	10. 1²

Block VII

8 ——	8342		t96e57 ——		70 ——	01	
	1569		4 ——		4t832		
2076//9543e—et70		681	2//		5 ——		
t			3//01 ——	16 ——		682743e9t5//	
1		2793	8	540te ——	e6//9		
		et045		83972	1//		
9 1³	4³	543	63 1³	5² 2	532 1²	10.2	

Block VIII

	892 ——	24 ——	4t3 ——	30e7 ——	7	5 ——	561
10 ——	0	75 ——	5e69 ——	9 ——	9t	2438	
54e ——	e	93t1		1	26 ——	6	870
276 ——		6	801	4 ——	4e53	t ——	t9
983 ——	317 ——		72	256t	0 ——	0e ——	e4
t ——	t564	0e8 ——		8	81 ——	179	23
3³ 21	4 3² 1²	43 2² 1	4 3² 2	4² 1⁴	4 2³ 1²	432 1³	3² 2³

Ars Combinatoria

Block IA

	0	01	e		3	38t	
5		5	5	4	6	6297	7
6	6	37	8	t	5		
140e	e		9	9	9		2
98	8	t	t	61	e	e	
			4	73	2		05
2	2		31	5	t	0	
7	7				4	4	489e6
3	3	42	6	e	1	1	1
	9		0	08	7	5	t
t	t	9e	72	2	0		
	415	68			8		3
421^6	31^9	2^51^2	2^21^8	2^31^6	1^{12}	431^5	521^5

Block IB

4	4	9	7	76	6		25
1	8	8t	t		e	3	30
e	9		9	402	1		1
8t3	3	7			75	6	6
502	2	3				74	4
	e1	6				t	t89
6		e	e	98	84		7
	0t5	5	1		32		
7		0	0		t9	958	
		4	6	e31		12	
	6	1	3485	5			
9	7	2	2	t	0	0e	e
3^21^6	321^7	21^{10}	41^8	$3^22^21^2$	2^41^4	32^31^3	32^21^5

Ars Combinatoria

Block IIA

4^221^2	62^3	543	621^4	6321	5^22	52^21^3
6954			e8013t	t		27138
78 0		6t35 0e194	2			
	t1 32		4	98 075		6e 5
1t23	50 897e46		6			
		287	79	2e3461	50	t4
e			5		e2t97 64813	0 9

Block IIB

52^31	4^3	631^3	642	5421	63^2	5321^2
t		429576 80t			te6	
e4219 83		3		0 356t7		7
		e	68		570423 891	
60	4e79 532t	1		98		1
75				4e12		508t9 263
	0681		1534 920e7t			4e

Ars Combinatoria

Block IIIA

	67	75924	et0		831	1
7t6538 09124e				8 e		
	te9	16 t30		4572	2	68
	102	8e	764		t5 49	53
			213 859	9t0	e6 07	4
	5843			316		e0t279
6^2	43^22	532^2	3^4	4321^2	321^4	62^21^2

Block IIIB

t		72459 3108e				60 e5
			2491e0 53t68	7		71
27540 8	619			3	e	t4
9 3	4 5t	6	7	e8 20	1	82
1e6		t			57809 6243	93
	38 027e			6514 9t	t	
531^4	43^221	5^21^2	651	4^231^2	541^3	2^6

Ars Combinatoria

Block IVA

3^22^3	4321^3	4^231	3^31^3	3^321	641^2	3^221^4
o3e		t		526	6794	t81
12	0	49e	657	3t8 e	e	5
45	96		te1 3	70	8	02
768	2		4		2510t3	3 4e9
9t	8	3621 8057		1e4		7
	t7e 4351		029 8	9		6
3^22^3	4321^3	4^231	3^31^3	3^321	641^2	3^221^4

Block IVB

	792	64 t8	4 8	3e10		5 0
t		29			e041 t873	1 36
5		0735 1e	e	t	69	4
2 8				4867	52	
9	e		3t015			
71643e	t05		9 2	2		78
0	31846		6 7	5 9		9t2e
61^6	53^21	42^4	51^7	421^4	42^22	4^221^4

Piano Concerto

Block IA

e2t	970	0				
	564					813
	1t2	2			3	506
		7684e				9
879		9			50t	4
		3		3621		e
45			537028			
			96te		e18	
		1	14	40e9		2
63				78t5		
		5			46297	7
01	e38	t				t
$3^2 23$	3^4	51^7	642	4^3	$53^2 1$	$32^1 6$

Block IB

6		8			1	534
9		9		20		0e7t
		64e7				98
3t0152					2	
e	126	3	3			
4		t			t05978	
			81et	69		
8		2	0	7354	4	
	8t375	5			6	6
	e940	0				21
7		1		18te	e3	
			497625			
61^6	543	41^8	641^2	$4^2 2^2$	621^4	$432^2 1$

Piano Concerto

Block IIA

t	9 41	e	e 56	720 83		0 3
2 8e	76	31 6		5 4	5 49	t
3	85	9 4	t0			7 26e1
47 9		7 8	3	t61	20 e	5
1 65	2	0	49 7	9e	3t8	8
0	03et	52 t	2 81		67 1	94
2^316	42^31^2	2^21^8	2^41^4	$3^22^21^2$	32^31^3	421^6

Block IIB

613	4 9	72	t0	85	5	e
0	6 3	e9 5t	84		7 2	7 01
	1 70		e6		6 t	243 t958
e	e 5	1 0	1	6t 237	89 4	
5t 8	8 2		7 29	9e041	3	6
4 792	t	83 64	3 5		e10	
3^221^4	21^{10}	2^51^2	2^41^4	532^2	321^7	4321^3

Piano Concerto

Block IIIA

5t e4		7e	0	2 435186	29		9
72 18	5		8	97e	510t3 e4		3 460
39			t 2e3461		7		8 7
	324 t198				86	075 6e	5
	0 7	09124 t6538					e 2
06	6 e		759	t0		924t 831	t 1
2^6	431^5	5^2	631^3	6321	52^31	43^22	31^9

Block IIIB

607	31 9t	t2			8 e		465e
39e48		05		6 32t1			17
	8057	71643e		7508		2	8t92
5	e6	89		9	91t 570423		3
2	24			4		53t687 491e0	0
t 1			t3108e 724596	e	6		
531^4	42^4	62^3	6^2	421^4	631^3	651	42^21^2

Piano Concerto

Block IVA

e5843	e 1		16	e0t27		9
	0 7	0 786t	t		e1942 35	
9	9 2	213e	087	5 64	t	
	3 t		e9	1	0 6	4572
102t 7	5 4		53	3 89		e6
6	6 8	954	42		7 8	8013t
541^3	1^{12}	4^231	32^41	52^21^3	521^5	5421

Block IVB

	0	386	65 027e9t			514
		e42190	83	356t	7	
46e	e31 t	t57	1	2 780	2 9	9
827	86			19e	59	t 03
9 0t5			4	4	6 13	7e8 2
13	42957				80te	6
3^321	5321^2	63^2	62^21^2	43^21^2	42^21^4	3^221^4

Consortini

Block I

$2^4\,1^4$	$3\;2^2\,1^5$	$3^3\,21$	$4\;2^3\,1^2$	$4\;2^4$	$32\;1^7$
63	7 0e1	94			8t5 2
8e	2		31 7649	5t	0
21	9t	805		3e	7 64
0	5 3	e	2 t8	6794	1
t7 5	64		e	02 81	9 3
9 4	8 732	te1	05		e

$3^2\,1^6$	$3^3\,1^3$	$3\;2^3\,1^3$	$4\;2^2\,1^4$	$5\;2^2\,1^3$	$43\;2^2\,1$
e 8		940	21 3		56t7
	6 3	5t	e984	7 2	01
164	t57	8	0	9	3e2
t 7	9	2	6	83e10 45	
3 9	184 02e	6	5 7t		
502		37 e1		6t	4 89

Consortini   Block II

	78	6	t ——	t	3
		1	40	e	9
1		t23	5	0	
768 ——			8	4	e
9	0	8	7	5 ——	5
2			e	3	46
5	46		2	9	7 ——
0	1	e	3	8	t
e	2t	9 ——	9	7	0 ——
4	35			1 ——	1
t	e9		16 ——	6	8
3		0457		2 ——	2
$3\ 1^9$	$2^5\ 1^2$	$43\ 1^5$	$2^2\ 1^8$	1^{12}	$2\ 1^{10}$

5e ——	e4	2			190	
2					8t3756	
						64e798//2
93 ——	3t0	1	52			
t		46e3				1
1		7508t9 ——				
7	18		t	e		30
4	9		7	6	2	5
0	6			81534 ——	4	
86				079t2	e	
	275		403			
			8619e			t
$2^3\ 1^6$	$3^2\ 2^2\ 1^2$	$64\ 1^2$	$532\ 1^2$	$5^2\ 1^2$	$63\ 1^3$	$72\ 1^3$

Consortini

6				6573t829 0	e04	9124e53t6
510t3	8 ——	89	7e460532			
2//87 9//	3					
e ——	6954271			1 e		8
4 ——	e0t			4	15683972t	0
		t1 324075e6	891t ——			
53 1^4	73 1^2	8 2^2	84	8 1^4	93	9 1^3

	1	87			
	t		9e4867 1		
		950t4e1263	3		
	4		2 ——	26	e170t958
013t42			380te 957		6
	2793865 ——		5	14	
	e				
986e57	0 ——		0		423
			t		
6^2	7 1^5	10.2	6 1^6	53 2^2	831

Consortini

Block IV

	12049e5t87				
				102t	
				7	48 —
85		9t071e	6		
		362 —			
	6		75924t3108e		
				e —	
t9e720613 —3		485			
				5843	16027e9-
				96	t —
4					53
9 2 1	10.2	6 3^2	11.1	4^2 2 1^2	7 2^2 1

	7		t6			538249	1e0//7 —
	36 —						6
53946						7e	8
	8	9e60t51 —				1	32
		243					
	21e4t059	78					
							//5 —
					et0831724596	//0 —	
			9				t
te18207			354 —				4
			70281e			t6	9
7.5	82 1^2	732	6321	12		6 2^2 1^2	42 1^6

Consortini Block V

$4^2 2^2$	$5 1^7$	$4^2 1^4$	3^4	$3^2 2^3$	$52 1^5$
	7	786t		35	
	1	40e9			2
		1		t2	35
76	684e9				
9t80		5			7
	2		213	e64	
	5	2	679		4
	0	3	et8	81	
e2	t			970	0
4351					8
					te916
	3		045		

$54 1^3$	741	$6 2^3$	5421	$62 1^4$	$4 3^2 1^2$	$3 2^4 1$
		e42190				
				8t	3	756
0					64e7	98
9		3t		0	152	
1643e			2			
t	t	57			809	
			4t83e	1		10
				792645		
		68	15			43
			6079		t	2e
8275	5403			3		
	728619e			e		t

Consortini

63		378t			5e9	4
		0e1942				
	2			315t0		
				8e764		
	9087		75		t	
2e	3		461			7508t
54	6			29		
01	1		e38t			
t7	e		029			
	5	56			6481	392
98	t					61e
	4				7320	
2^6	$4\ 1^8$	642	$4\ 3^2\ 2$	$5^2\ 2$	$4^2\ 31$	$5\ 3^2\ 1$

	02	2	1		
	8			356t7	
		6		e984	7
	93	5t		201	
t46e					e312
		9			
9718			8te30		0
		4	497625		
		318			465
		0e7			t
5023	74				
	5e16t				89
4^3	$5\ 2^3\ 1$	$3^2\ 2\ 1^4$	651	543	$432\ 1^3$

NOTES

CHAPTER 1

1. See, for example, Lerdahl 1988.

2. This may be traced to his longtime work with soprano Bethany Beardslee; see, for example, Beardslee Winham 1976.

3. See Morris and Alegant 1988.

4. See Babbitt 1976d and 1974.

5. For a discussion of Schoenberg's use of the twelve-tone system in tonal forms, see Mead 1987b and Peles 1983–84.

6. For a comprehensive overview of the properties of the diatonic collection see Browne 1981.

7. The profound differences between tonal and twelve-tone music are implicit in all Babbitt's writings but are particularly well presented in "Since Schoenberg" 1974.

8. Babbitt describes his early contact with Schoenberg's music in 1976d and 1987.

9. Schoenberg's own discussion of his development of twelve-tone music may be found in Schoenberg 1984.

10. Ibid.

11. See Forte 1973 and Rahn 1982 for discussions of music of this period.

12. The whole issue of hearing in twelve-tone music has generated a number of interesting writings, including Dubiel 1990b, 1991, and a forthcoming essay; Lewin 1987; Mackey 1985 and 1987; Morris 1987; Rothstein 1980; Samet 1987; and Straus 1986, to mention the more prominent ones.

13. The study of the restrictions of the sorts of relationships found in Example 1 is fascinating and extensive. Clearly, Example 1 is a very simplified illustration of the possibilities inherent in relations among aggregates. Much more information may be gleaned from most of the writings found in the bibliography, including Babbitt 1974, 1976d, and 1987; Bazelow and Brickle 1976; Forte 1973; Howe 1965; Kassler 1967; Martino 1961; Mead 1988; Morris 1987; Morris and Alegant 1988; O'Connell 1968; Perle 1981; Rahn 1976 and 1982; Starr 1978 and 1984; Starr and Morris 1977 and 1978; Westergaard 1966; and Zuckerman 1976.

14. See Schoenberg 1984.

15. See Babbitt 1987.

16. See, for example, Babbitt 1960c, 1961b, and 1962.

17. Various persistent and annoying canards regarding Babbitt's degree of awareness of the differentiations among musical dimensions are alive today, despite the efforts of many to clear them up. In Perle 1990, for example, Babbitt is taken to task for his use of dynamics, despite the fact that the accusations are leveled against a technique that Babbitt not only does not employ but also has criticized in others (Babbitt 1960c and 1962). Perle's criticism is repeated with neither a comment nor an explanation of Babbitt's actual com-

positional practice (described as early as Arnold and Hair 1976) in a brand-new textbook, Elliott Antokoletz's *Twentieth-Century Music* (Englewood Cliffs, N.J.: Prentice-Hall, 1992).

18. Both Forte 1973 and Rahn 1982 contain extensive and detailed accounts of unordered pitch class collection theory. Additional useful informaion may be found in Starr 1978, Howe 1967, and Morris 1987. The term *index number* was coined by Babbitt and first used in Babbitt 1962.

19. The term *mosaic* was coined in Martino 1961. Additional study of mosaics may be found in Mead 1988 and Morris and Alegant 1988.

20. See Babbitt 1961.

21. See Morris 1987 for an extended study of interval strings.

22. Babbitt has on several occasions described himself as daring "to presume to attempt to make music as much as it can be rather than as little as one can get away with" (Babbitt 1987, p. 183).

23. See chapter 1 of Babbitt 1987.

24. The term *array* is first used in Winham 1970.

25. The term *lyne* was first coined by Michael Kassler.

26. Robert Morris has made extensive compositional use of arrays formed from unusual overlappings of rows, as have Donald Martino and Richard Swift, to mention a few others. Some of Morris's approaches are detailed in Morris 1987.

27. See Babbitt 1961, and Starr 1978 for additional discussion.

28. These hexachords are discussed in Babbitt 1955 and Martino 1961; Babbitt's aversion to the whole-tone hexachord is expressed in Babbitt 1987, p. 116.

29. See Babbitt 1961 and 1987.

30. See also Example 139 in Perle 1981.

31. See Bauer-Mengelberg 1965; also, see Morris and Starr 1974.

32. See Starr 1984.

33. See Babbitt 1974 and 1987.

34. See Babbitt 1971a and 1987, as well as Pouser 1964.

35. Example 9 is a 4 × 4 Latin square, with the additional constraint that the contained 2 × 2 squares also contain all four elements. Latin squares are discussed in Morris 1987 and O'Connell 1968. I am grateful to Nancy Rao for several discussions concerning the application of Latin squares to Babbitt's music.

36. Babbitt's characteristic practice creates rows that are degenerate, in the sense that the retrograde forms are the same as the inversions; however, the use of two blocks allows the four orientations of the hexachordal interval pattern to traverse both transpositions of the hexachordal collection in the course of an array.

37. See Babbitt 1974, Martino 1961, and Morris and Alegant 1988.

38. Aspects of this are detailed throughout the first four chapters of Babbitt 1987.

39. An extensive discussion of this may be found in Westergaard 1966.

40. Babbitt discusses the dispositions of trichords in arrays in Babbitt 1974 and 1987.

41. The same point is made with the same passage in Dubiel 1990b.

42. Babbitt discusses all-partition arrays in Babbitt 1974 and 1987; additional discussion may be found in Arnold and Hair 1976b, Dubiel 1990b, Lake 1986, Mead 1983, and Peel and Cramer 1988.

43. Exceptions include the array of the String Quartet no. 3 and that of *Post-Partitions* and *Sextets*; additional discussion of the former is contained in Arnold and Hair 1976b and of the latter in Kuderna 1982, Capalbo 1981–82, and Dubiel 1990b, as well as in Chapter 3 of the present volume.

44. The format duplicates that in Example 4 of Mead 1984.

45. The definition of conjugates appearing in the example is taken from John Riordan, *An Introduction to Combinatorial Analysis* (New York: John Wiley and Sons, 1958).

46. A few complete all-partition arrays used by Babbitt have been published, including a four-part array in two transpositionally related versions in Mead 1983 and Lake 1986; a six-part array from several pieces in Mead 1987; the unusual eight-part array of the String Quartet no. 3 in Arnold and Hair 1976b; and a complete twelve-part array used in *Reflections* in Peel and Cramer 1988. The list of all-partition arrays in this volume contains two additional six-part arrays and certain other twelve-part arrays.

47. See Babbitt 1974 and 1987.

48. The operation is discussed in a number of places, including Howe 1967, Morris 1987, Starr 1978, and Star and Morris 1977–78.

49. Richard Swift details the significance of vowels in *Phonemena* in a forthcoming volume on the music of Babbitt and Roger Sessions.

50. I am indebted to Robert Morris for this observation.

51. See Babbitt 1961b; also, for examples from Schoenberg, see Haimo and Johnson 1984, Mead 1985 and 1989, Peles 1983–84, and Samet 1987.

52. As Babbitt notes in 1962, the twelve-tone system already creates certain qualitative rhythms through the projection of order in time.

53. See Borders 1979 and Westergaard 1965 for descriptions of duration rows in the *Composition for Twelve Instruments*.

54. The rhythmic structure of the *Composition for Four Instruments* is discussed in Swift 1976. I am also indebted to Joseph Dubiel for a number of observations concerning the rhythmic aspects of this work.

55. More general discussions of consistent abstract general transformations and their perceptual consequences are found throughout Lewin 1987.

56. See Westergaard 1965. Griffiths 1981 raises similar issues.

57. The time point system is first described in Babbitt 1962; additional useful discussions include Arnold and Hair 1976b, Batstone 1972, Johnson 1984, Morris 1977 and 1987, Rahn 1975, and Swift 1976, as well as Mead 1987a.

58. See Babbitt 1955 and 1960c.

59. This is discussed in Babbitt 1962.

60. See Rahn 1975 for additional discussion, and Mead 1987a for techniques for investigating relationships peculiar to rows of elements ordered in their own dimension.

61. See Babbitt 1962, pp. 71–72.

62. See Arnold and Hair 1976b.

63. The degree to which this is hearable is questioned in Lester 1986.

64. For an extensive analysis of this piece in all dimensions, see Wintle 1976.

CHAPTER 2

1. See Babbitt 1976d.

2. See Babbitt 1984b and chapter 6 of Babbitt 1987.

3. See also Morris and Alegant 1988 and Mead 1988.

4. The opening of the piece is analyzed in Swift 1976, and a number of interesting facets of the work are discussed in Dubiel's forthcoming essay.

5. See Wittlich 1975.

6. This aggregate is discussed by Babbitt in some detail in chapter 1 of Babbitt 1987 and is also found in Swift 1976.

7. These rows are the same as those discussed in Babbitt 1976d in conjunction with the *Composition for Four Instruments*.

8. This is discussed in Swift 1976.

9. I am grateful to Joseph Dubiel for pointing this out to me.

10. See Swift 1976 and chapter 1 of Babbitt 1987.

11. This was initially drawn to my attention by Joseph Dubiel.

12. For a somewhat different approach to progression through the piece as a whole, see Dubiel's forthcoming essay.

13. Such a compositional strategy allows multiple interpretations of the work's underlying structures. For a different description of such a passage, see Rothstein 1978.

14. For an extensive analysis of the latter work, see Borders 1979; Westergaard 1965 addresses interesting rhythmic issues in the same piece.

15. Another interesting feature entails one of the hexachords derived from the mosaics. [0, 1, 2, 3, 4, 6] may be generated from a pair of [0, 1, 4] trichords, and it may also be generated from the combination of a [0, 1, 4] and a [0, 1, 5] trichord, the two trichord types found as discrete segmental trichords in the work's row class.

16. See also Borders 1979.

17. Babbitt comments on this point in 1976d.

18. This row is illustrated in Babbitt 1976d.

19. Babbitt comments on the difference between the Woodwind Quartet's strategy and that found in the String Quartet no. 2, which is more akin to that of the *Composition for Viola and Piano*, in Babbitt 1976d, by contrasting the earlier work's efferent structure with the later one's afferent structure.

20. Swift notes the first of these in his forthcoming book on the music of Sessions and Babbitt.

21. Babbitt mentions this ordering of the chromatic hexachord in Babbitt 1987.

22. This is mentioned in passing in Swift 1976.

23. Discussions of all-combinatorial tetrachords may be found in Martino 1961, Starr 1978, and Morris and Starr 1977, as well as others.

24. See Babbitt 1987, chapter 3.

25. Nevertheless, some of the simultaneities generated in the two passages

are of the same collectional type, producing a nice linkage between the two spots.

26. Consider, for example, Zuckerman 1976a and b.

27. As Zuckerman demonstrates in 1976a and b, the dyadic passages may also be construed as arising from trichordal combinations, projected by dynamics. Babbitt also discusses this in 1987.

28. See Morris and Starr 1974.

29. See Zuckerman 1976a and b for a detailed accounting. I am also grateful to Nancy Rau for conversations concerning her work on the String Quartet no. 2.

30. For a more detailed discussion of some of the trichordal aspects of *Du*, see Morris and Alegant 1988.

31. See Babbitt 1987, chapter 1; and Zuckerman 1976a and b.

32. Babbitt, in 1976d, describes the process as "picking up and putting together ever larger pieces of the set, rather than evolving or disclosing it."

33. Described in the score as "from the volume 'DU,' published by Verlag der Sturm, Berlin." See also *August Stramm: Das Werk* (Wiesbaden: Limes Verlag, 1963). Analyses of portions of the work are found in Morris and Alegant 1988 and in Rahn 1976.

34. This duplicates some of the information in the charts at the end of Rahn 1976, pp. 79–80.

35. Morris and Alegant 1988.

36. See Babbitt's comments on the work in Babbitt 1976d, p. 14.

37. Morris and Alegant 1988 discusses a similar structure in later songs of the cycle.

38. Additional discussion of a listener's progression through the work is found in Babbitt 1976d, pp. 16–17.

39. This and the rows for works up through the String Quartet no. 3 may be found in Arnold and Hair 1976b.

40. Discussions of swapping may be found in Starr and Morris, 1977.

41. Babbitt mispeaks himself on this passage in Babbitt 1987, pp. 97.

42. A highly detailed account of the opening bars of *Partitions* may be found in Dubiel 1990b.

43. Private conversation.

44. Riordan 1958, p. 107.

CHAPTER 3

1. See Babbitt 1960a, 1962, and 1964a as well as Ussachevsky 1976.

2. See, for example, Babbitt 1970c.

3. See Borders 1979 for an account of the array of the *Composition for Twelve Instruments*; the basic structure of the array is also dealt with in Babbitt 1961b.

4. Babbitt hints at this in 1976d.

5. For an elaborate account of this work, see Blaustein and Brody 1986.

6. See, for example, Arnold and Hair 1976b, Blaustein and Brody 1986, Borders 1979, Mead 1987a, and Scotto 1988 for various accounts of time point structures in instrumental works.

7. See Arnold and Hair 1976d; an extensive analysis of the *array* of *Sounds*

and Words is found in Dubiel 1990a. I emphasize *array*, as Dubiel is quick to point out that the analysis of an array is *not* the analysis of a composition—a point that I hope is implicit, if not explicit, in the present volume.

8. This hexachord type has also been extensively used by Elliott Carter, as described in David Schiff, *The Music of Elliott Carter* (London: Eulenburg Books, 1983 reprint, New York: Da Capo Press, 1983.

9. Babbitt 1976d, p. 7.

10. Swift 1976.

11. See Babbitt 1987, chapter 4; and 1988 for an account of his encounter with Stravinsky's technique. See also Babbitt 1971b for more general remarks about Stravinsky.

12. For example, the need for every nonzero integer to appear on one side of the diagonal within a corner of the twelve-by-twelve row matrix guarantees, by the dual nature of those integers as both pitch classes and intervals between adjacent and nonadjacent elements of the row, that there can be no excluded interval in the segmental hexachord, a requirement for transpositional combinatoriality. See Babbitt 1988 for more on the dual nature of matrix integers, as well as Morris 1987.

13. This array is found in Arnold and Hair 1976b.

14. See Borders 1979.

15. The complete arrays of *Reflections* are found in Peel and Cramer 1987, and portions thereof are found in Babbitt 1974 and 1987. Sections of the circle-of-fifths transformation of the array are found in Dubiel 1991.

16. See also Peel and Cramer 1987.

17. Detailed accounts of *Post-Partitions* may be found in Kuderna 1982 and Lieberson 1985; *My Complements to Roger* is examined in Mead 1983.

18. See Babbitt 1974 and 1987.

19. Ibid.

20. See Mackey 1985 and Mead 1987a.

21. Richard Swift has explored the possibilities of retrograde weighting in a number of his own compositions.

22. See Mackey 1986 and Scotto 1988 for a more detailed discussion.

23. See, for example, the rapidly changing registers of *My Complements to Roger*, illustrated in Example 3.7 of the present chapter.

24. Example 3.6 replicates aspects of Example 6a in Arnold and Hair 1976b, p. 162.

25. This example reproduces information contained in Mead 1983.

26. See also Borders 1979.

27. But not identical, either. While both designs are Latin squares, they are not isomorphic:

Trichordal arrays:	A B C D	Instruments:	A C B D
	C D A B		B A D C
	B A D C		C D A B
	D C B A		D B C A

28. See Dubiel 1991.

29. Babbitt intimates the rich variety of restrictions imposed by partial or-

derings in 1976d, and the issue is further discussed in the opening portions of Samet 1987.

30. See, for example, Mead 1985, Peles 1983–84, and Samet 1987, as well as Babbitt 1987, chapter 3.

31. An extensive analysis of the complete work is found in Borders 1979, while an extraordinarily detailed account of the opening bars is found in Dubiel 1991.

32. See also Capalbo 1981–82 for a discussion of aspects of the work's array.

33. I am indebted to Milton Babbitt for this observation.

34. See bar 10, second violin part.

35. An account of the details of the work and their source in the array may be found in Mead 1983.

36. In *Dual*, a series of aggregates composed to represent the four classical forms of an ordered trichord are followed by a series of aggregates composed to replicate members of the work's underlying row class; in the opening passages of *Paraphrases*, the reverse is true.

37. Additional examples may be found in Dubiel 1990b and 1991, Lake 1986 and Peel and Cramer 1987, to mention a few.

38. See Scotto 1988.

39. Ibid.; also Mackey 1986 and Mead 1987a.

40. I am indebted to Joseph Dubiel for this particular example.

41. Cirro Scotto compared the opening portions of *Melismata* and *Playing for Time* in a presentation to the Society for Music Theory's national conference in Baltimore, 1988. His observations concentrated on considerably different aspects of the music.

42. A complete example of this array type is found in Mead 1987a.

43. See chapter 4.

44. Babbitt, in 1976d, comments briefly on the correlations between the pitch and rhythmic domains of *Tableaux* and *Arie da Capo* (p. 19).

45. See Mackey 1986.

46. This pairing by dynamics is also used in the String Quartet no. 4; later in *An Elizabethan Sextette* the pitch class lynes are separated and assigned to different voices.

47. See Mead 1987a.

48. Analyses of the work are found in Kuderna 1982 and Lieberson 1985.

49. The basic premises of the rhythmic structure in *Post-Partitions* are outlined in Griffiths 1981, p. 156. Lieberson 1985 also discusses the rhythmic structure of the composition.

50. See also Morris and Alegant 1988.

51. The Schoenberg work is closely examined in Peles 1983–84.

52. Babbitt himself discusses properties of the row of the Schoenberg work in Babbitt 1960c.

53. Analogous observations about the row class of *My Complements to Roger*, based on the circle-of-fifths transformation of the array, are found in Mead 1983.

54. This is discussed in greater detail in Mead 1987a.

55. Examples of this same array type, transformed by the circle-of-fifths mapping, are found in Mead 1983 and Lake 1986.

56. In a presentation on the work at the Midwestern Theory Conference in Iowa City, 1988, Jason Gibbs noted the constant presence in the surface of the work of segments of the row class. See also Gibbs 1989, in which he approaches the work through the surface, showing how it only gradually reveals its underlying structures.

CHAPTER 4

1. Some of the observations here are also made in Mead 1984.

2. But in the way that the weighted notes are always parts of local aggregates, the effect is quite dissimilar.

3. See Peel and Cramer 1987.

4. These are, respectively, the initial and final elements of the pairs of lynes in each instrument.

5. This is similar to the double lists of partitions of four found in his trichordal arrays, involving both all combinations of lynes and all combinations of trichordal transformations.

6. As noted in chapter 1, I am indebted to Robert Morris for this way of looking at superarrays and their relation to arrays.

7. See, for example, the discussion of modes of projection for the String Quartet no. 5 in Lake 1986.

8. Robert Morris has called this (in a private conversation noted in Lake 1986) "pitch articulating pitch."

9. Lake 1986.

10. Example 4.4 duplicates information in Lake's Example 5.

11. This is noted in Lake 1986.

12. For a detailed analysis of this work, see Dubiel's forthcoming essay.

13. The hexachords, for example, are B-type hexachords, which may also be found registrally at the outset of *Playing for Time* (see the preceding chapter).

14. See Dubiel's forthcoming essay.

15. Babbitt's most recent compositional period finds him even more humorous with his titles, but his decision not to use *Serial Killer* after some consideration indicates at least a modicum of restraint.

16. I am indebted to Dave Hollinden for sharing with me his work on *Four Play*. Example 4.8 is based on his analysis of the composition.

17. The array is represented in the list provided in this volume.

18. Unlike the array of *Reflections*, that of *Fanfare* contains the fifty-eight partitions of segments up to length six in up to twelve parts.

19. An earlier example of dynamics indexing pitch class lynes was noted in the *Canons for Clarinet* section of the Woodwind Quartet, a feature observed in Swift 1976.

20. This duplicates information from Mead 1987a, Example 31.

21. The order of partitions is slightly shuffled through exchanges across aggregate boundaries.

22. Example 4.23 duplicates material from Mead 1987a, Example 31.

23. See Dubiel's forthcoming essay.

24. I am indebted to Richard Swift for his comments on *Lagniappe*.

25. According to Babbitt's own program notes for the work; it is based at the outset on a trichordal superarray.

26. See Babbitt 1988.

27. Poem 157 in *The Complete Poems of Emily Dickinson*, ed. Thomas H. Johnson (Boston: Little, Brown, 1960).

28. See Schiff 1983.

29. Ibid.

30. This is a major point implicit in a number of Babbitt's writings and made most explicit in Dubiel 1990b.

31. Babbitt himself makes this point in Babbitt 1962.

32. To carry this a little further, one might say that the sorts of shifts one follows against a steady meter in the earlier time point practice are akin to the variety of displacements found in Brahms's music, the exposition of the Second Symphony being a particularly notorious example, while the shifting distances between downbeats in the later practice are reminiscent of the stretching and compressing of bar and beat lengths in Stravinsky. What is particularly vivid in Babbitt's recent music is the effect of steady pulses elongated or curtailed by a sixteenth-note, shifting the listener to a new metrical position in the temporal flux. One senses in his newer music a slower, statelier progression underlying the welter of surface rhythmic detail.

BIBLIOGRAPHY

WRITINGS OF MILTON BABBITT

1945. "Battle Cry." *Politics* 2, no. 11: 346.

1946. "The Function of Set Structure in the Twelve-Tone System." Ph.D. dissertation, Princeton University (1992).

1949. "The String Quartets of Bartók." *Musical Quarterly* 35: 377–85.

1950a. Review of *Schoenberg et son école* and *Qu'est ce que la musicque de douze sons?* by René Leibowitz. *Journal of the American Musicological Society* 3, no. 1: 57–60.

1950b. Review of *Polyphonie, Quatrième cahier: Le système dodécaphonique. Journal of the American Musicological Society* 3, no. 3: 264–67.

1952. Review of *Structural Hearing* by Felix Salzer. *Journal of the American Musicological Society* 5, no. 3: 260–65.

1953. Review of *The Life and Music of Bela Bartók* by Halsey Stevens. *Saturday Review* 36, no. 30: 23.

1954. "Musical America's Several Generations." *Saturday Review* 37, no. 11: 36.

1955. "Some Aspects of Twelve-Tone Composition." *The Score and IMA Magazine* 12: 53–61.

1958. "Who Cares if You Listen?" *High Fidelity* 8, no. 2: 38–40. Reprinted in *The American Composer Speaks*, ed. Gilbert Chase, pp. 234–44. Baton Rouge: Louisiana State University Press, 1966. Also reprinted in *Contemporary Composers on Contemporary Music*, ed. Elliott Schwartz and Barney Childs, pp. 243–50. New York: Holt, Rinehart, and Winston, 1967.

1960a. "Electronic Music: The Revolution in Sound." *Columbia University Magazine* (Spring): 4–8. Revised and reprinted as "The Revolution in Sound: Electronic Music" in *Music Journal* 18, no. 7 (1965): 34–37.

1960b. Review of *A Short Introduction to the Technique of Twelve-Tone Composition* by Leopold Spinner. *Juilliard Review* 7, no. 3: 25.

1960c. "Twelve-Tone Invariants as Compositional Determinants." *Musical Quarterly* 46, no. 2: 246–59. Reprinted in *Problems of Modern Music: The Princeton Seminar in Advanced Musical Studies*, ed. Paul Henry Lang, pp. 108–21. New York: Norton, 1962.

1961a. "Past and Present Concepts of the Nature and Limits of Music." *Congress Report of the International Musicological Society* 8: 398–403. Reprinted in *Perspectives on Contemporary Music Theory*, ed. Benjamin Boretz and Edward T. Cone, pp. 3–9. New York: Norton, 1972.

1961b. "Set Structure as a Compositional Determinant." *Journal of Music Theory* 5, no. 1: 72–94. Reprinted in *Perspectives on Contemporary Music Theory*, ed. Benjamin Boretz and Edward T. Cone, pp. 129–47. New York: Norton, 1972.

1962. "Twelve-Tone Rhythmic Structure and the Electronic Medium." *Perspectives of New Music* 1, no. 1: 49–79. Reprinted in *Perspectives on Contemporary*

Music Theory, ed. Benjamin Boretz and Edward T. Cone, pp. 148–79. New York: Norton, 1972.

1963a. "An Introduction [to the Issue]." *Journal of Music Theory* 7, no. 1: vi–vii.

1963b. "Mr. Babbitt Answers [in response to George Perle's preceding "Babbitt, Lewin, and Schoenberg: A Critique"]." *Perspectives of New Music* 2, no. 1: 127–32.

1964a. "An Introduction to the RCA Synthesizer." *Journal of Music Theory* 8, no. 2: 251–65.

1964b. "Remarks on the Recent Stravinsky." *Perspectives of New Music* 2, no. 2: 35–55. Reprinted in *Perspectives on Schoenberg and Stravinsky*, ed. Benjamin Boretz and Edward T. Cone, pp. 165–85. Princeton: Princeton University Press, 1968; 2d ed., New York: Norton, 1972.

1964c. "The Synthesis, Perception, and Specification of Musical Time." *Journal of the International Folk Music Council* 16: 92–95.

1965a. "The Structure and Function of Music Theory." *College Music Symposium* 5: 49–60. Reprinted in *Perspectives on Contemporary Music Theory*, ed. Benjamin Boretz and Edward T. Cone, pp. 10–21. New York: Norton, 1972.

1965b. "The Use of Computers in Musicological Research." *Perspectives of New Music* 3, no. 2: 74–83. Reprinted in *Conference on the Use of Computers in Humanistic Research*, Rutgers and IBM, 1966.

1966a. "Edgar Varèse: A Few Observations of His Music." *Perspectives of New Music* 4, no. 2: 14–22. Reprinted in *Perspectives on American Composers*, ed. Benjamin Boretz and Edward T. Cone, pp. 40–48. New York: Norton, 1971.

1966b. Panel discussion: "What Do You, as a Composer, Try to Get the Student to Hear in a Piece of Music?" Mod. Peter Westergaard. *Proceedings of the American Society of University Composers* 1: 59–81.

1968. "Three Essays on Schoenberg: Concerto for Violin and Orchestra, *Das Buch der hängenden Gärten*, and *Moses and Aaron*." *Perspectives on Schoenberg and Stravinsky*, ed. Benjamin Boretz and Edward T. Cone, pp. 47–60. Princeton: Princeton University Press, 1968; 2d ed., New York: Norton, 1972. (Originally appearing as notes for: Columbia M2S-679, Son-Nova 2, and Columbia K31–241).

1970a. Contribution to "The Composer in Academia: Reflections on a Theme of Stravinsky." *College Music Symposium* 10: 63–65.

1970b. Contribution to "In Memoriam Matyas Seiber." *Musical Times* 111: 886.

1970c. "On *Relata I*." *The Orchestral Composer's Point of View*, ed. Robert Stephan Hines, pp. 11–38. Norman: University of Oklahoma Press, 1970. Reprinted in *Perspectives of New Music* 9, no. 1: 1–22.

1971a. "Contemporary Music Composition and Music Theory as Contemporary Intellectual History." *Perspectives in Musicology*, ed. Barry S. Brook, Edward O. D. Downes, and Sherman J. van Solkema, pp. 151–84. New York: Norton, 1971.

1971b. Contribution to "Stravinsky (1882–1971): A Composers' Memorial." *Perspectives of New Music* 9, no. 2: 58, 103–7.

1972. Contribution to "In Memoriam: Stephan Wolpe (1902–1972)." *Perspectives of New Music* 11, no. 1: 5–6.

1973. "Present Music Theory and Future Practice." *IRCAM Conference: Abbaye de Senanque.*

1974. "Since Schoenberg." *Perspectives of New Music* 12, nos. 1–2: 3–28.

1976a. "Celebrative Speech." *Journal of the Arnold Schoenberg Institute* 1, no. 1: 6–13.

1976b. Letter. *In Theory Only* 2, no. 5: 35.

1976c. Contribution to " 'Maximally Scrambled' Twelve-Tone Sets: A Serial Forum." *In Theory Only* 2, no. 7: 9.

1976d. "Responses: A First Approximation." *Perspectives of New Music* 14, no. 2/15, no. 1: 3–23.

1979a. "Ben Webber (1919–1979)." *Perspectives of New Music* 17, no. 2: 11–13.

1979b. Foreword to *Beyond Orpheus: Studies in Musical Structure* by David Epstein. Cambridge: MIT Press.

1981. "The Next Thirty Years: The Future in Audio, Video Music, and Recordings." *High Fidelity/Musical America* 31, no. 4.

1982. "Robert Miller (1930–1981)—In Memoriam." *Perspectives of New Music* 20, nos. 1–2: 26–27.

1984a. "Composer Survey, Opinions on Solo Vocal Literature." *Perspectives of New Music* 22, nos. 1–2: 631–38.

1984b. "The More Than the Sounds of Music." *Horizons '84.* New York Philharmonic program book. Reprinted in *In Theory Only* 8, no. 3: 7–10.

1985a. "I Remember Roger (Memoirs of Roger Sessions)." *Perspectives of New Music* 23, no. 2: 112–16.

1985b. "All the Things They Are: Comments on Kern." *Institute for Studies in American Music* 14, no. 2: 8–9.

1986a. Foreword to *Musings: The Musical Worlds of Gunther Schuller* by Gunther Schuller. Oxford: Oxford University Press.

1986b. "Memoirs. Hans Keller: A Memorial Symposium." *Music Analysis* 5, nos. 2–3: 374–76.

1987. *Words about Music.* Ed. Stephen Dembski and Joseph N. Straus. Madison: University of Wisconsin Press. Reviews by Jason Gibbs in *In Theory Only* 10, no. 8 (1988): 15–23; Andrew Mead in *Journal of Music Theory* 32, no. 2 (1988): 366–79; Bayan Northcott in *Musical Times* 129 (April 1988): 189–91; and Arnold Whittal in *Music and Letters* 69, no. 3 (1988): 418–21.

1988. "Stravinsky's Verticals and (Schoenberg's) Diagonals: A Twist of Fate." *Stravinsky Retrospectives*, ed. Ethan Haimo and Paul Johnson Lincoln: University of Nebraska Press, 1988.

1989. "On Having Been and Still Being an American Composer." *Perspectives of New Music* 27, no. 1: 106–12.

1991. "A Life of Learning." Charles Homer Hoskin Lecture, *American Council of Learned Societies Occasional Papers*, no. 17.

WRITINGS ABOUT MILTON BABBITT AND RELATED TOPICS

Arnold, Stephen, and Graham Hair. 1976a. "A List of Works by Milton Babbitt." *Perspectives of New Music* 14, no. 2/15, no. 1: 24–25.

————. "An Introduction and a Study." 1976b. *Perspectives of New Music* 14, no. 2 and 15, no. 1: 155–86.

Barkin, Elaine. 1966. Letter. *Perspectives of New Music* 5, no. 1: 170.

————. 1967. "A Simple Approach to Milton Babbitt's 'Semi-Simple Variations.'" *Music Review* 28: 316.

————. 1976. "Conversation Piece." *Perspectives of New Music* 14, no. 2/15, no. 1: 83–84.

————. 1980. *The New Grove Dictionary of Music and Musicians*, ed. Stanley Sadie, s. v. "Babbitt, Milton." London: Macmillan, 1980.

Batstone, Philip Norman. 1972. "Multiple Order Functions in Twelve-Tone Music." *Perspectives of New Music* 10, no. 2: 60–71; and 11, no. 1: 92–111.

Bauer-Mengelberg, Stefan, and Melvin Ferentz. 1965. "On Eleven-Interval Twelve-Tone Rows." *Perspectives of New Music* 3, no. 2: 93–103.

Bazelow, Alexander R., and Frank Brickle. 1976. "A Partition Problem Posed by Milton Babbitt." *Perspectives of New Music* 14, no. 2/15, no. 1: 280–93.

Berger, Arthur. 1976. "Some Notes on Babbitt and His Influence." *Perspectives of New Music* 14, no. 2/15, no. 1: 32–36.

Berry, Wallace. 1976. "Apostrophe: A Letter from Ann Arbor." *Perspectives of New Music* 14, no. 2/15, no. 1: 187–98.

Blaustein, Susan, and Martin Brody. 1986. "Criteria for Grouping in Milton Babbitt's *Minute Waltz (or)* $\frac{3}{4} \frac{+1}{-8}$." *Perspectives of New Music* 24, no. 2: 30–79.

Borders, Barbara Ann. 1979. "Formal Aspects in Selected Instrumental Works of Milton Babbitt." Ph.D. dissertation, University of Kansas.

Boretz, Benjamin. 1963. "Music." *Nation* 196, no. 14: 294–96.

————. 1974. *Dictionary of Contemporary Music*, ed. John Vinton, s. v. "Babbitt, Milton." New York: Dutton.

Brooks, Richard James G. 1981. "Heard in Selected Instrumental Compositions of the Twentieth Century: A Graphic Analytic Method." Ph.D. dissertation, New York University.

Browne, Richmond. 1963. Review of *Perspectives of New Music* 1, no. 1. *Journal of Music Theory* 7, no. 2: 262–65.

————. 1976. "Re the Babbitt Mallalieu Fully Cyclically Permutational Row." *In Theory Only* 2, no. 7: 10–14.

————. 1981. "Tonal Implications of the Diatonic Set." *In Theory Only* 5, nos. 6–7: 3–21.

Brunner, L. W. 1981–82. "Bowling Green State University Second Annual New Music Festival: A Review." *Perspectives of New Music* 19, nos. 1–2: 484.

Bulow, H. T. 1984. "Problems and Issues Facing a Young Composer." *College Music Symposium* 24, no. 2: 115.

Capalbo, Mark. 1981–82. "Charts." *Perspectives of New Music* 19, nos. 1–2: 311.

Carter, Elliott. 1976. "To Think of Milton Babbitt." *Perspectives of New Music* 14, no. 2/15 no. 1: 29–31.

Davis, P. 1982. "Milton Babbitt: Special Pulitzer Citation." *BMI: The Many Worlds of Music*, no. 2: 20–21.

Dominick, L. R. 1983. "The Eighteenth Annual Festival-Conference of the American Society of University Composers: The Composer in the University Reexamined." *Perspectives of New Music* 21, nos. 1–2: 383.

Dreyer, M. 1981. "Glasgow: Musica Nova." *Musical Times* 122: 766.

Drone, J. 1983. "American Composer Update: The 1982 Premieres, Performances, Publications, Recordings, News." *Pan Pipes* 75, no. 2: 20.

Dubiel, Joseph. 1990a. "Review Essay: Robert D. Morris, *Composition with Pitch-Classes: A Theory of Compositional Design.*" *Journal of Musicological Research* 10, nos. 1–2: 47–80.

———. 1990b. "Three Essays on Milton Babbitt": "Part One: Introduction, 'Thick Array / of Depth Immeasurable.'" *Perspectives of New Music* 28, no. 2 (1990): 216–61; "Part Two: 'For Making this Occasion Necessary.'" *Perspectives of New Music* 29, no. 1 (1991): 90–123; and "Part Three: The Animation of Lists." *Perspectives of New Music*, forthcoming.

Eaton, J. 1976. "Neue Musik seit 1950 in den Vereinigten Staaten: Ein Ueberlick." *Oesterreichische Musikzeitschrift* 31: 476–81.

Francome, L. 1985. "1985–86 Premieres and Season Highlights." *Symphony Magazine* 36, no. 5: 45.

Forte, Allen. 1964. Review of *Perspectives of New Music* 1, no. 1. *Journal of the American Musicological Society* 17, no. 1: 110–13.

———. 1973. *The Structure of Atonal Music.* New Haven: Yale University Press.

Fowler, Charles. 1968. "An Interview with Milton Babbitt." *Music Educators Journal* 55, no. 3: 57–61, 127–33.

Gamer, Carlton, and Paul Lansky. 1976. "Fanfare for the Common Tone." *Perspectives of New Music* 14, no. 2/15, no. 1: 228–35.

Gibbs, Jason. 1989. "Prolongation in Order-Determinate Music." Ph.D. dissertation, University of Pittsburgh.

Griffiths, Paul. 1973. "Oxford." *Musical Times* 114: 173.

———. 1976. "New Music." *Musical Times* 117: 1018–19.

———. 1981. *Modern Music: The Avant-Garde since 1945.* New York: George Braziller.

Grimes, E. 1986. "Conversations with American Composers." *Music Educators Journal* 72: 52–53.

Haimo, Ethan, and Paul Johnson. 1984. "Isomorphic Partitioning and Schoenberg's Fourth String Quartet." *Journal of Music Theory* 28: 47–72.

Hamilton, D. 1986. "Babbitt at Seventy." *Opus* 2, no. 6: 28–30.

Hasty, Christopher F. 1987. "An Intervallic Definition of Set Class." *Journal of Music Theory* 31: 183–204.

Hirschfeld, J. G. 1982. "Milton Babbitt: A Not-So-Sanguine Interview." *High Fidelity/Musical America* 32, no. 6 (1982): 16–18.

Hollander, John. 1967. "Notes of the Text of *Philomel.*" *Perspectives of New Music* 6, no. 1: 134–41.

Howe, Hubert S. 1965. "Some Combinational Properties of Pitch Structures." *Perspectives of New Music* 4, no. 1: 45–61.

Hush, David. 1982–83 and 1983–84. "Asynordinate Twelve-Tone Structures: Milton Babbitt's Composition for Twelve Instruments." *Perspectives of New Music* 21, nos. 1–2 (1982–83): 152–208; and 22, nos. 1–2 (1983–84): 103–16.

Jarmon, Douglas. 1988. "Review: *Words about Music.*" *Music Review* 48–49: 157–58.

Johnson, William Marvin. 1984. "Time Point Sets and Meter." *Perspectives of New Music* 23, no. 1: 278–97.

Karpman, Laura. 1986. "An Interview with Milton Babbitt." *Perspectives of New Music* 24, no. 2: 80–87.

Kassler, Michael. 1967. "Toward a Theory That Is the Twelve-Note-Class System." *Perspectives of New Music* 5, no. 2: 1–80.

Kostelanetz, Richard. 1967. "The Two Extremes of Avant-Garde Music." *New York Times Magazine*.

———. "Notes on Milton Babbitt as Text-Sound Artist." 1987. *Perspectives of New Music* 25, nos. 1–2: 280–84.

Kowalski, David. 1987. "The Construction and Use of Self-Deriving Arrays." *Perspectives of New Music* 25, nos. 1–2: 286–361.

Kuderna, Jerome George. 1982. "Analysis and Performance of Selected Piano Works of Milton Babbitt (1916–)." Ph.D. dissertation, New York University.

La Barbara, J. 1980. "New Music: Running the Gamut." *High Fidelity/Musical America* 30: 14–15.

———. 1981. "Babbitt's *Dual:* A World Premiere." *High Fidelity/Musical America* 31: 15.

Lake, William E. 1986. "The Architecture of a Superarray Composition: Milton Babbitt's String Quartet No. 5." *Perspectives of New Music* 24, no. 2: 88–111.

Lerdahl, Fred. 1988. "Cognitive Constraints on Compositional Systems." *Generative Processes in Music*, ed. John A. Sloboda, pp. 182–235. Oxford: Clarendon Press.

Lester, Joel. 1986. "Notated and Heard Meter." *Perspectives of New Music* 24, no. 2: 116–29.

Lewin, David. 1976a. Contribution to "'Maximally Scrambled' Twelve-Tone Sets: A Serial Forum." *In Theory Only* 2, no. 7: 9.

———. 1976b. "On Partial Ordering." *Perspectives of New Music* 14, no. 2–15, no. 1: 252–57.

———. 1987. *Generalized Musical Intervals and Transformations.* New Haven: Yale University Press.

Lewin, Harold. 1965. "Aspects of the Twelve-Tone System: Its Formation and Structural Implications." Ph.D. dissertation, Indiana University.

Lieberson, Peter G. 1985. "Milton Babbitt's *Post-Partitions.*" Ph.D. dissertation, Brandeis University.

———, E. Lundborg, and J. Peel. 1974. "Conversation with Milton Babbitt." *Contemporary Music Newsletter* 8, no. 1:2–3; and 8, no. 2:2–3; 8, no.3:2–4.

Mackey, Steven. 1985. "The Thirteenth Note." Ph.D. dissertation, Brandeis University.

———. 1987. ". . . what surfaces." *Perspectives of New Music* 25, nos. 1 and 2: 258–79.

Martino, Donald. 1961. "The Source Set and Its Aggregate Formations." *Journal of Music Theory* 5: 224–73.

Maus, Fred. 1989. "Review: *Words about Music.*" *American Music* 7: 476–79.

Mead, Andrew W. 1983. "Detail and the Array in Milton Babbitt's *My Complements to Roger.*" *Music Theory Spectrum* 5: 89–109.

――――. 1984. "Recent Developments in the Music of Milton Babbitt." *Musical Quarterly* 70, no. 3: 310–31.

――――. 1985. "Large-Scale Strategy in Arnold Schoenberg's Twelve-Tone Music." *Perspectives of New Music* 24, no. 1: 120–57.

――――. 1987a. "About *About Time*'s Time: A Survey of Milton Babbitt's Recent Rhythmic Practice." *Perspectives of New Music* 25, nos. 1–2: 182–235.

――――. 1987b. "'Tonal' Forms in Arnold Schoenberg's Twelve-Tone Music." *Music Theory Spectrum* 9: 67–92.

――――. 1988. "Some Implications of the Pitch-Class/Order-Number Isomorphism Inherent in the Twelve-Tone System: Part 1." *Perspectives of New Music* 26, no. 2: 96–163.

――――. 1989. "Twelve-Tone Organizational Strategies: An Analytical Sampler." *Intégral* 3: 93–170.

Moog, R. A. 1984. "The Columbia-Princeton Electronic Music Center: Thirty Years of Explorations in Sound." *Contemporary Keyboard* 7: 22–24.

Morris, Robert. 1977. "On the Generation of Multiple-Order-Function Twelve-Tone Rows." *Journal of Music Theory* 21: 238–62.

――――. 1987. *Composition with Pitch-Classes: A Theory of Compositional Design.* New Haven: Yale University Press.

――――, and Brian Alegant. 1988. "The Even Partitions in Twelve-Tone Music." *Music Theory Spectrum* 10: 74–101.

――――, and Daniel Starr. 1974. "The Structure of All-Interval-Series." *Journal of Music Theory* 18, no. 2: 364–89.

O'Connell, Walter. 1968. "Tone Spaces." *Die Reihe* 8 (English ed.): 35–67.

Packer, R. 1986. "An Interview with Judith Bettina." *Perspectives of New Music* 24, no. 2: 112–14.

Paulson, J. C. 1987. "Electronic Pioneers." *The Instrumentalist* 41: 40–54.

Pazur, Robert. 1976. "A Babbitt Bibliography." *Perspectives of New Music* 14, no. 2/15, no. 1: 26–28.

Peel, John, and Cheryl Cramer. 1988. "Correspondences and Associations in Milton Babbitt's *Reflections*." *Perspectives of New Music* 26, no. 1: 144–207.

Peles, Stephen. 1983–84. "Interpretations of Sets in Multiple Dimensions: Notes on the Second Movement of Arnold Schoenberg's String Quartet #3." *Perspectives of New Music* 22, nos. 1–2: 303–52.

Perle, George. 1963. "Babbitt, Lewin, and Schoenberg: A Critique." *Perspectives of New Music* 2, no. 1: 120–27.

――――. 1981. *Serial Composition and Atonality: An Introduction to the Music of Schoenberg, Berg, and Webern.* 5th. ed. Berkeley and Los Angeles: University of California Press.

――――. 1990. *The Listening Composer.* Berkley and Los Angeles: University of California Press.

Philippot, Michel P. 1976. "Ear, Heart, and Brain." *Perspectives of New Music* 14, no. 2/15, no. 1: 45–60.

Pousseur, Henri. 1966. "The Question of Order in New Music." *Perspectives of New Music* 5, no. 1: 93–111. Reprinted in *Perspectives on Contemporary Music Theory*, ed. Benjamin Boretz and Edward T. Cone, pp. 97–115. New York: Norton, 1972.

Powell, Mel. 1960. Review of *Problems of Modern Music: The Princeton Seminar in Advanced Musical Studies*, ed. Paul Henry Lang. *Journal of Music Theory* 4, no. 2: 259–69.

Rahn, John. 1975. "On Pitch or Rhythm: Interpretations of Orderings of and in Pitch and Time." *Perspectives of New Music* 13, no. 2: 182–203.

———. 1976. "How Do You *Du* (by Milton Babbitt)?" *Perpsectives of New Music* 14, no. 2/15, no. 1: 61–80.

——— et. al. 1977. "Quaestionis Gratia: Milton Babbitt's *Du*: A Query." *In Theory Only* 3, no. 2: 32.

———. 1982. *Basic Atonal Theory*. New York: Longman.

Rosen, Charles. 1976. "Homage to Milton." *Perspectives of New Music* 14, no. 2/15, no. 1: 37–40.

Rothstein, William. 1980. "Linear Structure in the Twelve-Tone System: An Analysis of Donald Martino's *Pianississimo*." *Journal of Music Theory* 24: 129–65.

Salzman, Eric. 1967. "Babbitt and American Serialism." *Twentieth-Century Music: An Introduction*, 2d ed., pp. 146–47. Englewood Cliffs, N.J.: Prentice-Hall.

Samet, Bruce. 1987. "Hearing Aggregates." Ph.D. dissertation, Princeton University.

Sandow, G. 1982. "Music: A Fine Madness." *Village Voice* 27: 76.

———. 1984a. "Music: An Open Letter to Milton Babbitt." *Village Voice* 29: 81–82.

———. 1984b. "Music: Lost Generation (Conservatives, Modernists, and Experimentalists)." *Village Voice* 29: 78–79.

Schoenberg, Arnold. 1984. "Composition with Twelve Tones." *Style and Idea*, ed. Leonard Stein, trans. Leo Black. Berkeley and Los Angeles: University of California Press.

Schwartz, E. 1985. "Directions in American Compositions since the Second World War: Part I, 1945–1960." *Music Educators Journal* 61: 29–39.

Scotto, Ciro. 1988. "Preparing a Performance of Babbitt's *Arie da Capo*." *Perspectives of New Music* 26, no. 2: 6–24.

Starr, Daniel. 1978. "Sets, Invariance, and Partitions." *Journal of Music Theory* 22: 1–42.

———. 1984. "Derivation and Polyphony." *Perspectives of New Music* 23, no. 1: 180–257.

———, and Robert Morris. 1977 and 1978. "A General Theory of Combinatoriality and the Aggregate." *Perspectives of New Music* 16, no. 1 (1977): 3–35; and 16, no. 2 (1978): 50–84.

Straus, Joseph N. 1986. "Listening to Babbitt." *Perspectives of New Music* 24, no. 2: 10–24.

Steinberg, Michael. 1963. "Some Observations on the Harpsichord in Twentieth-Century Music." *Perspectives of New Music* 1, no. 2: 189–94.

Sward, Rosalie La Grow. 1981. "An Examination of the Mathematical Systems Used in Selected Compositions of Milton Babbitt and Iannis Xenakis." Ph.D. dissertation, Northwestern University.

Swartz, A. 1985. "Milton Babbitt on Milton Babbitt (Interview with the Composer)." *American Music* 3, no. 4: 467–73.

Swift, Richard. 1976. "Some Aspects of Aggregate Composition." *Perspectives of New Music* 14, no. 2/15, no. 1: 236–48.

Taub, Robert. 1986. "An Appreciation of Milton's Piano Music." *Perspectives of New Music* 24, no. 2: 26–29.

Treibitz, C. H. 1983. "Substance and Function in Concepts of Musical Structure." *Musical Quarterly* 69, no. 2: 209–26.

Ussachevsky, Vladimir. 1976. "A Bit of History and a Salute to Milton." *Perspectives of New Music* 14, no. 2/15, no. 1: 43–44.

Varga, B. A. 1984. "Three Questions on Music." *New Hungarian Quarterly* 25/99: 199.

Westergaard, Peter. 1965. "Some Problems Raised by the Rhythmic Procedures in Milton Babbitt's Composition for Twelve Instruments." *Perspectives of New Music* 4, no. 1: 109–18.

———. 1966. "Toward a Twelve-Tone Polyphony." *Perspectives of New Music* 4, no. 2: 90–112. Reprinted in *Perspectives of Contemporary Music Theory*, ed. Benjamin Boretz and Edward T. Cone, pp. 238–60. New York: Norton, 1972.

Winham, Bethany Beardslee. 1976. "Thoughts on 'I. B.' from 'L. W.'" *Perspectives of New Music* 14, no. 2/15, no. 1: 81–82.

Winham, Godfrey. 1970. "Composition with Arrays." *Perspectives of New Music* 9, no. 1: 43–67. Reprinted in *Perspectives on Contemporary Music Theory*, ed. Benjamin Boretz and Edward T. Cone. New York: Norton, 1972.

Wintle, Christopher. 1976. "Milton Babbitt's *Semi-Simple Variations*." *Perspectives of New Music* 14, no. 2/15, no. 1: 111–54.

Wittlich, Gary E., et al. 1975. *Aspects of 20th Century Music*, ed. Gary Wittlich. Englewood Cliffs, N. J.: Prentice Hall.

Wolpe, Stefan. 1983. "On New (and Not-So-New) Music in America." *Journal of Music Theory* 27, no. 2: 16–22.

Wuorinen, Charles. 1976. "An Appreciation." *Perspectives of New Music* 14, no. 2/15, no. 1: 41–42.

Zuckerman, Mark. 1976a. "Derivation as an Articulation of Set Structure: A Study of the First Ninety-Two Measures of Milton Babbitt's String Quartet No. 2." Ph.D dissertation, Princeton University.

———. 1976b. "On Milton Babbitt's String Quartet No. 2." *Perspectives of New Music* 14, no. 2 and 15, no. 1: 85–110.

DISCOGRAPHY

About Time (1982).

Alan Feinberg, piano. Composers Recordings CRI CD-521.

All Set for Jazz Ensemble (1957).

Modern Jazz Concert. Gunther Schuller and George Russell, conductors; Brandeis University Festival of the Arts. Columbia Wl-127, recorded 18 June 1957; released 1958. Rereleased in 1964 as CL 2109-10 in C2L-31/CS 8909-10 in C2S-831. Deleted 1970.

Arthur Weisberg, conductor; Contemporary Chamber Ensemble. Nonesuch H-71303; released 1974.

Arie da Capo (1973–74).

Harvey Solberger, conductor; Group for Contemporary Music at Columbia University. Nonesuch H-71372; released 1980.

Ciro Scotto, conductor; *Perspectives of New Music* PNM 26.

Canonical Form (1983).

Robert Taub, piano. Harmonia Mundi HMC-5160; released 1986.

Composition for Four Instruments (1948).

John Wummer, flute; Stanley Drucker, clarinet; Peter Marsh, violin; Donald McCall, cello. Composers Recordings. CRI 138; released 1961.

John Heiss, conductor; New England Conservatory Chamber Ensemble. Golden Crest NEC-109; released 1979.

Composition for Guitar (1984) (also called *Sheer Pluck*).

New Music with Guitar, vol. 3. David Starobin, guitar. Bridge BDG-2006; released 1985.

Composition for Synthesizer (1961).

Columbia-Princeton Electronic Music Center. Columbia ML-5966/MS-6566; released 1964. Deleted 1979.

Composition for Twelve Instruments (1948).

Ralph Shapey, conductor; Hartt Chamber Players. Son Nova 1/S-1; released 1962. Deleted 1967.

Composition for Viola and Piano (1950).

A. Loft, viola; Bernhard Weiser, piano. New Editions 4; released 1951.

Walter Trampler, viola; Alvin Baumann, piano. Composers Recordings CRI 138; released 1961.

John Graham, viola; Robert Black, piano. Composers Recordings CRI SD-446; released 1981.

Concerto for Piano and Orchestra (1985).

Alan Feinberg, piano; Charles Wuorinen, conductor; American Composers Orchestra. New World NW-346-2

Consortini (1989).

Griffin GM 2032

Du (1951).

Bethany Beardslee, soprano; Robert Helps, piano. Son Nova 1/S-1; released 1962. Deleted 1967.

Duet (1956).

Stephen Gerber, piano. Opus One 67; released 1982.

Robert Taub, piano. Harmonia Mundi HMC-5160; released 1986.

An Elizabethan Sextette (1979).

Harvey Solberger, conductor; Group for Contemporary Music. Composers Recordings CRI CD-521.

Groupwise (1983).

D. Shulman, conductor; Group for Contemporary Music. Composers Recordings CRI CD-521.

The Head of the Bed (1981).

Judith Bettina, soprano; Anthony Korf, conductor; Parnassus. New World Records NW-346-2.

It Takes Twelve to Tango (1984).

Alan Feinberg, piano. Composers Recordings CRI CD-521.

The Joy of More Sextets (1986).

R. Schulte, violin; A. Feinberg, piano. New World NW-364-1, and NW-364-2

Lagniappe (1985).

Robert Taub, piano. Harmonia Mundi HMC-5160.

Minute Waltz (or $\frac{3}{4} \frac{+}{-} \frac{1}{8}$) (1978).

The Waltz Project. Alan Feinberg, piano. Nonesuch D-79011; released 1981.

Alan Feinberg, piano. Composers Recordings CRI CD-521

Paraphrases (1979).

Anthony Korf, conductor; Parnassus. Composers Recordings CRI SD-499; released 1984.

Partitions (1957).

New Music for the Piano. Robert Helps, piano. RCA Victor LM-7042/ LSC-7042; released 1966. Deleted 1971. Reissued in 1972 as Composers Recordings CRI SD-288

Alan Feinberg, piano. Composers Recordings CD-521.

Robert Taub, piano. Harmonia Mundi HMC-5160.

Philomel (1964).

Bethany Beardslee, soprano. Acoustic Research 0654.083; released 1971. Reissued in 1980 as New World NW-307.

Phonemena (with piano, 1969; with synthesized tape, 1975).

Lynn Webber, soprano (with tape) and Lynn Webber, soprano; Jerry Kuderna, piano. New World NW-209.

Playing for Time (1977).

Alan Feinberg, piano. Composers Recordings CRI CD-521.

Post-Partitions (1966).

Robert Miller, piano. New World NW-209.

Robert Taub, piano. Harmonia Mundi HMC-5160.

Quartet No. 2 (1954).

Composers Quartet. Nonesuch H-71280.

Quartet No. 3 (1969).

Fine Arts Quartet. Turnabout TVS-34515; released 1973. Deleted 1978.

Quartet No. 4 (1970).

Julliard Quartet. Composers Recordings CRI CD 587.

Quartet No. 5 (1982).

Composers Quartet. Music and Arts Programs of America CD 606.

Relata I (1964).

Paul Zukofsky, conductor; Julliard Orchestra. New World Records 80396-2.

Reflections (1974).

Robert Miller, piano (with synthesized tape). New World NW-209.

Robert Taub, piano (with synthesized tape). Harmonia Mundi HMC-5160.

Semi-Simple Variations (1956).

Stephen Gerber, piano. Opus One 67.

Robert Taub, piano. Harmonia Mundi HMC-5160.

Sextets (1966).

Music for a Twentieth-Century Violinist: An Anthology of Three Decades of American Music, 1940–1950–1960. Paul Zukofsky, violin; Gilbert Kalish, piano. Desto DC-6435-37 (3 discs); released 1975.

R. Shulte, violin; A. Feinberg, piano. New World NW-364-1 and NW-364-2.

A Solo Requiem (1976–77).

Bethany Beardslee, soprano; Cheryl Seltzer and Joel Sachs, pianos. Nonesuch H-78006; released 1982.

Tableaux (1973).

M. Kriesberg, piano. Spectrum SR-324

Robert Taub, piano. Harmonia Mundi HMC-5160.

Three Compositions for Piano (1947).

Robert Taub Plays Music by Milton Babbitt, Béla Bartók, Leon Kirchner, and Seymour Shifrin. Robert Taub, piano. Composers Recordings CRI SD-461.

Robert Taub, piano. Harmonia Mundi HMC-5160.

Vision and Prayer (1961).

Columbia-Princeton Electronic Music Center Tenth-Anniversary Album. Bethany Beardslee, soprano. Composers Recordings 2-CRI SD-268.

Bethany Beardslee, soprano. Composers Recordings CRI CD-521.

INDEX

Andrew Mead is Associate Professor of Music Theory
at the University of Michigan